Now and Then

Now and Then

From Coney Island to Here

JOSEPH HELLER

SIMON & SCHUSTER
A VIACOM COMPANY

First published in Great Britain by Simon & Schuster, 1998
An imprint of Simon & Schuster Ltd
A Viacom Company

Simon & Schuster Ltd
West Garden Place
Kendal Street
London
W2 2AQ

Simon & Schuster Australia
Sydney

A CIP catalogue record for this book is
available from the British Library.

ISBN 0–684–81968–6

3 5 7 9 10 8 6 4 2

Printed and bound in Great Britain by
Butler & Tanner Ltd, Frome and London

For my sister, Sylvia

ACKNOWLEDGMENTS

*The author would like to thank Donald Kaplan,
Judy Walsh and the staff of the Brooklyn Public Library,
and the entire staff of the East Hampton Public Library.*

Now and Then

1

The Gold Ring

THE GOLD RING on the carousels was made of brass. Even
as kids in Coney Island we didn't believe it was the real
thing. By the time we'd grown old enough to ride the outside horses and lunge out sideways to grasp the metal rings
that swung toward us for the final few rotations, the
carousel was no longer enchanting and we had no deep
desire for the free ride that the last, lucky gold one awarded.
By then we had nickels enough to go around again if we
wanted to, but we tended to spend them on attractions that
were higher and faster, more spectacular—roller coasters—
and, for fun, the electric bump-cars.

We were luckier with the staying power of our craving
for things like pretzels, potato chips, jelly doughnuts, and
chocolate bars. Mark Twain is said to have remarked that by
the time we're tall enough to reach the jar of jam on the high
shelf of the cupboard, we find that we've lost our taste for
jam. No such rueful fate struck me or my friends or any in
the small family of four of which I was the youngest, not
with edibles like halvah or salted peanuts, ice cream, kosher
corned beef and hot dogs, or even salami sandwiches. When
we found ourselves with enough cash to obtain as much of
these delicacies as we wanted, we still had a hearty appetite

for them, and we tended to indulge ourselves, and still do, by eating as much as, sometimes more, much more, than we truly did, and do, want.

Of late, my best defense against corpulence has been to keep out of the house supplies of things to eat that reason cautions I shouldn't be stuffing into myself. Pistachio nuts, for instance, whether in petite jars or five-pound bags, have a feeble chance of extended survival once I discover them close at hand. If there's ice cream in the freezer, I feel a commanding moral responsibility to move it out of the house as quickly as I'm able to swallow as much as is there. Lately, I've discovered that salty pretzels go very well with just about any dessert I am likely to have at home. They're also good by themselves. If, before going to bed, I happen to remember we have sliced turkey breast in the refrigerator, the odds are heavy that I'll put some in my mouth as I find my way into the bathroom to brush my teeth—on a couple of crackers, of course, or half a flat of pita bread, with salt and mustard.

But it's ice cream that still tastes most wonderful and is richest in evocative associations extending backward in time almost to the formation of memory itself, to brands and items long extinct—to Dixie cups, for example, with their prized photographs of cowboy movie stars on the inside of the lid under a transparent waxed-paper seal. Like the evocations of the cookie to Proust, a meditation on ice cream soon takes me back to the age of eight or nine and into a family setting in which a small container is shared with bliss by the four of us, a mother, a sister, a brother, and me. (I was by many years the youngest.) In summer, ice cream was everywhere. In autumn, though, after the change back from daylight saving time, and even in winter on a black night after dinner and before bedtime, the idea of ice cream might be voiced, taking on a sacramental meaning to our small family in our small apartment—four rooms, looking out on West 31st Street near Surf Avenue in Coney Island. My mother—finally relaxing in front of the radio with the rest of us, after shopping for dinner, preparing dinner, serving dinner, and cleaning up in the kitchen after dinner—might say with her Jewish intonations that she would certainly very much welcome the taste of a little ice cream. We had no refrigerator then, no freezer—no family living in our apartment building did—and there would be no ice cream in the house. At that late hour only the soda fountain in a drugstore two blocks away was open. I was the one who would volunteer to go. I would be given a dime to bring back a container. The flavor of our unanimous choice in those years was called Golden Glow. It's hard today to believe that just half a pint of bulk ice cream could have been so satisfying to the four of us, but that's all, as I recall, that a dime paid for. More than a dime for ice cream they couldn't bring themselves to spend. We were prudent with money because we didn't have much, but I, the "baby" in the family, was never allowed to feel that.

MY SISTER, SYLVIA, was seven years older than I. My brother, Lee, originally Eli, born in Russia and brought to this country at the age of six, was seven years older than she was. In reality, they were only my half brother and half sister, the children of my father and his first wife, who had died. My mother was therefore a stepmother to them. They were, I realize only now, technically orphans, and although they never said so, they must have felt at least a little like orphans. I was, then, the baby in the family, treated by everyone, in effect, like an only child, which in some ways I was.

I had no inkling of these family relationships until I was well into my teens, and I was shocked nearly speechless when confronted by the discovery, which unfolded at my brother's wedding. There, my mother's role in the procession down the aisle was to walk behind him, alone, and I listened dumbfounded to the officiating rabbi praise her so generously for the loving care she had given the groom, the son who was not biologically her own, and the daughter, too. I felt victimized, disgraced. My response to rage then, as it chiefly is still, was to break off speaking to the person offending me. I stopped speaking to my sister one time when she took up cigarettes and another time when she bleached her hair. And this time I may have fallen silent with all three of them, possibly with so deep and vindictive a hurt that I would obstinately refuse to tell any of them the cause, for that would be speaking. My oldest friend in the world, Marvin Winkler, with whom as an infant I had often been lodged together in a playpen, was amazed not long ago when I recalled the incident and related my stunned reaction. He was puzzled by my surprise, for he had been informed of the relationship by his mother when he was still a child and cautioned against hurting my feelings by bringing it up. My sister, too, was taken aback to read my account of this event in a biographical piece about me for which she had also been interviewed. She, along with my mother and my brother, had simply assumed, she claimed, that I'd known all along. It was not a scandal, not even a secret. They didn't talk about it because there was no need to.

On the other hand, I know it is true that neither my brother nor my sister ever said anything at all to me about my father, least of all about an earlier marriage, until out of curiosity as an adult I began to inquire. And only once did my mother talk to me about him, volunteering the information that my father could eat a whole chocolate cake at a single sitting—as a delivery driver for a wholesale bakery firm, cakes were easy for him to obtain—and that before he went into the hospital with a bleeding gastric ulcer, his stool was as black as coal. She told me this as an admonition against my own appetite, for I could always eat as much cake as was given me, and still want more. I discovered early in life that shelled walnuts in a bowl of raisins make a lovely late-evening treat for uninterrupted munching till bedtime. I once overheard my mother recounting that when I was a nursing infant, she had to tear me away from the breast, for I would never finish, and I can believe her.

DIFFERENT AS EACH OF US was from the others, and however much there was inside us that we didn't want to talk about, we were, and functioned as, a close family. It was not in our nature to complain, quarrel, demand, or gossip. I remember a number of tantrums I discharged as a juvenile, but I believe that from the time I was an adolescent, I had acquired the family's stoic, resigned, and undemanding nature and didn't complain, quarrel, or gossip, either. My mother, finding herself after six years of marriage a widow with three children, two of them not naturally her own, had brought us up as the mother of us all, and my brother and sister had related to her as such. My brother, I learned, had at one time saved up money enough to buy her a better radio. The gift was poignantly apt, for my mother loved melodic music, Puccini arias in particular. And in those days of radio entertainment, amid the glorious profusion of comedy and variety shows, there was an opulence of weekly broadcasts featuring short selections from opera and other light classical pieces.

Although the period was one of severe economic depression, everybody sooner or later seemed able to find employment. By the time I started school, my brother, fourteen years older than I, was already working at a brokerage in Wall Street as a customer's man, a job for which he was to prove ill suited by his modest manner and unaggressive temperament, and by a disposition to be continually obliging to others. My sister, after graduating from high school and encountering a number of startling rebuffs at employment agencies, would eventually find herself starting at R. H. Macy's department store, where she would remain for something like forty years. And I at sixteen, after classes at high school, would be cutting a dashing figure in a khaki quasi-military uniform as a part-time messenger boy delivering telegrams for Western Union, in office buildings in Manhattan weekdays, on a bicycle weekends to residences in Brooklyn, and mostly exulting in my duties with a sense of adventure and attentive curiosity. My mother, who had been a seamstress and something of a dressmaker before her marriage, worked steadily at home at her sewing machine mending garments for neighbors and doing alterations for a cousin, Sadie Pacon, who owned a dress shop on Gravesend Neck Road in lower Flatbush nearby. She also found steady work at home from laundries, turning frayed collars on men's shirts so that, from the outside and at the neck at least, the shirts looked almost good as new. Some weekend nights, mainly Saturdays, my brother would find extra income filling in at a catering hall for some banquet, dressing up appropriately for his suave role in the cloakroom or as one of the hall's hosts greeting and directing arriving guests. Neighbors outside the apartment building seeing him depart in a tuxedo or a natty, double-breasted, summer sport jacket might remark that he was off on a heavy date. But I knew he was going to work.

My mother liked to read. In Europe, her family had been bookbinders. From the Coney Island public library I would bring her Yiddish translations of novels. She enjoyed Tolstoi, especially *Anna Karenina,* with which she had long been familiar, and thought Dostoyevsky was crazy. Her brother (my Uncle Sam) late in life was employed repairing books for the library of Brandeis University, where his son, Harry Stein, a varsity player in James Madison High School in Brooklyn and City College in New York, was one of the athletic coaches.

When my mother noticed an apple turning soft she would briskly plan a noodle pudding that made use of it rather than have it go to waste. She took threadbare bedsheets to her scissors and her sewing machine and converted them into window curtains. (Often, as her eyesight weakened with age, I would help with the sewing by threading her needle. Today I would not be able to.) If brother and sister had quarreled, she wouldn't let them go to bed until they had talked it out and made peace. She was never more happy than when a friend from the old country appeared unexpectedly. The visit to Coney Island of a Mrs. Rosen filled her with joy.

My sister's clothing as a teenager in high school, she recalls, came to her mainly as hand-me-downs from an older first cousin, who, because she was already at work in a business with her father, favored dresses of dark color, which my mother altered to fit. She also remembers feeling endlessly self-conscious, because she wore dresses rather than the skirts with blouses or sweaters fashionable among her schoolmates. Widowed twice, she is esteemed by a step-daughter from her first marriage and by the three children from her second, all of them grown now.

For a little while, far back before the age of sixteen, out of eagerness more than need, I hawked newspapers in the early evening, peddling the next morning's editions the night before, crying, "'Merican, News, and Mirror, morning pape'!" The *American,* a Hearst newspaper more reactionary than his *Mirror,* was thicker than the others, cost more, and had few readers in the Italian and Jewish neighborhoods I traversed in my desperate hurry to keep ahead of other newsboys who were trying desperately to keep ahead of me. I soon dropped that heavier paper from my inventory, and my sales cry became "Hey, get your morning *News* and *Mirror,* morning pape'!" At best this was very small stuff, and I was lucky if I earned as much as a dollar. I bought the papers for a penny and a half, I think I remember, and sold them for two cents each, hoping for an occasional tip of a penny or two. People who wanted both might give me a nickel. I bought the papers from trucks near the subway station at Stillwell Avenue, usually eating a frankfurter while I waited for them to arrive, and wended my way home on a route along the boardwalk and the populous avenues of Surf and Mermaid in the hope that my last batch would be entirely gone by the time I got there. If not, a humorous, audacious plea to neighbors sitting outside their houses might do the trick. "Extra, Extra! Hitler dies . . . his mustache!" was one shouted ploy to command immediate attention. Any papers that remained I might give away to mothers and fathers there who were my favorites.

A wondrous incident remains indelibly alive—it occurred only one time. At a boardwalk Irish bar one night, a thin man sitting alone at a table beckoned to me and reached out for one of my papers. As I stood there and waited in suspense, he opened it from the back, studying the racing results a few moments, and then returned it. And then he gave me a dime and wanted no newspaper. I was in heaven, strolling on air as I went back outside. I was in love with a world that had such humans in it.

From repeated personal experience I've learned that few pleasures are so thoroughly reinforcing to the spirit as the arrival of unexpected money. Not long ago, I was amazed to receive in the mail, with no advance word, a royalty check from my literary agent for almost $18,000, representing cumulative royalties over the years from the publication of one of my novels in East Germany. I had long since forgotten that I'd even had a novel published there, and for the next hour or so I found myself grinning and humming a happy show tune or two. But I doubt very much that the sensation of well-being I experienced from this relatively huge windfall surpassed the joy brought me by that ten-cent gift I once received as a newsboy. It feels now as though that dime meant enormously more to me, and perhaps it did.

Each of these benign surprises affecting me was a rapture someone born rich is not likely ever to enjoy. There are some pleasures money can't buy.

OUR STREET AND neighborhood felt safe, insular, and secure, to a child an ethnic stronghold. Just about all the parents were immigrants, the majority from Eastern Europe. There was nothing and no one to fear physically.

I did not really know who Hitler was. Our elders did, but I doubt that even they, or anyone, could have guessed at the evil immensity of the brutal destruction he was going to set loose. I remember a day: It is late afternoon, and I can hear again the newspaper vendors tearing through our street with their high-pitched cries and their "extra" editions of the papers with glaring headlines announcing that Hindenburg had resigned as president of Germany to make way for Hitler as chancellor. They knew they would sell every copy that day, whereas I didn't know who Hindenburg was. Until much later, I thought he was a zeppelin.

There was just about no fear of violence in that part of Coney Island where I lived and grew up. And there was practically no crime, unless one considers the peddling of ice cream or soft drinks on the beach a criminal activity—the police did, but we didn't—or later on, approaching the years of the war and to a broader extent afterward, the possession and smoking of marijuana. I didn't consider using marijuana a crime, either, although I never wanted to become "schooled" to be what was called a "viper." I doubt that my brother or sister even knew about the increasing prevalence of this activity, and my mother would have been of a disapproving mind toward anything thought wrong. Then after the war came heroin.

In the nineteen years I lived on that street before going into the army—except for two months away as a blacksmith's helper in a southern navy yard, I lived nowhere else—I never heard of a rape, an assault, or an armed robbery in our neighborhood. I do recall having heard of a bookmaker shot to death in a poolroom, but that was on West 25th Street, six blocks away, on the very border between the Jewish and Italian sections. It wasn't really in our neighborhood, although we were eventually using that spot as a meeting place and the most convenient site for placing our bets on professional baseball games. It was run by a short, squat man called Sammy the Pig. The poolroom nearer my home was owned and run by a man we knew as Weepy. Nicknames were legion in Coney Island. *Foofson* is the Yiddish word for the number fifteen. Sammy Foofsen, an older youth, was already Sammy Fifteen by the time I heard of him. A little while later, even his nickname acquired a nickname: He was referred to as Six-Six-Three. These mutations in title appeared to arise and take hold quite naturally, as though by spontaneous generation; no one person originated them. A guy called Chicago was Chi, then Shy. Mursh the Cripple had a leg in a clumsy metal brace from polio. In time, Mursh the Cripple matured into Mursh the Hopper. He was older, too—one of the first guys we knew in Coney Island to own a car; it was an automobile with just hand controls. And a prank of his was to sit in the space beside the driver's seat, staring straight ahead with a placid smile and, with no person behind the wheel, operate the car with manual movements below the dashboard that weren't visible to disbelieving other drivers or pedestrians, who, startled, usually looked twice. My friend Marvin Winkler was Beansy for some reason, which seems almost preferable to Marvin. Murray Rabinowitz was Rup since childhood, in honor of his early surgery for a hernia, known then as a "rupture." Danny Rosoff was Danny the Count. Squeezy and Frenchy were two girls—I don't know how they came to merit such racy monikers. Danny the Bull, another fellow my age, was given that name before the war because of his broad chest and muscular shoulders. After the war, he was soon rendered frail and woeful by an addiction to heroin. His father, a barber named Max, gave him a cruel new title, derogating him to customers in his shop as My Son the Junkie.

THE LONE ACT of violence affecting me was one I unconsciously took pains not to find out much about until I was well into my thirties, and that was the death of my father in a hospital—from internal bleeding after surgery for a condition that today I imagine would likely be considered almost routine, his bleeding ulcer. I prefer to believe that these days, with such protective facilities as intensive-care units and surgical recovery rooms standard, the falling open of his stitches would have been detected in time and that he would have survived.

I was just past five. I knew he was gone—I don't remember that I was ever told, I just knew—but I had no notion of the cause. For thirty years I didn't care to ask. I didn't dare? It wasn't a secret. I didn't know, I eventually recognized in one startling moment—and it came to me in an illuminating burst of understanding—because I had never wanted to ask; they didn't tell me, I guess, because with the passing of years they simply assumed I knew. It was not a gratifying subject for family discussion. The impact upon my brother and sister—losing both parents in so short a time and finding themselves in the care of a stepmother they had known only six years—would have been enormous. But not only did we not complain much in my family, we didn't talk much about anything deeply felt. We didn't ask for much, either. Only one time ever was I present when one of us shed a tear, at the funeral of a spouse. And that's about all it was, a tear.

About my father, I simply lost interest in him after he was gone. Later on—outside the family, of course—it became a conceit of personality to assert impertinently when the subject arose that I never missed him, and I don't believe I did. I didn't have that tender admiration for a large and generous nature that Nabokov expresses for his father. I hardly knew mine at all. If anything, the passing away of Mr. Isaac Daniel Heller was for me more a matter of embarrassment than anything else. At the beginning of each term in elementary school, it was the procedure of the teacher to call the children one by one to the desk in front of the classroom to obtain information that included the father's name and perhaps his occupation. Someone, teacher or sister, taught me the word *deceased*. I said it always in a repentant murmur brought low by a burden of shame and humiliation, and I hoped none of my classmates would hear.

I did not feel I missed him. In later years, I might even wisecrack irreverently when hearing someone talk of an appalling home life caused by a father that I was fortunate mine was gone before he could inflict much damage. But I was biting my fingernails at the age of seven. And except for two hospital confinements very much later, during which my anxieties were focused on inescapable concerns, I have gone on biting them and I still do. In my late teens and afterward, I was suffering headaches before I understood what headaches were. Earlier, when someone spoke of a headache, I had no grasp of what was meant; once I did get the idea, I realized that I had been having them all along, usually on weekend mornings and afternoons. They've stopped. I studied my face in the mirror excessively. I had overheard that I was a good-looking child, mostly from repeated comments by my sister's girlfriends, and I wanted to reassure myself that I had not changed for the worse. I suffered boils more often than what was considered normal and had a school year of warts: There were seventeen on my hands and arms, including one large flat one on an elbow that didn't disintegrate with the others and had to be burned off by Dr. Abe Levine (who charged two dollars for the office visit and the treatment). I had a crazy fear I was going bald, because the hairline at my forehead was so much higher than at my ears. I did what I conceived I could to "train" my hair, and I moved the part from one side to the other, and then to the center and then off again to the side, and then tried it without a part, plastered flat with a stiffening hair tonic, and then with waves. I did other little things I still wouldn't want to tell anybody. I measured my height by the level of my eyes and therefore believed dismally that I was half a head shorter than I indeed was—that I was much shorter than boys who were shorter than I. It was vanity, of course, but I'm inclined now to believe that it was a very anxious vanity founded on a wobbly formation of what R. D. Laing might have called "ontological insecurity."

I was prone to fantasizing, daydreaming—and to good effect: I brought my rather overworking imagination into the classroom in book reports and compositions, and in this schoolwork I excelled. I can think of these examples: For a book report on *Tom Sawyer* in one of the earliest grades I donned the mantle of Tom Sawyer tasked with the assignment of writing a book report on the work in which he is the principal personality; in the seventh grade, when I was about twelve, for an autobiographical written assignment supposedly by a subject in history, I became, in a first-person account—not Abraham Lincoln, which would have been ordinary, others would have chosen him—but the *metal* in the gun that was used to shoot him. I was born, I remember, in a mine in Chile, in a shovelful of iron ore. Papers like these were read aloud as outstanding, which was the reward I aimed for. I very strongly did want to excel and be noticed.

And one time I used some savings to surprise my brother with a gift for Father's Day. I bought him a carton of cigarettes, Camels, and it cost a dollar then. And I still am unable to decide, aware now of unconscious motivation, whether the deed was one of sincere gratitude and affection or merely a stunt contrived to excite comment and win me some complimentary attention. Or both. Another time, nearing the age of sixty, while experimenting with psychoanalysis as a remedy for alleviating stressful moods in the throes of a rancorous divorce, I had a coherent dream in which my brother, Lee, who then was living and in good health, was dead and resurrected from the grave to rejoin the family in the old apartment house in Coney Island, where my mother, who had long since died, was alive and active. On my back on the analyst's couch, I protested astutely that I probably wouldn't have had that dream of my father-as-brother the night before were I not in this treatment and if I hadn't known I would be coming to see him that morning. And he, chuckling in his upholstered armchair, didn't disagree, and conceded that the psychoanalytical process was indeed to a large extent "neurogenic," a word I had not heard before and have not heard since.

NOT LONG AFTER my father died, we moved from our old apartment into one of equal size directly across the street, and that is the one I think of as the home in which I grew from childhood. It had four rooms. All of the apartments seemed to have four rooms, one a full kitchen, one a living room that routinely also functioned as somebody's sleeping place. In spring, with us as with others, the ROOM FOR RENT sign went up, the notice went out to neighbors, and we took in a boarder for the summer, usually a single adult or an adult couple with friends or relatives nearby. None of us, not my brother or sister or I, could recall with certainty how we disposed of ourselves for the period in which we gave up that room. My sister does remember a situation in our first apartment with two parents and a child boarding in one room, while one of us slept in the kitchen. She can't remember which one of us it was.

It was to one of these boarders that I owe my first exposure to classical music. He politely requested permission to tune in to station WNYC on our radio when it wasn't in use (in use by me, usually, listening—to the despair of my mother—to big-band swing). WNYC was a classical music station. I didn't have to listen when he played the music he preferred, but I did have to hear. And I was overwhelmed when I recognized in these classical performances so many melodies already familiar to me as popular songs from *Your Hit Parade* and other radio programs: "Our Love," "I'm Always Chasing Rainbows," "You Are [perhaps "This Is"] My Song of Love," "The Lamp Is Low," and a host, more than one host, of others ("The Isle of May," "April Showers," "No Star Is Lost in My Blue Heaven," Tchaikovsky again, and what appeared to be a genuine Negro spiritual and was, in fact, astonishingly, the largo from Dvořák's *New World* symphony, "Going Home"). And it was while I was listening alertly to discover more of these that other strains I hadn't heard before were played and repeated and became recognizable and appreciated.

When families moved from one flat in Coney Island to another, it was mainly to take advantage of the usual "concession"—a rent-free first month or two given to the new tenant. When they moved away from Coney Island into areas of loftier economic standing, it was because they could at last afford to. The clearest memory I preserve of our earlier apartment was of my brother, after all our belongings had been transferred, going back with me and bringing a broom to sweep out, still one more time, the corners of all the rooms. He didn't want the new tenants, he explained, to think that the ones preceding them, us, were slobs. He would retain this conscientious and considerate trait, this regard for comportment, till the end of his life.

In the new apartment, after being put to bed, I would frequently and furtively imagine, or hope, that a policeman was stationed at each end of our segment of the dark block, keeping vigilant watch on my building and window to safeguard me from—I cannot imagine what. Except for the threat of true poverty, against which I was protectively kept ignorant, there were no dangers. Both inside and outside the house we were safe. There were no kidnappings or burglaries, and always in decent weather there were scores of kids on the street to play with, and grown-ups to watch and keep an eye on us. From the earliest grades on, we were encouraged, boys and girls, to walk on our own to the grade school close to half a mile away, crossing streets. We walked home for lunch at noon, walked back to school for the afternoon session, returned on foot when classes ended at three, without fear, without harm. Except in summer, there wasn't much danger from automobiles; this was a low-income neighborhood during the Great Depression, and there weren't many automobiles. From about the age of nine or ten, we could play in the street at night or roam the board-walk until we sagged with sleepiness or someone came to fetch us.

The two apartments I spoke of were in buildings on a side street that ran between Surf Avenue, the thoroughfare that was closest to the boardwalk and seashore, and, receding from Surf Avenue in a direction opposite the beach, the tracks of a trolley line running in a straight sand-and-stony trench we called Railroad Avenue. Once across these tracks on my walk to school, I might be joined by my friend Albie Covelman, a classmate from the second half of first grade on, or, a few years later, by Seymour Ostrow, who had moved to our block from Sea Gate, a sequestered, private settlement a few streets past the other side of the school, after his own father died. At Mermaid Avenue, we would join a thickening pedestrian flow of other friends and acquaintances from school who were coming from homes a few streets past my own. At the school, waiting on line as instructed or romping about the spacious yard, there would be many more boys and girls from kindergarten classes through eighth grade. They had come from all directions. I must note that I remember no blacks in my elementary school, and none in my high school, not even on the football or basketball teams. The high school, several miles away, drew its students from a number of surrounding areas of diverse populations, but not yet so diverse as to include "Negroes." I recall no discussions of the subject before World War II.

The streets in Coney Island were divided into three residential segments, sometimes four, by Surf Avenue, by the trolley line, and by Mermaid Avenue, which had the most stores. Some of the streets had apartment houses between the beach and Surf Avenue, others didn't. On one whole block of prime property between the boardwalk and Surf Avenue and open only in summertime was a Catholic orphanage for boys, who came, I think, for short stays. With fair hair and milky, freckled skin they looked sickly to us when we passed and stared; and we, with our suntans and dark complexions, must have seemed peculiar and exotic to them. The avenues paralleled each other on linear courses from the high fences and guarded entrances of Sea Gate at one end of Coney Island to the final station of the BMT subway train routes in the amusement section in the middle, and each of the three segments between them was thickly populated, each block of each street a close-knit miniature village in its own right. Surf Avenue, the largest of them, ran past the train stop into and through the amusement area, past the games and rides and other sidewalk attractions; a Surf Avenue trolley line that began outside Sea Gate ran well past Coney Island and came to its last stop at Sheepshead Bay.

Despite its bustle, solid population, and long eminence, Coney Island is not impressive in size and not really an island but part of a Brooklyn sand spit hardly more than half a mile wide, with the ocean on one side and a bay, Gravesend Bay, bordering the other. In that small span of street in which we lived, surely no more than two hundred yards between Surf Avenue and the Norton's Point trolley tracks, there were four apartment houses of three or four stories each and a sprinkling of smaller dwellings for one or two families, and there were always enough other boys of the right age to play our street games with, the older boys training us to catch and throw a ball when they needed more players to complete a team. Girls, too. My sister, near eighty now and living in Florida, is still friendly with several women she met on the block in those days. And there were always parents, mostly smiling mothers, happily overseeing us from the windowsills of their apartments as we played ball or tag or roller-skated. When weather and domestic chores permitted, they sat outdoors on chairs carried downstairs and placed alongside each other in front of the apartment houses on both sides of the street, conversing with each other in Yiddish, with us in English, or in a patois of both.

Regularly on pleasant afternoons as they sat there, a Mrs. Shatzkin who lived near us would trudge by, carrying in a sack of black oilcloth a large covered kettle holding homemade potato knishes—thick, circular, good-sized dumplings of mashed potatoes richly seasoned with pepper and browned onions in pockets of a special dough of her own invention which were deep-fried in vegetable oil— freshly made and still warm, and from which she strived to eke out her living. She made another kind, too, with a filling of a buckwheat grain called kasha. Both kinds were unusually good, and sold for a nickel apiece. My mother was among those who relished them, and would call me to her to share one with me. A Mrs. Gelber, who lived around the corner on Surf Avenue, made in her kitchen what we called "jelly apples" and carried them around to sell. They cost a nickel, too. Soon she was making them in quantity to supply food stands in the amusement area. And soon Mrs. Shatzkin had leased a large storefront on the corner, with a staff of middle-aged women—probably relatives, because they all resembled her—making her knishes in full view and selling them to customers on the street; then she expanded into a much larger outlet on the more crowded boardwalk and supplied food stands in other locations, too. At least four generations of Shatzkins, all with the same florid faces, stippled with large brown and gray freckles, earned their keep from the knishes originated by the maternal founder of that thrifty dynasty.

Other women came by frequently with trays of sesame candies and the like, which sold for two pennies apiece. Some early evenings in spring, summer, and fall, a hearty black woman would appear in the street and in the courtyards of the summer bungalow colonies—a street singer singing Yiddish songs with accurate Yiddish pronunciation. If we were upstairs, my mother invariably would wrap a few pennies in a scrap of newspaper and toss them down from the window, as she did with others who arrived to serenade us with accordions or violins. My mother had the same keen appreciation for food that I am blessed with, though not nearly my capacity. She was particularly fond of certain salty, smoky flavors. Toward the final years of her life she surreptitiously came upon bacon and instantly found the taste delicious. Who wouldn't? She adored smoked whitefish, too.

So do I. I look like her, though I'm taller. High forehead that is broad and flat, large face with prominent cheekbones, a determined, sometimes surly mouth. Not long ago, my friend Marvin, who lives a distance away, exclaimed on the resemblance after we hadn't seen each other for a couple of years. My sister and brother grew more and more to look like each other as they aged. Their wide eyes were a clear, bright blue. Mine, like my mother's, are brown.

ALL OF US in Coney Island did whatever we legally could to earn what money we needed, and somehow everyone I know of managed to fare pretty well. The fathers all worked, as did the older brothers and sisters as soon as they had liberated themselves from high school by graduating. Almost none of us then thought seriously about going to college or wanted to go, or could have afforded to. (My brother did want to go, would have given anything to have been able to, my sister, Sylvia, tells me.) For me, years before the time for decision, Lee was sending away for catalogs and applications to colleges such as MIT, Oberlin, Harvard, Yale, and others of that elevated level for which I could not possibly have paid and to which I could not then conceivably have gained admission. At New York University after the war, when I was selected in my junior year for membership in Phi Beta Kappa—as much for success with the publication of a few short stories as for classroom distinction—I didn't know what Phi Beta Kappa was. But Lee did and was flushed with pleasure in the pride he took in me. "Some Phi Beta Kappa," was his happy comment on that ignorance of mine. But for him it was already too late for college, and I couldn't be sure whether a longing for a university education was another painful disappointment he suffered or merely a whimsical reverie in which he indulged. He owned a tennis racquet, which he kept in a wooden press in a closet and which I never saw him use. I don't know where that came from, if not from a few summers when he was away as a camp counselor. He had a Red Cross badge for lifesaving which he earned in those days. At times as he aged he could be arbitrary, critical, and argumentative over very small matters—what bread was best for what kind of sandwich. But he was instinctively obliging and well-mannered, especially with strangers.

For a while, a very short while, when I was just eighteen, in a concession to respectable conformity I did accede to the plan of applying for admission to night school at Brooklyn College. My high-school transcript was better than average, and I was accepted. However, I decided impulsively one evening before term began, while sleepily registering for classes, that I much preferred my nighttime social life, unremarkable as that was, and I dropped out before attending. When the time arrived that I was able to go, felt realistically that I *could* go, to college, I wanted to and did. I was twenty-two when I started, and I enrolled like a million or two other recent American war veterans, with the federal government paying a monthly subsistence allowance and just about all my educational costs.

Most of the fathers I knew of had salaried jobs in Manhattan in what was called "the garment center," performing one specialized function or another in the sequence essential to the manufacture of clothing. None advanced to salesmen. But a number of friends in the expanding circle I acquired as I grew up came from families with small businesses of their own right there in Coney Island, mostly stores: Louie Kessler, Solly Mirror, and Lenny Karafiol owned bakeries.

Esther Dessick's family owned the fish store—none of these retail shops on Mermaid Avenue filled premises roomy enough to be called markets. Lily Dashevsky came from fruits and vegetables, Murray Singer's father was the butcher. Louie Berkman's father owned a lucrative junk-yard. Marvin Winkler's father prospered as a bookmaker and eventually was able to move his family into the richer milieu of Sea Gate. In the flat just below our apartment lived Irving Kaiser, a year younger than I but a friend from early childhood who was one of the three people I grew up with who were killed in the war, and just below him on street level was the tailor shop owned by his father. And the father of Danny the Bull was a barber.

LOOKING BACK, I find it something of a miracle that from such a beginning the four of us in my family separately and independently eventually found ourselves through most of our lives with enough money to satisfy our needs and our material wants. Our expectations, while varying considerably, were disciplined. We did not want what we could not hope to have, and we were not made bitter or envious by knowing of people who had much more. The occasional neighborhood Communist proselytizer got nowhere with us. Neither, I must record, did the dedicated anti-Communist ideologue, not then or later. We worked at what we could because we never doubted we had to work, and we felt fortunate indeed that we could find work.

In time, both my brother and sister with their spouses were able to retire comfortably to modest dwellings in West Palm Beach, Florida, with savings and pension benefits from companies with which each had been working many years, Sylvia from her employment with Macy's as a minor executive, a sales supervisor in one department or another, my brother as head of the mail room at MCA, the thriving talent agency that eventually acquired the Universal Pictures motion-picture studio. People I've run into who worked with my sister invariably speak of her with tremendous affection. Men I've met who worked for my brother describe him as a gracious, generous, helpful, and kind boss. It has proved impossible for me to give either one of them anything. Once I tried to buy my brother a better car than the one he was driving in Florida, and was not allowed to.

Right or wrong, I'm convinced that no one in the family lied to the others about anything, or to anyone else. If they did, it would only be to say they were feeling all right when they weren't, or that there was nothing they needed when there might be something they did.

Following the success of my first novel, published when I was thirty-eight, there was a considerable financial return from my second, *Something Happened,* and I was able to retire from my own salaried position, which was with the English Department of the City College of New York, where I had spent the previous four years. I went on writing, of course, but I thought of this work—think of it now, at this very moment!—not so much as working for money but as a challenging and eternally and increasingly harrowing (and remunerative) application of the mind to leisure, in much the same way I imagine a rock climber or mountain hiker contends with his pastime or an amateur bridge player or golfer tussles with the frustrations and adversities of his particular obsessive recreation. I make a living from mine.

ELSEWHERE DURING MY CHILDHOOD, in the world and in this country, there was turmoil. There were violent strikes. Blacks were lynched, and photographs of these heartless crimes seemed invariably to picture among the lynchers men wearing the American Legion field caps of veterans of World War I. Labor organizers in rural communities were beaten, jailed. A bonus army of veterans descended on Washington, D.C., with demands for a promised payment and was forcibly dispersed by military units commanded by officers soon to be honored in World

War II. In the weekly newsreels in movie theaters we watched infuriated dairy farmers spill into streams milk they couldn't sell at a profit; countless people who would have wanted the milk lacked money to buy it. There were no jobs for huge and growing numbers. For the evicted and other homeless there were shantytowns across the country called Hoovervilles, so named for the sitting president, Herbert Hoover. Men stood on breadlines, families were fed in soup kitchens. Banks failed.

Somehow, we, on that minute parcel of seashore at the lower tip of Brooklyn that was home to separate but overlapping neighborhoods mainly of Jewish and Italian families, managed to escape the worst of the consequences of the stock-market crash and the Depression. And so, it seemed, did most of the nearby districts of Brooklyn, one of five boroughs in New York City, which, with approximately two million residents, had as it does now a population greater than all but the few largest cities in the country.

I don't know how that happened or why we were so lucky.

I do know that the prevailing sympathy in our locality was always automatically for all strikers, and for the poor and the downtrodden. This meant we were not Republicans. Chanting with others "Hoover, Hoover, rah, rah, rah/Put him in the ashcan, ha, ha, ha!" in a torchlight parade on election eve in November 1932 was my first political action, taken at the age of nine years, six months.

THE HEALTH OF the four of us was generally very good. I remember no illness of significance striking any of us until well past the age of fifty. It would have been hard to tell if our health hadn't been good, since no one in our family made a fashion of ailments or talked much about the distress they brought. My brother, even in his last years, even with one excruciating foot infection that swelled the tissues until the flesh seemed ready to explode, would consistently

attempt to minimize his condition; he put off going to a doctor *for anything* until further postponement was no longer
humanly, humanely, possible, until symptoms or someone
forced him to go.

Late in my mother's life, however, there was one accident of permanent and drastic consequence. While I was
away in preflight training at aviation cadet school in Santa
Ana, California, she, at home alone, tumbled from a stool
while hanging kitchen curtains and broke a hip. She
dragged herself to the kitchen window and, spying Jeannie
Goldman, a girl my age who lived in a facing apartment
just across the street, shouted out to her for help. Jeannie
rushed upstairs—apartment doors then were never locked
in the daytime, there was no need—and telephoned for the
ambulance.

Perhaps it was that crawl across the floor that did it:
Emergency treatment and surgery as a ward patient in
Coney Island Hospital left her with one leg shorter than the
other, and she was reduced to walking in one heavier, built-
up shoe and with a limp and a cane.

She went on doing everything in the house she had done
before, including shopping on Mermaid Avenue and climb-
ing the stairs to our apartment two floors above street level,
but the cane and the observable limp were humiliations over
which she never stopped grieving for as long as she lived.
She had my vanity, or I inherited hers. If ever she needed
assistance for anything unusual or just wanted to talk, she
would bang with her cane on the floor, and Mrs. Rose
Kaiser would come up from below to accommodate her.
When Mrs. Kaiser, by then also a widow, died and unknown new tenants moved in below, my mother's spirit
seemed to ebb, and she lapsed more and more into that
hopeless, emotionless state of resignation we recognize so
often in the aged. But from her, there was never a plea or
complaint. In my fifties I grew friendly with the novelist
James Jones, whose mother was alive and ailing, and one
time in answer to his question I told him that both my

parents had long since passed on. Grimly, he responded: "You're lucky." Grimly, I understood him.

BUT FARTHER BACK, in better days, I can find a deeply satisfying episode that bonded us closely to each other; this was the time when I, so much younger than the others, was nevertheless able to cooperate with Sylvia and Lee to help teach my mother sufficient English to qualify her to vote.

She voted for Roosevelt, of course, for Franklin Delano Roosevelt, as did everyone else in the neighborhood, if not, as it felt to us, the world. And then, for the office of New York State governor and later of U.S. senator, for Herbert Lehman, who possessed the double virtue of being not only a New Deal Democrat but also a Jew. These candidates always won. I couldn't vote until the election of 1944, while still overseas in the service, and I voted for Roosevelt by absentee ballot. He won again. I wasn't wounded in the war. I wasn't killed, either, or taken prisoner, and those were the good old, gone-but-not-forgotten days when the candidates I favored most had the best chance of election. That never happens anymore. Even now, though I know this is an illusion, it feels improbable to me that there should have been any such curious things back then as Jewish Republicans, and perhaps there weren't any. The brass ring seemed good as gold.

2

Coney

CONEY ISLAND, with its beaches, crowds, commotion, and couple of hundred entertainments, has always been magical to children and a gaudy magnet for adults. People came from everywhere. Early in this century, even Sigmund Freud dropped in for a look on his trip to the United States; the Russian author Maxim Gorky was a sightseer, too. The milling crowds through the 1930s included soldiers on leave and sailors in port, crewmen in the American and foreign merchant marine. Whole families, sometimes clans of extended families, would journey from Manhattan and the Bronx and other parts of Brooklyn to spend the day and early evening. Those who eschewed the lockers and other facilities of the bathhouses would make camp on blankets under the boardwalk, changing in and out of bathing suits, eating from tubs of cooked foods prepared at home before setting out. The place was better known than we who lived there realized and had been a famous, and notorious, playland and summer resort far longer than we could appreciate—at its most wicked when its first recreational community was established at Norton's Point just after the Civil War at the western tip of what later came to be called Sea Gate. Visitors came by ferry. So infamous for vice did

Norton's Point grow—for pickpockets, prostitutes, gamblers, hoodlums—that numbers of tough and cunning rogues with schemes of their own began moving eastward for safety into what eventually grew to become Coney Island proper.

The founding of Luna Park and George C. Tilyou's Steeplechase Park dates back to the last years of the 1890s. Both had been long established and were already in decline by the time I grew aware of them. Although I didn't know it until I began this history, at one period there were three prominent horse-racing tracks in the area: one in Sheepshead Bay close by, another in the district called Gravesend, to which all of Coney Island is joined; and another in Brighton Beach, closer still.

Notable stake races of the present day like the Suburban and Futurity Handicaps were features of the season and were better known nationally than the Kentucky Derby; the Preakness for its first fifteen years was in Coney Island too. Prizefighting also: The first contest in New York State for the world heavyweight title took place at the Coney Island Athletic Club (in 1899, between Bob Fitzsimmons and James Jeffries. Jeffries triumphed, though a three-to-one underdog). The racing season brought socialites with names like Whitney, Vanderbilt, and Belmont into this home area of mine, as well as big spenders of lesser pedigree. The socially correct visitors preferred the sedate environment of Manhattan Beach and Oriental Beach at the eastern end of what was then called the Island. But the trainers and jockeys as well as the touts, gamblers, and other raffish drifters who followed the horses, and the prizefights, too, also came in thick crowds and brought business and action into the lively center, to the hotels and eating places and to the beer gardens with their singing waiters and female entertainers, to flirtatious beer-hall waitresses hustling customers to drink more, and to freelance prostitutes as well, of whom, I now learn, there were continually growing numbers. A New York State antibetting law of 1909 put an end to Coney

Island as a center of horse racing in the East. All three tracks were gone by the time I came along, and the only horseflesh we knew belonged to the iceman, the milkman, and the man at the reins of the Brighton Laundry wagon.

Surviving into my time was the spacious, elegant German beer garden Feltman's, a famous meeting place for fun-loving celebrities of the Gay Nineties, but it was on the way out by the time I discovered it. It was the original Mr. Feltman himself who is credited with inventing the frankfurter, a small boiled sausage that he served on a roll. Also in operation in my time as a Coney Island amusement was an exhibition of premature babies in incubators. I swear to God it's true! I now find out that the facility was the enterprise of a European physician of some international reputation, staffed with nurses, containing up-to-date equipment, and devoting more effort to preserving the lives of these infants than hospitals at the time were inclined to do. Nonetheless, it does seem grotesque.

CONEY ISLAND WAS generously extolled in hit songs that are still sung: in Rodgers and Hart's "Manhattan" and "The Lady Is a Tramp," and in Cole Porter's "You're the Top," in which a night at Coney is up there with the Colosseum and the Louvre museum, the Tower of Pisa and the Mona Lisa. In film, too, the place was celebrated. Year after year, those weekly newsreels typical of the 1930s never failed to highlight the opening of the season each Decoration Day weekend with a shot of a flat-bottomed boat accelerating down the watery slope of the Shoot-the-Chutes in Luna Park, and another of one of the circular rides in operation in Steeplechase Park, or of a woman's skirt blown above her head by an unexpected blast of air from a hidden jet in the floor. In the movie *Manhattan Melodrama* of the early thirties, characters played by William Powell and Myrna Loy go to Coney Island on a date. In *The Devil and Miss Jones,* Robert Cummings and Jean Arthur join the Coney Island crowds for pleasure on a day off from work, accompanied by Spring Byington and Charles Coburn. William Powell and Myrna Loy and Robert Cummings and Jean Arthur might all well have gone there as their natural selves, too, for celebrities were continually reported by people who knew people who swore they had spotted them.

Celebrity sightings were most common after the Labor Day holiday during a series of nightly parades called Mardi Gras, which were contrived to signal the close of the season on the one hand while, on the other, prolonging it by several days. Oddly, this postseason celebration also claimed the high moral purpose of providing money to rebuild the Coney Island Rescue Home, a shelter for wayward girls that had burned down. Predictably, the effect of those parades was to attract hopeful floods of yet more wayward girls to the area.

In the 1920s, lawmakers finally began bringing about reforms that eventually transformed Coney Island's character. These changes were accelerated by improvements in electric trolley-car service and in the extension of the subway system into the Island itself, right to a busy crossroad on Surf Avenue. For a fare of only a nickel, rapid transport brought in multitudes of people seeking safe and inexpensive varieties of recreation, and by the thirties, my era, the sinful prestige of the notorious beach resort was unearned and all but gone.

At the Mardi Gras parades from then on, for those of us quickly bored by the marchers, the greatest joy consisted of nothing more exciting than throwing handfuls of confetti into the faces of girls, who appeared flattered by these attentions. It was not much fun. In rowdier days, I've read, rougher sports would stuff the confetti down and up their dresses and into their mouths. That doesn't seem like much fun either.

Noticeable in almost all the sophisticated tributes to Coney Island I've cited is a more than faint aura of the patronizing, of people going slumming for fun. They are making a fashion of the unfashionable, in much the same jaunty spirit in which chic and adventurous New Yorkers would safely voyage up to Harlem before the war, my war, for the music and the food (mainly spareribs) and also to buy marijuana. I don't know where those Coney Island addicts on the needle like Danny the Bull, Raymie Glickman, Philly Penner, George Weiss, and others went for their heroin after the war, for I had married shortly after my discharge and moved from Brooklyn, and that was not something I could have found out from my mother.

It didn't take long for me or any of the others migrating into the broader world to learn that one widely used way of deprecating a place was, and still is, to scoff that it is just like Coney Island. And, for the record, no one I've known from Coney has ever referred to Coney Island by just that abbreviated term "Coney."

BY 1920, soon after the BMT subway company extended four of its lines into Coney Island, huge masses of people were arriving—first, tens of thousands on summer weekends, then hundreds of thousands, finally a million and more. Most came now from the working classes and the newly emerging lower-middle class. Many belonged to immigrant groups recently settled in the East, especially from Eastern Europe (Jews) and Southern Europe (Italians). The Irish were already there, as were the Germans and Scandinavians. Witness the names of enterprises already established: Hahn's Baths, Scoville's, Feltman's, Stauch's, Paddy Shea's Saloon, Shannon's. A man named Handwerker, first name Nathan (a nephew went to high school with me), had fortuitously opened a small hot-dog stand on Surf Avenue just across the street from the corner on which the terminal of the new subway station arose, selling his savory product from a griddle for only five cents, in contrast to Feltman's costlier boiled ones for ten cents. Feltman may have invented the hot dog, but Nathan's perfected it, and soon customers stood in packs five deep, clamoring to be served.

Probably it was about then, with the subway now granting convenient access to just about anywhere else in the city, that the wood bungalows, brick homes, and apartment houses I knew began to be built and immigrant families to move in. As early as 1921, a progressive reformer, Bruce Bliven, was complaining in the progressive *New Republic* about a new population that was displacing "native American Stock." He had noticed that just about all of the people he saw on the Coney Island beach now seemed to have "black hair."

EVEN AT THIS LATE DATE, people I meet with a large stock of memories of visits to Coney Island still express surprise upon hearing that I grew up there, that families lived there, and still do, and that children were brought up there, and still are.

The single image they retain is of a gigantic, sprawling, fenced-in amusement area with an abundance of games and rides, of sideshows and food stands, that is closed down and locked up at the end of each season until the following spring. In fact, though, the amusement area was perhaps only fifteen blocks long, on a strip only one block deep from Surf Avenue to the boardwalk, in a seaside community that is about two and a half miles long and about half a mile wide and which, by contemporary suburban standards, was densely populated with year-round residents. Even back in 1929, when I entered kindergarten, there were sufficient families with young children living in Coney Island to overcrowd the two elementary schools there—and each of these stood five stories high and a full block wide. One was in the Jewish area, the other in the Italian, but this division into Jewish and Italian was anything but absolute. There were Bartolinis, Palumbos, Salimeris, and a Charlie Anderson in my school, P.S. 188, and a Klineline (German) and Bannon

on my street, and there were Mandels, Goldbergs, and
Kesslers in the other school, P.S. 80, which rose near both
the Catholic church and a synagogue of yellow brick on
Mermaid Avenue that was perhaps the largest of the several
in Coney Island. A Julia Revelli was in my class all the way
through elementary school.

The second apartment house in which we lived was
owned for a few years after we moved in by the Provenzano
family. They dwelled on the second-floor front, opposite the
Kaiser family across the large landing, which sometimes
served as a play area. Tony Provenzano was a year older
than I, proportionately larger, and probably stronger. I
never had to find out. Tony was disconcertingly rigid in his
unwillingness to cooperate in automatically allowing me to
take the lead in deciding the games to be played or to
assume the captainship of the team, as all the others of our
approximate age group in the street were inclined to do.
There was in the Provenzano apartment a player piano with
a wealth of piano rolls. I was endlessly fascinated and would
listen as long as they would let me. Tony had a large collection of lead soldiers, too, the first I'd seen, and we played
with them also, although there isn't much one can do with
lead soldiers except stand them up and look at them and try,
without much gratification, to play at war. Across that first-
floor hall in Irving Kaiser's apartment was an early phono-
graph—a Victrola, as all phonographs were then called
generically. It was wound up and powered by a hand crank.
The favorite record, preferred even to a couple by Enrico
Caruso, was one called "Cohen on the Telephone," a comic
monologue by a man with a Yiddish accent attempting with
ineffectual desperation to place a phone call. The records,
like those in our cellar clubs much later, were made of shel-
lac; they were played with a metal needle, and they shat-
tered if dropped. There was a complete set of volumes in the
Kaiser apartment called *The Book of Knowledge* that held
our interest for hours. (For a short while, the Kaisers had a

summer boarder who also held my interest: She was a snappy young lady from Pennsylvania who walked about freely in a half slip and brassiere, and I would drop downstairs and hang around casually with Irving in the hope of again seeing her half undressed. In a week or so she had a man of middle years as a gentleman caller, a man who owned a concession in the amusement center. And a week or so after that, she was removed by the police.) *The Book of Knowledge* contained not only simple information about almost everything in the world; it also provided instructions for making and doing things. Howie and Henny Ehrenman, brothers in an apartment house on Surf Avenue just around the corner, still remember that I ruined their mother's best frying pan one afternoon, demonstrating how to make perfect butterscotch from *The Book of Knowledge*. They remember I ruined the butterscotch, too.

When Nettie, one of the two Provenzano daughters (the other was Rosemarie), had her church wedding, the Hellers attended as a family, possibly excepting my brother, who tried to avoid all such ceremonial events as assiduously as I attempt to avoid them now. That was the first time any of us had been inside a Christian church of any kind. I wouldn't bet that any of us felt we had a right to be there.

After the Provenzano family surrendered ownership of the apartment house, they moved down into the Italian section of Coney Island, on Surf Avenue just about opposite one of the several stretches occupied by Steeplechase Park. I went at least once to visit them in their new quarters. The next time I passed that way, Tony had a food stand in the building and we waved. The last time I passed, the food stand was gone. So was Steeplechase Park, all but the framework of the defunct Parachute Jump, which still towers as a mournful landmark, presumably because the cost of demolishing it would be higher than anyone might wish to spend to be rid of it. And Irving Kaiser, as I've said, was killed in the war, in Italy. If, as I've heard, his life was ended by an artillery shell, it could be that he never knew what hit him. In that one respect, just that one, it might be said he was lucky.

Today, the Italian neighborhood remains; the Italian restaurants best known then, Gargulio's and Carolina, are still functioning. But the Jewish section, right up to the barrier gates of Sea Gate—which are guarded more vigilantly today than ever before by a private security force—has given way almost wholly to a population mainly Hispanic and African American. There are fewer stores; possibly no supermarkets; and, I am given to believe from newspaper reports, a higher crime rate than in my day. When last I looked, the storefronts on Mermaid Avenue still stood, but most were boarded up at the windows and had nothing going on inside. I wondered then what residents did for a convenient drugstore, tailor, or shoe-repair shop. People in Sea Gate today must drive a good distance to a mall for all their marketing. At Surf Avenue and West 31st Street, where my two old apartment houses had been, two tall modern units of a housing project stand.

Coney Island is, of course, in lower Brooklyn, at the lowest tip, lying laterally along the southern front of that borough like an inverted anvil facing the Atlantic Ocean just outside the mouth of New York Harbor. It is attached to Brooklyn at the Gravesend section and runs from Norton's Point at the western end of Sea Gate, which it includes, eastward in a descending order of numbered streets that now contain the city's Aquarium at West 8th Street and end at Ocean Parkway. There Coney Island terminates at the beginning of a contiguous locality called Brighton and/or Brighton Beach. Past Brighton is Sheepshead Bay, thriving in past days with seafood restaurants and flotillas of public, party-fishing boats. And on the south side of the bay along that same unbroken stretch of shorefront lies the smaller community of Manhattan Beach. Manhattan Beach was once prized for its formal hotels and upper-class residents and vacationers, who came mainly for the horse races in

Sheepshead Bay. In a later life it had a pair of fancy casinos; these were not gambling places but dance halls presenting famous bands and singers of the time. Brighton Beach was known for its handball players and handball competitions. Manhattan Beach was considered the most well-to-do section; Sea Gate was next; then Brighton. Coney Island was the lowest in income level but by far the best known and most exciting. People from the other sections frequently came to ours to dance at our social clubs and ride the rides. We did not often go to theirs.

While certainly not a slum, Coney Island was in my time a depressed area for its year-round dwellers, except for Sea Gate, and this is even truer today than in the past. It appears to me today a rather squalid scene, and it must have seemed so back then to others better off than we who weren't living there. The older my mother became, the more she detested the place for its harsh and rowdy intrusions, especially in summer, when the streets were constantly filled with people and noise, often late into the night. Screened apartment windows were open at night, for this was before the days when air conditioners were ubiquitous. My mother liked the bathing and, before the accident of the broken hip, would go to the beach on sunny days, taking along an empty milk bottle to fill with ocean water for washing the sand from her feet when she returned. But she was distressed and angered by the vulgar turmoil and ceaseless, turbulent motion, the sheer volume and activity, of the crowds everywhere. Bitterly she would denounce our part of the world as a "*chozzer* mart," a pig market. I might feel secretly chastened when I heard her, but I was also secretly unsympathetic, for I was part of the restless commotion and, once old enough for membership in one of the local social clubs, thoughtlessly helped contribute to the din and disorder of the street with our late-night banter and our club room's outdoor loudspeakers blasting away with "jump" music from the unrelenting record players within.

We were children from poor families, but didn't know

it. I don't think I have ever in my life thought of myself as underprivileged, as unfairly deprived of something I might reasonably wish to own and didn't. Although incomes were low, everyone's father did seem to have a job, and later everyone's older brother and sister; finally, we, too, were out of school and working. It was a blessing of our childhood to be oblivious of our low economic state and of how others might regard us. We had our beach and our boardwalk, our safe streets, the food and clothing we needed, and I don't believe the circumstance of moderate poverty was too upsetting to our parents either. Nearly all were immigrants and living on a roughly equal level. This was the nature of life; they had learned that in Europe. It was not stylish to bemoan. They expected life to be hard, and most were living better than they had been able to in the Old World. I doubt that many had known the luxury of running water, central heating, and indoor plumbing before they arrived in America. Until my mother and my brother, the latter a child of six, set out on the sea journey to New York from somewhere in western Russia—they sailed separately on different voyages, for my father's first wife was still alive, and he and my mother had not yet met—neither had seen an orange. My brother was offered his first one on the steamship carrying him across the Atlantic. Because it was an object alien to him, he refused it. The next day, after hearing from others how wonderful the flavor was, he was eager to try, but the supply was exhausted; there were no more.

That was life, too.

The elders in our families worked hard, both the men and the women, and did not often quarrel. Quarreling was not how things got settled. They didn't drink to excess and seldom divorced, and, unless they were more artfully circumspect than my own generation, they didn't fool with the wives or husbands of their friends and neighbors.

I once heard George Mandel, an early friend from Coney Island and the first of the people I knew to succeed in becoming a novelist, present in a television interview a description of Coney Island I wouldn't try to improve upon: If a person did have to grow up in a slum (he used that word *slum* for comic exaggeration) he could imagine no better one.

THERE WERE apartment houses on just about every side street in my section of Coney Island and on every block of the avenues they crossed. All of the larger ones were brick buildings with three or four landings of apartments above the ground floor, which might contain a row of stores like Mr. Kaiser's tailor shop downstairs and, for a while as in mine, a corner grocery store, later remodeled into another couple of apartments. On every street were narrower, lower houses made for the most part of dull yellow brick, with porches up a stoop of stairs and basements below street level, and these could be dwelling places for two or three families, though many were owned and occupied by single families. Of the larger apartment houses, none but a few of the newer ones provided elevators. These were self-service, and for a while were baffling contraptions of great interest as well as places for restful, occasionally mischievous, play on rainy days. Pressing all the buttons to slow the passage of the elevator and irritate the next passengers was one of our tricks. A scene from this time I still preserve in my memory is of aging men and women (eventually the old men and women were our fathers and mothers, and my own mother was among them) laboring up the steep flights of stairs, the women usually with arms filled with brown bags from the grocer or butcher. Anyone in our family going downstairs from our second-floor domicile was reminded to "take down the garbage" to the covered metal pails always waiting in the alleyway of our house. There were wooden houses, too, some with small yards in front and back, meager gardens, with an architecture of clapboard walls and sloping, shingled rooftops instead of the flat tops with the clotheslines and radio antennas of our building.

Scattered everywhere about the Island, mostly in neighborhoods near the beach, were complexes of bungalows and frame buildings called "villas" or "courts" or "esplanades," which might all have been there before we were. Certainly, they were already in place when I came along to notice them, and were still there after the war when I married and moved away to attend college. These wooden structures of various sizes would lie silent and shut for nine months of the year and then teem with families who rented the cramped bedrooms and housekeeping units for the summer and came crowding into them excitedly with their bedding and baby carriages—almost all of them arriving, it seemed, in the same few days. They would pour in from other parts of Brooklyn such as Williamsburg and East New York, and from Manhattan, the Bronx, and New Jersey, to pass the next few months in a bustling proximity to each other that would have been intolerable to people more cultivated and less sociable, and likely *was* intolerable to the generation of young they reared. The summer renters would for the most part spend their months in these quarters happily, for the same families returned with bedding and growing children to the same rudimentary "villas," "courts," and "esplanades" year after year. Some of the boys came to be summer friends; their return was awaited and they grew acceptable enough to play in our card games for pennies or soda-bottle tops, or to qualify for a position on the Surf Avenue punchball team of West 31st Street, especially when we were short of players.

A small summer bungalow structure of two stories with a center courtyard stood on my side of the street between my apartment house and a lesser one at the corner of the Railroad Avenue trolley stop. This other apartment house had a candy store on street level, in which Mr. Moses and his wife and daughter worked; they lived in an apartment in the back. He sold newspapers, too, both Yiddish and English, and for a long time the telephone in the public telephone booth inside his store was the only one on the street and was used by every family, both for making calls and for receiving them. In those days, an unseen telephone operator was still on duty at what was called the switchboard, a woman who said "Number please?" Any of us hurrying to summon anyone to the candy store to receive a phone call could expect a two-cent tip, the going rate. My sister recalls now that any boy calling her for a date had to do all his courting and preliminary kidding around on the telephone in Mr. Moses's candy store.

Across the street from my house was an expansive facility called the West End Villa—a row of one-family bungalows. Off-season, we would play our games of tag on the porches and over the railings. Behind these, inside a development on two levels similar to those in today's motels, were strips of adjoining summer apartments, and it was due to one of these, probably, that my brother met the girl who would in time become his wife. Perhaps he didn't actually meet her there, but her family rented one of these apartments summer after summer, and I was familiar with her parents and her brother, Ben, before they became his in-laws.

Her name when we met her was Perle; then, for some reason, for one or two seasons she changed it to Lynn. There was something of a fashion then among young women—though in that period we said girls—for changing names. I remember seeing a girl named Gertrude whom I'd known all through primary school suddenly pointed out to me as Gail when she showed up as a potential date for one of the fellows in the "senior" group of a social club of which I was already, and only, a junior member. She was then in my French class in high school. The club was in a store with a back room on a side street two blocks away from my house and was called Club Alteo. What was unusual about the Alteo was that it was already second generation; many of the members, then in their twenties, were the younger brothers of the original organizers, who, maturing into full-fledged adults, had outgrown the social and athletic activities of the numerous "SACs"—social and athletic clubs—

always flourishing in Coney Island and in Brighton Beach, too. I was one of a group of neighborhood boys in our mid-teens already organized into the Alteo Juniors. We were permitted to use the club room for our weekly meetings and as a place to hang out during the day and into the early evening to listen to music, listen to the tall stories told by the older guys, and learn how to dance the lindy hop. We learned as well to distinguish between the very good music of bands such as Jimmy Lunceford's, Duke Ellington's, and Count Basie's, and the more popular "commercial" stuff of Glenn Miller and Tommy Dorsey, with Benny Goodman preferable to the latter two but not nearly as enthralling as the best, who without exception were black. In the evenings, when their own social activities got going, our elders showed us the door, outside which we often loitered awhile on the sidewalk just to watch.

Gertrude, now Gail, was brought to the club room by an older, pretty sister, and Gail was wearing lipstick and mascara, done up in a way none of us had seen her before. In short order she became the girlfriend of twenty-two- or -three-year-old Murray Beckerman. It was conceded by his peers that he was the best lindy hopper in the club and, along with a nonmember named Curly Klein, good enough to take the floor without shame at the Savoy Ballroom in Harlem. In all other ways he seemed unremarkable to us teenagers when compared to the George Mandels, Roy Roycemans, and Danny Rosoffs who were also members: George and Roy could talk of Beethoven as well as Basie; and it was from the lips of Danny the Count that I first heard the names Hemingway, Fitzgerald, Faulkner, Dos Passos, all uttered without a given name, as though they had long been familiars of his. He spoke to me about them because he knew I was already writing short stories (short stories that were spectacularly immature and inept). I confess that even back then I began to wonder whether Danny had actually read these authors or had merely read *about* them. I wonder still.

Neither Gertrude nor I could ever be at ease with each other after exchanging glances in the club room. She was Gail there and Gertrude in the French class. But she, with a nubile bosom dauntlessly accentuated by the tight sweater and uplifting undergarment cups then in style, could note with confidence that she was attractive to older men in their twenties; whereas we, poor things at fifteen, didn't know of any girls our own age who might be attracted to us. Young people then were slower to mature socially than they seem to be today; at least that was true of many of the teenage boys in Coney Island.

In a little while, my sister-in-law, Lee's wife, reverted to her original name of Perle, to the confusion of my mother. (I don't know what eventually happened to Gertrude/Gail.) When I got married, which I did at twenty-two, in October of 1945, it was to a young woman named Shirley. As my mother aged, the distinction between Perlie and Shirley was not always easy for her to preserve. With increasing frequency, and with exasperation, too, for she was always sufficiently alert to recognize her slip as she was making it, she would use one name when calling or referring to the other, much the same way that I now, as I age, occasionally blunder with my second wife by addressing her by the name of my first. This is not a sage thing for a husband to do.

JUST ABOUT AS NUMEROUS as the bungalow dwellings for summer renters were the bathhouses for people who came just for the day. There were bathhouses down the length of Coney Island, almost all of them between Surf Avenue and the boardwalk and beach, and on just about every street. Most of them were simple facilities with lockers and showers, such as Hahn's Baths just down the block from where we lived, and Ward's baths across the street facing it. The strongest appeal they exercised was their immediate access to the beach and the ocean. My sister remembers working at Hahn's one summer as the locker girl in the female section; while still a schoolgirl, she worked other summers at one of the many soft-ice-cream stands on the boardwalk—we called it "frozen custard"—and intermittently as a "shill" at one of the games of skill or chance, pretending to be playing as a paying customer in order to draw others to witness how she fared and thus be enticed to play, too. There was little need for kitchen services in any of these humble bathhouses, for an abundance of food stands on and underneath the boardwalk provided almost everything that might be craved in the way of fast food and soft drink.

Here and there, extending right up to the boardwalk, were a number of elaborate swimming establishments featuring outdoor pools with water slides and diving boards, together with a few simple sports activities like Ping-Pong, shuffleboard, basketball shooting, and, highly favored by those who knew how to use them, punching bags. Raven Hall (named after one of the prominent early developers, Ravenhall, I've just found out), which was far down in the amusement area and functioning long before I was, seemed by far the largest. Later on, Steeplechase augmented its myriad features by installing a pool that might have rivaled Raven Hall in size. Washington Baths seemed to have the most loyal following: People I've met through the years say they bought season tickets summer after summer. McLaughlin Baths, right in our neighborhood, drew its patrons from the Scandinavian, mainly Norwegian, and Irish populations in Bay Ridge, an area distinguished for a brawling toughness and the predictable anti-Semitism then generally common in America among groups that were not Jewish. The younger, high-spirited, rougher ones at McLaughlin's took occasional pleasure in loudly mocking the Jews on the beach by whom they found themselves surrounded, and once or twice each summer there was a report of some fracas brewing that, as far as I know, never did erupt into anything of large consequence. The war seemed to put an end to that kind of local friction.

The swimming pools at most of these establishments

were located right up against the boardwalk and always lured spectators from the throngs of curious strollers, who paused to watch through the openings in the enclosing fences. These were, after all, the only swimming pools ever seen by any of us except on the screens of movie theaters. It was good to have proof they were real. The swan dive and the quick jackknife from the low and medium diving boards were the favorites; perhaps they were also the easiest. Likewise, the men adept with the rhythms and variations of the punching bag happily worked up sweats performing for admiring viewers assembled on the boardwalk. On the beach, athletes who stood on their heads balanced on the abdomen and knees of supine girlfriends were so prevalent as to hardly command more than a glance. A disappearing species of beach gymnast was the athlete who stood on his hands and walked about a bit in jerky strides. I haven't seen any of these clumsy jokers perform that stunt in years, and I hope I never see one again. Pinochle games played by elderly Jewish men with vigorous gestures and impassioned discussions were more exciting spectator sports as we tried to learn the subtleties of the game and figure out what these characters from the Old World were gloating and disputing about. Portable radios made their appearance with huge batteries in large cases that seemed to weigh half a hundred pounds. Ukulele and banjo players abounded. It was on the beach in Coney Island that I first heard western ballads such as "Clementine" and "Red River Valley."

BACK IN THE EARLY THIRTIES, some shrewd speculators decided to erect a luxury hotel right at the boardwalk on West 29th Street, the Half Moon Hotel, and soon afterward they were tormented by shadows of insolvency. The Half Moon, so christened after Henry Hudson's vessel, remains the most majestic building in Coney Island, and I think I remember watching it going up from the window of my apartment. I knew nothing about Henry Hudson and his fatal voyage then, but I would have thought someone more knowledgeable might have proposed a name auguring better prospects for the venture than the end met by that seafaring explorer.

In retrospect, it's hard to guess what in the world it was that led those crafty real-estate operators to suppose that, with the charisma of Coney Island already fading among the swells, people with enough money to go somewhere else would choose to come to Coney Island. The Half Moon Hotel achieved a brief flare of notoriety in about 1940 with the death of one of the few figures acquiring some measure of fame through association with Coney Island, a man named Abe Reles. Although he never lived in Coney Island, Abe Reles, who hailed from Brownsville, a fiercer area of Brooklyn distinguished for its gangsters and a prizefighter named Bummy Davis, was secretly sequestered in the hotel in protective custody as a material witness while waiting to give crucial testimony at the trial of some men involved with a gang known as Murder, Incorporated. Reles broke into public notice with a fatal splash when he either fell, jumped, or was thrown from the window of his hotel room before he could testify. At the time very few people other than the police authorities knew he was there, and although it was never proved, the rumor existed, and still is believed, that he was helped out the window by the very policemen to whose protective custody he had been entrusted. Eventually, after the war, during which it was utilized by either the coast guard or the navy, the hotel became a Hebrew home for the aged, and this metamorphosis, though somewhat somber, was an apt symbol for the old and faltering Island itself, which had certainly seen more vital days. My mother in her last years spent some time there as a resident, following emergency surgery for a strangulated hernia from which she never regained her strength. The surgery also revealed that she had become diabetic. No doubt she would have greatly preferred living with one of us, provided her presence was welcomed warmly and no source of conflict; a cynical realist, she knew that wasn't possible and didn't expect it to happen, and, to my knowledge, she didn't ask. Consistent with modern convention, none of the three of us, all married by then and living in confining apartments, felt we could have her. The subject never arose, but I would guess that each of us secretly suffered at least some remorse. In our family, we did not often talk about sad things.

EVEN BEFORE WORLD WAR II, the Island as diversion and playground had been fading in verve and enterprise, its amusement area persistently shrinking. And since the end of that war, in 1945, with the exception of a few government-financed public housing projects, there has not (to my knowledge) been a single new residential dwelling of size constructed. The amusement area, once as up-to-date as any in the world and with a reputation for being just about the best, has not provided a spectacular new attraction since the Parachute Jump from the 1939–40 New York World's Fair was installed by Steeplechase.

Coney Island still presents a boardwalk that seemed then, and probably still does, the longest, widest, and most splendid boardwalk in the whole world. It has a wide beach of fine sand its entire length, a beach that continues well beyond Coney Island into Brighton Beach and Manhattan Beach. One has only to stumble with shock and lacerated arches upon the shorefronts of Nice or the English Brighton—and remember with a sense of affront that these are also called beaches—to begin to fully appreciate the spacious shorefront of Coney Island as a truly distinguished natural treasure.

And Coney Island also had for us those long, paved streets, almost entirely free of motor traffic except in summer, that were better playgrounds than any recreation engineer has ever devised.

Our favorite street game in spring and summer was punchball, a variation on conventional baseball played with a springy rubber ball—the "Spaldeen" was best, but it was costlier than the others. The ball was propelled from home plate by a fist rather than by the shaft of a broomstick or any other kind of bat, hence the name "punchball." In fall, we played hockey on roller skates and also a game with a football called association, involving passing, dodging, and tagging, with no tackling or blocking. In this I excelled as a receiver. Then, once we learned how, we played real football on the sand beach. The first time we played a team on hard ground, and that was in Sea Gate, I was astounded at just how hard the ground was when you fell and struck it. We wore no padding or helmets. Earlier, when we were still more juvenile than adolescent, there were games like "hango-seek" (hide-and-go-seek), tag, and follow-the-leader on the beach and around the empty summer bungalows, with me almost always the leader. For follow-the-leader on the boardwalk summer evenings, I originated a variation based on guile and impishness rather than agility. I would excuse myself with winning politeness to people standing in conversation, step between them, and move on. The second fellow was obliged to do the same. With the interruption from the third, suspicion was aroused, and by the fourth or fifth, the victims broke off to stare and caught on, usually with good-humored surprise. The longer the line, the broader the laughter. In barrooms, waiters and bartenders didn't tolerate us with such good humor. I, the leader (in follow-the-leader, one almost always remained the leader; if I fell in jumping from one porch railing to another, I insisted the others would have to fall, too) would enter innocently, make my way around as though in search of someone, and exit through another door, while the second young fellow was already coming in as though looking for me, and after him a third, innocently trailing both of us. It was the fourth or fifth who would be roared at and shooed out. And the one after him would hesitate to go forward and unhappily have to move to the end of the line, while, I of course, was always spared.

A typical Saturday morning in spring and summer

found us playing a punchball game against a team from another block—which more often than not we won—then coming home triumphantly for a well-earned glass of cold milk and hungering for lunch. Saturday early afternoon saw us going to the movies with a dime for admission and a nickel more for candy to see a double feature (two movies), the latest episode in a cowboy or Tarzan serial, a newsreel, and a Mickey Mouse or Betty Boop cartoon or travelogue thrown in, and then walking home afterward in serious discussion of plans for the rest of that day. Sunday usually was simpler, with most of the morning spent eating breakfast and perusing the colored funny papers and the advertisements of toys we'd like someday to own, such as two-wheel bicycles, and trips we'd dream of someday being able to take. From the beginning of time we had two large movie palaces to attend—the RKO Tilyou and Loew's Coney Island. Then, on an empty lot on Surf Avenue around my corner one block away, a new one, the Surf Theater, was constructed, and we had three. The opening of the Surf Theater was an event I remember. The picture was *One Night of Love* and starred the opera singer Grace Moore, who was killed in an airplane crash not many years later. Much of the music, including the title song, was based on melodies of Puccini, and my mother went, too.

THE AMUSEMENT AREA of Coney Island—that stretch encompassing the rides and the games, the food stands and the penny arcades—was of greatest interest to us in the cooler days of spring and late summer, or to break the routine even on hot days when one of us would get hold of some free passes to Luna Park or Steeplechase. These were the only two true amusement parks then existing, each charging an admission price and incorporating attractions exclusively its own, in name if not necessarily in originality: The slow boat ride through darkness was in one of the parks called the Tunnel of Love and in the other (I believe) the

Red Mill. All the individual attractions required a specific ticket of admission or a separate fee, and at Steeplechase everyone had to pay extra for the Parachute Jump. Stauche's indoor arena, one of the original large restaurants early in the century, was still standing, but now it was a place where prizefights were occasionally held and where marathon dance contests were for a while in vogue. For half a mile between Surf Avenue and the boardwalk, past Steeplechase almost to Feltman's, there was (and is) a pedestrian thoroughfare called the Bowery, the name appropriated, of course, from that earlier boulevard of fabled excess in lower Manhattan. Almost every inch of it was consecrated to some kind of attraction, and even the cross streets were crammed with sideshows, games, rides, and food stands, with the cries of barkers and ticket sellers, the sputtering of engines and the rolling turmoil of wheels, and the maniacal bedlam of amplified mechanical laughter crashing incessantly from the various spook rides. And famous Feltman's was still in business, though inexorably expiring, still large and garish but waning from neglect now that Diamond Jim Brady and other bigwigs from the Gay Nineties had themselves passed on.

At one point on the Coney Island boardwalk, a Howard Johnson's ice cream stand suddenly surfaced, with many very bright lights and twenty-six different flavors. Having overcome our surprise, we stared with wonder at this oddity and scanned the names of the flavors, musing on why, with vanilla, chocolate, and strawberry standard, and burnt almond and butter pecan available, and then pistachio for the plain novelty of color rather than for any particular excellence of taste, there was a need for so many more flavors. And who in hell was Howard Johnson, of whom we had never heard? On the boardwalk we preferred our soft ice cream, our frozen custard, to the true ice cream we normally enjoyed at home or in our street, and Howard Johnson's was soon gone. Twice there were bold ventures with outdoor bowling alleys on the boardwalk. These were exotic gambles, too. Bowling then was still *goyisheh naches,* (Gentile pleasure), and these didn't last long, either.

We learned early on that a boiled frankfurter anywhere is not as good as one broiled on a grill to the point of splitting—you only had to ingest a boiled one in a stadium at a professional baseball game to know you were tasting only hot water and mustard; that the Wonder Wheel with its rolling, swaying gondolas, which is one of the two mechanical attractions from our antiquity still in operation, was obviously superior to George C. Tilyou's Ferris wheel in Steeplechase Park, but that both were for sightseeing squares or for adults with children who were squares and still too young to be exposed to the terror of anything but height; that the Cyclone, which is the second old-timer still extant, was far and away the best of all roller coasters; and that it was futile to search anywhere in the universe for a tastier potato knish than Shatzkin's when they were still made by hand by old women who were relatives or friends of the family. (Although I still run into mulish people, hogs, who didn't mind the thicker, yellow Gabila's, and to people brought up in adjacent Brighton Beach who still salivate at the mention of Mrs. Stahl's, the queen of potato knishes there.)

All of this was practical, worldly knowledge that taught us always to look for fair value for money. We also learned at an early age a fact of capitalism that directed us toward the antithetical principle that it is usually impossible to obtain fair value. The difference, to Aristotle as well as Karl Marx, is known as profit. We learned this first of all from the Coney Island barkers who offered to guess your weight, guess your age, guess your name or occupation, the country you came from or the date you were born, guess anything at all about you including the color of your underwear, for a dime, a quarter, a half dollar, or a dollar, the prize at stake improving with the increase in the amount bet. The fact was that the barker could never lose. He knew no more about the tricks of this trade than you do, but he always came out ahead, right or wrong, because the customer could never win. Phrased more nicely, while the customer might walk away with a prize, the proprietor could never lose, because the prize at stake invariably cost him less, considerably less, than the patron had spent to win it. Of course, the customer also walked away with the satisfying emotional reward of having outsmarted the expert, while the proprietor in turn enjoyed the emotional reward of knowing he had just pocketed another piece of small change as profit.

But honest to God, a kid could win a whole coconut for a penny at the penny-pitch game and, once having acquired the know-how, knock a hole through the soft spot in the head of the shell with a hammer and nail to get at the milk, then smash the whole coconut into fragments to be distributed liberally to everyone around. The trick to winning a coconut was not to toss each penny at one of the metal button targets that would set off a ringing to announce a winner but to aim it into a patch of losing pennies already lying there and set several of them vibrating down the incline onto one of the buttons.

The catch to winning a coconut was that nobody really enjoyed eating coconut or drinking coconut milk. But we all had to pretend we did in order to savor the victory.

THERE WAS A COMPETITION between Luna Park and Steeplechase that dated back to the founding of both at the turn of the century. I forget the names of the two men involved with the spectacular opening of Luna Park a few years after Steeplechase, but Steeplechase the Funny Place was solely the creation of an individual named George C. Tilyou. Tilyou was a born entrepreneur. As a boy, he began accumulating capital by selling vials of Coney Island sand and bottles of Coney Island seawater to wide-eyed visitors. Even people from places with beaches of their own returned home with precious souvenirs of Coney Island sand and ocean water. His idea for a Ferris wheel, the first in Coney

Island, came from one he saw while on his honeymoon at the Exposition in Chicago in 1893. He undertook construction of a copy half its size and ballyhooed it from the day he broke ground as the largest in the world. When the first of his amusement parks burned to the ground in one of Coney Island's periodic fires, he promptly began recovering his losses by charging people ten cents to enter and see the smoking ruins. "If Paris is France," he is reported saying, "then Coney Island between June and September is the world." This was not wholly true. Tilyou died in 1914, nine years before I was born, and is buried in Green-Wood Cemetery in Brooklyn, and all that any of us knew about him was that his name was on Steeplechase Park and on one of our two capacious movie theaters, and that there was, or had been, a family home on Surf Avenue across the street from the amusement park. It was a wooden affair of a couple of floors set back from the street, with that family name, TILYOU, carved on the vertical face of a stone step at the bottom of a small entranceway with the letters already sunk almost halfway into the ground at the edge of the sidewalk. We would note the marker and the house on the way to his movie theater. It didn't occur to us then that he was already dead. It didn't cross our minds that he had once been alive. We never thought of him at all as somebody human, or thought of his name as any more of a family name than the equally improbable one of Loew.

Of the two amusement parks, there seemed to be a near unanimous preference for Luna Park, and we were inclined to be contemptuous of anyone, usually someone from someplace else, who raved about Steeplechase. The most we could feel about Steeplechase was that it was "all right"— we couldn't honestly say, "It stinks." Once we got inside Luna Park, there seemed to be a good deal more open space in the middle in which to meander and more interesting things to look at. The architecture was a fantastic, almost nightmarish corruption of the Moorish and the Byzantine in circus-clown colors of chalk white and cherry red with ornamental stripes of black and bright green on minarets, spires, and onion domes. Every few hours Luna Park offered a free circus in a small tented ring to everyone already inside the park. Its commencement was heralded by a short parade of a few listless elephants and other performers to the beat of a drummer and the notes of a trumpet and trombone. I remember a high-diving act outside in public view, I'll take my oath I do—someone diving from a tall platform into a thimbleful of water; and I'll swear to this one, too: a man or a woman shot from a cannon into a net a good distance away, maybe four or five times daily.

Luna Park began with the Shoot-the-Chutes, which was a pretty good ride to go on and to watch, a flat-bottomed boat sliding down a high incline slippery with water into a bouncing splash in a large pool at the bottom and coasting to a stop. The best part, sadly, was waiting for your turn. It also had the Mile Sky Chaser, the highest roller coaster in Coney Island. God, it was high. And something to stare up at from the ground, that long pull of the cars to the top of the first descent. With wonder and dread, I mustered enough nerve to approach it as a customer for the first time at the age of eleven or twelve. It was taken for granted that as a step toward maturity every boy would sooner or later have to ride the Mile Sky Chaser, as older ones already had; this was another in the progression of rites of initiation. I contemplated this looming challenge with the pragmatic and stoic frame of mind that has stood me in good stead in other perilous situations since then and with which I long ago came to face the necessary act of dying itself: If others could go through it and survive, I could, too.

As it turned out, the Mile Sky Chaser was a cinch—after the first time. Though high, it was tame, not nearly as fast or as twisting and jolting as the Tornado or the Thunderbolt, or, grandest of all, the Cyclone, which was reserved by everyone for last, the consummation of the roller-coaster agenda. I worked up to the big event of the Cyclone over one or two summers by growing used to and scornful of the lesser rides. The easiest of all the roller coasters was the rather childish one in Steeplechase. It was nothing much, and not intended to be in that rather mannerly playground, and except for a series of rapid bumps at the conclusion— they were bumps, not dips—it provided no surprises. Luna Park had a better, minor one, called the Dragon's Gorge, which, inventively, was partly indoors and partly in darkness. I'm not sure how much later I mastered the Tornado and the Thunderbolt; these were speedy and rattling variations of each other, with women screaming in true or pretended fear and men with their mouths gaping, pretending to grin. But first came the day of my induction to the Mile Sky Chaser, accompanied for morale, as was usual, by a couple of friends who had already been and guaranteed that it was nothing.

As it turned out, it was not only a cinch, it soon proved a bore. After experimenting over time with a seat at the very front, the back, the middle, I could anticipate accurately every dive and turn of the Mile Sky Chaser with my eyes closed better than, years later, I was ever able to read an aerial map in the air corps with my eyes open, or am able even now to read a road map. As a matter of fact, we often would take this whole ride, and others, with our eyes closed in attempts, mainly futile, to amplify our sensations of thrill and fright. Soon the only excitement the Mile Sky Chaser yielded was the chance to display to marveling strangers how coolly we braved its apparent perils.

None of us, then or afterward, was ever able to be that casual about the Cyclone or to chance the same liberties. I was discharged from the army in May of 1945—the war against Japan was still on when our government began demobilizing—and found myself back home during a spell of beautiful weather in spring with little idea of what to do with myself during the day. My cellar clubs had passed away from attrition. In an ardor of liberation, I went hurrying down Surf Avenue in civilian pants and my army field jacket, looking for any old friend to rejoice with. Through a coincidence of good luck emanating from bad, I was among the first to be released from the service under the point system newly in effect. The bad luck was that I had lost most of my pocket money in a dice game or card game on a base in San Angelo, Texas, and thus happened to be on hand that weekend when an order arrived to discharge a certain number of officers. That last part was the good luck. Back home, it seemed that just about everyone I knew from the neighborhood was still away. Suddenly, on Surf Avenue, I spied Davey Goldsmith, whom I hadn't seen in three years, home on furlough and doing the same thing I was, looking for someone to pal around with. We embraced each other jubilantly and then hurried, almost running, down into the amusement area in search of old times, our receding childhood. I was better at schoolwork than Davey, but he was smarter and more self-assured than I was in just about all other ways. (The last time I saw him he was prospering as the owner of a division of a hatband manufacturing company for which he had worked since finishing high school.) At Nathan's Famous, we gulped down some hot dogs and a couple of bags of their unrivaled fried potatoes, and that indeed was exactly like old times. It was *better* than old times, because we now had cash in our pockets for everything we might feasibly want. (As an officer with flight pay on combat duty overseas, I had been able to send home plenty.) When we went on the Parachute Jump, I was tense again for just the few seconds of suspense that preceded the unexceptional drop along protective guide wires. But coasting down, I had to wonder why anyone would want to ride it a second time. The Cyclone, it turned out, hadn't diminished with age—its age or mine—or with familiarity. We rode it once. I don't know what Davey was doing, but I was holding on for dear life through the racing plunges and veers, and I tottered off with a thumping ache in my head and a wrenched neck. And all at once I understood without needing to put anything into words that this was a part of

my life that was definitely over. After sixty missions overseas, I was now selective in my adventures, and I had no
doubt that I would never want to ride that or any other
roller coaster again. Davey Goldsmith might love to, but
Joey Heller wouldn't. I was twenty-two and would soon be
engaged to be married and I was too old. And like someone
very much older, for I have crossed similar thresholds of loss
since, I felt with sadness that something dear was behind me
forever, but I also felt that loss with tremendous relief. It is
often pleasing to be free of even good things, and childhood
is one of them. Youth is another.

Following the Cyclone, Davey guided me by trolley car
to a fantastic clam bar in a Sheepshead Bay restaurant called
Lundy's to teach me how to eat raw clams on the half shell. I
had never before even looked a clam in the eye. I didn't
think it could be done. Davey showed me it could, and I've
been eating them ever since.

WHILE STEEPLECHASE, "the funny place," was also
always the lesser place, it was not all that bad. Much of it was
indoors under a vast roofed pavilion, away from the sun,
shielded from rain. For ten or fifteen cents you could purchase entry to the park but not admittance to any of the
rides, and many wise people did just that. There were food
stands inside—cotton candy, frankfurters, ice cream—and
games of skill and chance, like the penny-pitch for the
coconuts. There were people to watch, and of best value
were those people who had bought tickets to all the rides
and used up very few of them; if asked, they might give you
the rest of their tickets as they were exiting. There was,
without fee, a theater with comfortable seating for about
three hundred, on whose stage unsuspecting patrons who
had just taken the Steeplechase ride and were exiting on
foot suddenly found themselves in the spotlight as spectacles
before an audience. They would have to cross that stage to

escape, braving the pranks of two or three jesters in wait for them, one a stunted clown; the second costumed as a farmer, or a New Yorker's stereotyped image of a hick farmer; and the third as a rangy cowboy. There were several shaky vertical columns of painted barrels strung along ropes, and these might abruptly begin to move, as would various shuttling sections of the floor. Also waiting to surprise them were mild electric shocks and upward gusts of air to raise the skirts of women and blow off men's hats. Those were the days in which men still wore hats, even to amusement parks in summer—straw hats and panama hats. One of the costumed figures sported a long wooden clapper with which he threatened to whack fannies, another brandished a metal wand at the end of a wire cord connected to an electrical outlet, openly threatening shocks. People coming upon them onstage without warning and with an audience watching must surely have been stricken, if only for a second, with the bewildering terror that they had somehow dropped into a chamber containing some of the milder tortures of the first level of hell.

For twenty-five cents in Steeplechase you could buy a circular pink ticket with numbers 1 to 25 that entitled you to twenty-five attractions. The tickets came on a loose white string that went about the wearer's neck to protect against loss. For fifty cents you bought a blue ticket that allowed you thirty-one attractions, the added six being the premium rides that were judged the best of the lot. Our practice was to get inside any way we could and then to politely ask well-dressed ladies and gentlemen moving in the direction of the exits if they were leaving and if so, could we have the remainder of their tickets. There was little reason to refuse us. Many of the elderly would use hardly any of their tickets, sometimes riding only on the elegant carousel—created originally for some German king by a master bridge-builder in Leipzig—on which they could smoothly circle for several minutes seated on the benches in one of the ornate gondolas. And in this way we could accumulate enough tickets to go on any ride as many times as we wanted, with the result that we soon didn't want to go on any.

LUNA PARK, as I've said, seemed to us much the better of the two competitors. Yet Luna Park closed first, a few years after the war ended, following a few fires and some desperate and futile attempts to arrest the critical decrease in customers. A housing project of complex design built by private developers for people of middle income now stands in its place.

Steeplechase held on gamely into the sixties before it gave up the battle and closed shop.

A few years before that, I went there one afternoon with my friends George Mandel and Mario Puzo on what proved to be a final trip. Mario had by then published two novels, *The Dark Arena* and *The Fortunate Pilgrim,* but not yet *The Godfather.* George had published *Flee the Angry Strangers* and *The Wax Boom.* My *Catch-22* had appeared shortly before, in 1961. I had met Mario years earlier through George. It was a lazy, drowsy day, and the three of us had come from the city with our children, I with my two, George with his two, and Mario with one or two of his five.

The very qualities that had disappointed us in the past made Steeplechase now ideal for languid fathers in their forties there with young children. It was clean, it was orderly, it was safe. While the children chased about in gawking exploration and enjoyed themselves first on one ride that moved slowly around in a circle, then on another that did exactly the same thing, the three of us could rest calmly on a bench and talk quietly about such things as publishers, book advertising, advances, and royalties, and that lousy Book-of-the-Month Club that had paid no attention to any of us. Luckily for us, the kids didn't want to go on many rides that would have necessitated our going with them, and we weren't really eager to go on any. Coming in, Mario, who was not from Coney Island and was rather portly, had chanced the Magic Barrel. He sank down slowly to the revolving floor and was unable to right himself, presenting a ludicrous picture as he rolled around there helplessly for a minute, laughing, with an unlighted long, long cigar in his hand, until finally the attendant in crimson coat and green jockey cap walked in and helped him through. After that he wanted no more. The place was very still and rather empty that bright afternoon. After a couple of pleasant hours, we prepared to leave, and a thought about the passing of generations occurred to me as we walked toward the exit: It struck me that if a kid like the one I used to be approached and asked for our tickets, he would have gotten from us three blue ones that were just about complete, except for the number-one ride punched for Mario. The next time I visited Coney Island, Steeplechase was no longer there, and only the red skeleton of the old Parachute Jump marked the spot, like a funereal obelisk.

EACH YEAR AFTER LABOR DAY, the traditional end of the summer season at most American resorts, there was that week of parades on Surf Avenue quaintly mistitled Mardi Gras by promoters who didn't know or didn't care that the title was traditionally connected with spring and Lent. If you hate parades as much as I did then and still do, you would have loved to hate the ones at the Coney Island Mardi Gras, for they represented everything about parades that is sordid, tawdry, and synthetic. They were long and they were tiresome. They were intended to draw crowds to the Island for that extension of the summer's business, and this they did. Celebrity attendance was most prevalent during Mardi Gras, and the city's daily newspapers, which then numbered about seven, often printed smiling shots of someone from the movies who had been snapped there the day before as though having a good time.

Negative as we felt, we nevertheless would go to the Mardi Gras just about every night, more for the rides and the food than the parades. Merely mixing with the crowds was diverting. Every night it was just about the same parade. One might be called "Firemen's Night," another "Policemen's Night," and so forth, but the floats were mostly identical, the same marching bands with honking brass and clarinets would go clumping by, and there was a goodly sprinkling of the ladies' auxiliaries to almost every group that marched. (Just about everything that marched had a ladies' auxiliary, and I'm still not sure what they are.) And we always had a nickel for at least one hot dog. The droves of people moving on the sidewalk in both directions and for the most part paying little heed to the marchers were potentially more interesting than the parades. On Saturday afternoon there was a different kind of procession called the "Baby Parade," an utterly grotesque competition for which mothers prepared their helpless offspring for weeks in advance and paraded them along in strollers past judges in the passionate hope of winning distinction and a prize for their efforts and their tot. I doubt that the first prize was a scholarship to West Point.

One night I did see Mayor La Guardia ride by in a car in the Mardi Gras. He was wearing a brown fedora with the rolled brim of a cowboy hat. I confess I was thrilled. I was young and I was thrilled and I'm glad, for our vision of Fiorello H. La Guardia as a figure of exceptional integrity for one holding political office endures. Except for FDR, I cannot think of many since then I've felt worth a second look.

Back when the area's permanent residential and seasonal population was almost entirely white, it was standard campaign procedure for political candidates for local or national office to make a stop in Coney Island. Then as now, the purpose for a politician was less to hobnob with voters than to be photographed with a frankfurter while on a leisurely stroll along the boardwalk, always smiling as though merry, introducing himself to people easily excited by the prospect of seeing their picture in a newspaper. Even before I turned impenitently cynical about all American contenders for elective position, I began to feel that this was too much of a condescending insult to impose on a low-income neighborhood already distressed with signs of unmistakable and irreversible decline. One of the more offensive images I still hold in memory is a newspaper picture of Nelson Rockefeller, campaigning either for himself or in support of some other Republican, sinking his good-natured teeth into a Coney Island hot dog. And one of the more ridiculous memories is of Henry Cabot Lodge, patrician scion of the impeccable New England line of Lodges, lending himself to that same demeaning ritual—demeaning to himself and demeaning to the local electorate he was humoring. Because of his innate good taste, one—this one—can still take sadistic pleasure from the thought of the piercing abhorrence he no doubt was suffering and pray, with abiding malice, that some of the mustard dripped off his hot dog and ran down into his shirtsleeve. I remember remarking at the time that it was sufficient to have people like these in public office without having to put up with their fellowship as well, and that they wouldn't be walking through Coney Island smiling if they had to live there.

THE YEARS OF MY CHILDHOOD were the years of the Great Depression, although in childhood we didn't have a firm idea of everything that term signified. In our wonderful streets, we could play our games. Also wonderful was that our street was right outside the doors and windows of our apartment houses. We could see in an instant which of our friends were already out there and what kind of game was about to start. If in doubt, we could call down and ask. Possibly the most valuable of our resources were all the other children. Almost always there were enough children nearby of all ages to organize any kind of activity and field any kind of team.

This, then, was the block—a section of a street between avenues that teemed with all the companionship we young ones needed, both boys and girls, and in the beginning our interests were centered almost exclusively on the block (not the whole street) that was our own. Our closest friends in school might be from other blocks on other streets, but outside school we didn't have much to do with them unless it was to challenge *their* blocks to a game of punchball or hockey. When a family moved from one street to another, the children almost invariably attempted at first to maintain affiliation with the old block and resisted assimilation into the new. Occasionally, two blocks would decide to have a fight; when that happened, we would mobilize our respective forces a safe distance apart, throw stones at each other for a few minutes, and then break off to return to our customary diversions without antagonism, which probably hadn't existed in the first place.

The beach as much as the street exerted a strong influence on our daily activities. In summer we were there much of every warm day. What better place to be? In autumn we played football there, which meant we were spoiled and tenderized by the soft sand and unconditioned for the real game when the time came to play on standard terrain. I take it as a cause for some negative pride that not a single one of the fellows I grew up with ever amounted to much as an athlete, or tried to.

There was a rhythm to our sequence of play activities that was both seasonal and intuitive. One mild day in early spring the sun would be out and suddenly the kids on every block were punching grounders to each other in the middle of the street, and the punchball season was awakening. The girls were skipping rope on the sidewalk or playing hopscotch on numbered grids marked out in white chalk. There would come a certain moment after Labor Day when every boy seemed to understand that summer was definitely on the way out and it was time to start tossing footballs. The same was true of hockey—sooner or later everybody roller-skated: All over the Island, on virtually the same day on every block, the flocks of flying footballs would thin and the grinding of steel-wheel roller skates would be heard in the land. At the beach in the summer, of course, there was the swimming, along with the occasional games of tag in the water and fetching things up from the bottom and the sunbathing out at the end of the mossy rock breakwater, over which we trained ourselves early to sprint with eye-catching agility across the irregular crags of massive stones. At night the busier streets were much too cluttered for games, and we would drift to the boardwalk to roam for hours, enviously watching the gaudy, kaleidoscopic world of grownups, until our big brothers or sisters were sent to find us amid the sauntering throngs and pull us home to sleep.

Considering how loosely we were guarded, the late hours we kept, and the vast influx of strangers into the Island each summer, it's surprising how little harm befell us. Where we lived, as I've stated, there was practically no crime and few serious accidents. I can't, for example, recall hearing of a single murder (other than the one occurring long before, outside a poolroom) in Coney Island up until the time I left to enlist in the army. I was not aware of any incident of child molestation or domestic abuse of any kind in any combination. One time, a strange male attempted to lure into his automobile Norma Goldman, who lived across the street with her family in the apartment we had formerly occupied; the street buzzed with that one for a day or so, and the net effect was an emphatic caution impressed upon all of us, boys and girls, against ever going off with a stranger. While still in my earliest grades of elementary school, a classmate who lived in my building, Jackie Keshner, was struck by a car at the corner and was out of school for a while with a leg in a cast; I would spend part of most afternoons keeping him up to date on our schoolwork, particularly on geography, which proved the easiest and most rewarding subject to transmit. In geography, I remember, we were gravely taught that bread is "the staff of life." We weren't taught what the phrase means, and I still don't know. (Sadly, I sense that geography as a subject for early study is probably obsolete everywhere. It surely is needed: While planning a family trip to Italy in the summer of 1966, one of my two children, a middle-class teenager midway through a costly private school in Manhattan, wanted to know why, instead of journeying by steamship, we couldn't travel there by car.) Robbery? I heard of just one: An armored car at the Rubel Ice Company, off a good distance from where we lived, was held up by armed robbers who made good their getaway across Gravesend Bay by speed-boat. But that still sounds like an industrial crime and, like most others of that class, had nothing to do with us. An interesting sidelight in our chronicle, though irrelevant, is that the Schechter chicken company, also a distance away, which supplied the freshly killed chickens that are still unmatched for flavor and texture by anything frozen or refrigerated for transport, was the small concern whose complaint against prevailing federal rules was the basis for the U. S. Supreme Court decision declaring the New Deal's NRA unconstitutional. The gangster Abe Reles, the Rubel Ice Company, and Schechter's chickens—the historical high points that brought newspaper fame to our realm at that time.

One summer when I was just into my teens, a younger boy from a family in my building drowned. A nonswimmer, he had ventured, it was reported, out along the safety ropes into water over his head and was swept away when his hold was broken by a wave unexpectedly large. I knew his sister, a girl two years ahead of me in school; before the season had passed, he seemed to me almost forgotten. He had another sister substantially older, mature. She was a slight, black-haired girl with dimples, and I remember her face more distinctly than the others, although I don't recall that we ever exchanged so much as a nod of recognition. She had a boyfriend, and because of her boyfriend I was too bashful to meet her eye. His name was Jack, and at the beach the two of them were always lying entwined in each other's arms on a blanket or the sand, dozing, talking, kissing, under the boardwalk mostly, separating themselves from others in her family group, which also was not the custom. Strolling there and back, they always held hands or walked with their arms around each other. In the Club Alteo was a boy named Herbie with a girlfriend named Teddy, and these two were always to be seen there lying on a couch, in the back room or the open one. And next door to my own Club Highlight later on, there was a member of the Club Amo Pharmacy named Arnie with a girlfriend called Bobbie, and these two also were always either dancing sensuously cheek-to-cheek or lying together in a sweethearts' embrace in full view on one of the couches. I have no idea what happened to any of this trio of ardent and loving couples. Did their unembarrassed affections endure? Did they marry and remain constant? If they're alive, they are older than I am and they are strangers I'd rather not meet. I can picture them only as young and still interlocked in their devoted snuggles and, with much misgiving, I succumb to temptation to repeat some stanzas from A. E. Housman:

> With rue my heart is laden
> For golden friends I had,
> For many a rose-lipt maiden,
> And many a lightfoot lad.
>
> By brooks too broad for leaping
> The lightfoot lads are laid;
> The rose-lipt girls are sleeping
> In fields where roses fade.

Rhymed lines about death or the lachrymose march of time are about as far as I ever was able to get in a struggle to like poetry, and I long ago gave up trying. Besides, of those three couples I've cited, just one of the performers, the girl

Bobbie, had golden hair, while another's was honey brown. I cannot swear that the boys were lightfooted. I didn't often see them standing.

ALTHOUGH I DID NOT at the time fully appreciate the degree of danger, at least three times before leaving home I came close to dying young, to being killed accidentally: once, for a kite; again when swimming out too far; and a third, by an automobile while being chased by my brother one night after refusing to come upstairs to bed when called from a window by my mother. I was swift on sneakers and dodged away from him in play, not fear, and I was still giggling to myself like a dimwit when the car squealed to a stop in the nick of time, as they say, and I found myself in sudden headlights, resting against its grille. I had turned the flight from Lee into a game; I had done the same thing several years before on the day of my father's funeral. Then, older boys on the block, who well knew what was taking place that day after I had succeeded in convincing myself I didn't, had to chase me over the railings of the porches and surround me in order to take me in hand and conduct me into the automobile carrying us to the chapel, which I remember not at all and from which, because I was just past five, I possibly might have been kept away, and then to the cemetery, which I recall only vaguely. In the military, I came close innumerable times to dying young, too, but didn't appreciate that either until I saw blood pouring from a man wounded in my plane. I expect my war experience in this regard corresponds to that of every infantryman, marine, paratrooper, etc., going into modern battle for the first time. I, luckily, was spared that dreadful recognition until I was far along in my tour of duty, on my thirty-seventh mission. But after that, I was in a state close to panic as we took off from the landing strip at the start of every one of those missions remaining.

As for the kite: Older young men at the beach with

unlimited funds would sometimes send batches of kites
aloft on strings tied to each other, with the result that the
central cord eventually developed quite a strong pull, and
the ancillary ones, too. Watching these grown-ups by myself
one time, I saw one string of kites tear loose and drift inland.
I moved up the street after them and saw them descending
limply above my apartment house. I bounded up the stair-
cases to the roof. There I found that the end of the string to
which they had been attached had caught on a radio aerial
wire strung a couple of feet out beyond the low protective
brick parapet around the roof of our building. The closest
one was dangling there by its cloth tail, but it wasn't close
enough; it was out of reach. I couldn't see that at first. I set
myself on that low wall of old stone and began carefully
stretching out toward it as far as I could, inching myself out
nearer and nearer the edge (while my mother sat downstairs
talking to some neighbors in front of the house; what a
ghastly surprise she might have received!). I still couldn't
take hold of the string or the tail of the kite. Then I glanced
down along the side of the building and saw myself perched
very high up above our alley and the garbage cans below. I
felt no fear. I went on leaning out farther, as though I hadn't
caught on that I was putting myself at precarious risk. A
moment's reflection could have reminded me that had I
asked my mother, sister, or brother for the nickel or dime
for a kite of my own, I probably would have had it; if not, I
could have pilfered still another coin from the secret cache
of my sister's I had discovered. But I wanted *that* kite. It was
a wish grown into a lust. I kept stretching and craving, craving and stretching. And then, for whatever obscure reason, I
stopped; in an instant I decided to give up. I turned yellow,
as they say, and, thank God, I simply quit. I straightened up
carefully and inched back from the edge as cautiously as I
had moved out, more frightened of a mistake in retreating
than I had been in exposing myself to danger just a few seconds before.

I feel now that I risked injury, could have been paralyzed or perhaps even killed, every time we played tag in an empty bathhouse and I vaulted from the top of one row of empty lockers to the top of another. And I *know* now that I was almost killed every time I swam out to the bell buoy off our block, even though nothing really threatened me the several times I did.

The summer would begin officially for us, I suppose, on that day in late June we called "promotion," when we would come running jubilantly home on that last day of school, waving our final report cards, me with my A in classwork and B+ in deportment, calling out to everyone we flew by that we had been promoted. "Over the ocean/tomorrow's promotion" was a refrain we chanted. Another was "No more classes/no more books/no more teachers'/dirty looks." By that day, we were already brown enough from the sun to be envied by every pale working adult and summer renter, for we would have been swimming in the ocean and capering in our bathing trunks for more than a month, since May. The Coney Island beach, then as now, was packed inhumanely on Saturdays and Sundays, but that didn't bother us as children, for we were almost never in want of a place to sit. Instead, we were always in and out of the water, jumping off the wooden jetty leading to that breakwater of large rocks or skipping nimbly out to the end of the rocks to rest or watch the strange adults who fished for hours with sinkers, reel, and rod and never seemed to catch a damned thing except an orange crab. We could catch crabs at will by cracking open a mussel torn from the rocks and lowering it into the water on a string through one of the openings. But once we had the crabs, we didn't know what to do with them. Only when an Italian family moved onto the block across the street did I discover with amazement and a momentary nausea that mussels and crabs could be eaten.

"Where are you going with those?" I inquired of Dolly Partini one day, when I came upon her returning from the beach with a pailful of black mussels.

It was many, many years before I could muster the

courage to try one, and today I well up with optimistic cheer whenever I spot them on the menu in a new restaurant, offered either in a white Normandy broth or in red marinara.

We learned to swim in shallow water by the age of seven or eight. The waves in Coney Island are seldom very high, and even when rough are never very rough, in comparison with other Atlantic beaches. The shore is shielded in part on one side by Sandy Hook projecting out from New Jersey and by Rockaway Beach jutting out from Queens on the other, and isn't fully exposed to the sea. From the day we found nerve enough to try the "dead man's float" and discovered we could remain bobbing for more than a stroke or two, we began preparing ourselves for the swim to "the third pole." This was not really to a pole but to the heavy rope connecting two of the poles farthest out and boxing in the protected swimming area at its outermost limit. The distance of each of the parallel lines of upright, sturdy wooden poles extending into the water from the first one, at the shore, to the farthest, third pole was at most between forty and fifty yards. At low tide we could walk more than halfway and, when we dared, pull ourselves out along the ropes for most of the rest. At the second and third poles, where the thick ropes of hemp were fastened above the waterline, we would have to let go and swim past the pole and take hold of the rope where it dipped down again. But the day we did get out to the third pole for the first time—no matter how—was a day on which we had accomplished a noble and heroic feat. To be able to swim there regularly back and forth without fear was to possess definite status in the young male community. After that, the only sea challenge left was the bell buoy, rocking and ringing about half a mile out, perhaps a quarter of a mile, maybe five hundred yards, past the rope at the third pole.

The buoy was of vivid red and bobbed and clanged so unremittingly that we soon turned deaf to the sound, as we did to the reverberations of the electric trolley cars rolling by on Surf Avenue practically in the apartment next door and

on Railroad Avenue not much farther away. Relatives who
came to spend a night for the first time would tremble in
shock at the volume of the various noises they had suffered
and to which our whole family had by then grown selec-
tively deaf. All of us in our innocence and ignorance spoke
freely of that bell buoy as a "bellboy." Not until after I had
my degree in English from New York University and a
master's degree from Columbia and after a year more in
English at Oxford on a Fulbright scholarship and two years
teaching English at Pennsylvania State University, then a
college, were my eyes opened upon meeting my friend Marvin Green, who then was selling artwork for slide shows at a
time when I was commissioning some as a writer in the promotion department of *Time* magazine and who had loved
sailing since a child: The letters "buoy" were not pronounced "boy" as in *buoyant* but more properly "boo-ey," as
in no other English word I know of. I laughed scornfully
the first time I heard him say it and thought he was crazy.
Of course I rushed to a dictionary to check. It still sounds
better my way.

The swim to the bell buoy was not especially dangerous
if, first, one knew how to swim, and, next, knew how to go
about reaching it. There was really no way to work oneself
up to the attempt through preparation. A day would simply
arrive when one of us who hadn't yet been there felt certain
enough that he could make it, and he would just tag along
tensely with a group of other boys who had been to the bell
buoy and survived. Valiant as we might prove, and young,
we were nevertheless too craven and too maturely wise ever
to try it alone.

Black-topped harbor poles far out in the water tilting
left or right would tell us which way the ocean was flowing.
We would move three or four blocks up or down the beach
in order to have the tide carry us toward, rather than away
from, the small, floating buoy with a circular platform for a
rim that was our destination. The tide was usually powerful
that far out; and if we had ever miscalculated and missed the

bell buoy, I think we would have drowned when exhausted. We were too young and not nearly hardy enough to make the trip out there and back without a rest.

Starting out, we would swim in a group directly to the safety rope at the third pole and there dawdle awhile to catch our breath, build up morale, and replenish what little energy we had expended. Then, with a unanimous nod, we would start swimming, not toward the buoy but heading straight out, banking on the flow of the tide to convey us horizontally toward the floating object that was our target. We would move leisurely, alternating a dog paddle with a comfortable variation of the sidestroke. We would talk in fragments of conversation as we progressed—conversation that had no purpose other than to tacitly supply mutual reassurance—and we would make sure we kept close together as we advanced outward. Gradually, we would find ourselves nearing the bell buoy. It was not a strenuous feat, really; it was more a matter of patience than endurance—cool patience. You simply kept paddling calmly and talking calmly, and after a while you could begin making out the markings on the red paint and were nearly there. The only moments of anxiety might arise when you looked back at the dwindling, now miniature shore and realized—if you had a haunted imagination like mine— how very far away help was. Suddenly, everything normally large there was so *small*! (Today, a mere revisit in memory to that Lilliputian picture is sufficient to chill.) But, of course, help of a sort was always near in the friends we were swimming with. And all the while, the tide was bearing us closer. When we found ourselves only fifteen or twenty yards away, we would turn over dynamically into the fashionable Australian crawl, as we then called it, and swim the rest of the way rapidly, to arrive in a racing splash. Once there, we would haul ourselves aboard onto our feet and, seesawing in tandem from one side to the other, clang that bell triumphantly to capture the attention of everyone on the beach. It was a revelation to observe the pressure with which the tide foamed against the base.

The swim back never had that keen thrill of drama that is often striking to a young boy taking a manful chance, mainly, I suppose, because each minute brought us closer to safety rather than away from it. And this time our target was a few miles of beach that would have been impossible to overshoot. One time, though, one boy in a group of four, tired badly and exclaimed that he didn't feel he could make it back. Without urgency, without even a sense of danger materializing, each of us simply took hold of a piece of him and cooperated in hauling him gently in, close enough to the rope at the third pole for him to manage the last few yards alone. It was not an occasion for exultation. I don't think we felt then that we had just saved a life; we didn't really believe he'd been in danger of dying.

But I don't recall that I ever set out on a swim to the bell buoy after that. I doubt that he did either. His name was Irving Kaiser, the same Irving Kaiser who lived in the apartment directly below ours—a year younger than I, he was thinner, too, and I was thin—and the same one who was killed by an artillery shell in Italy six or seven years later. I am more saddened by his death as I write about him now than I believe I let myself be at the time the news reached me, and even when I was back living in Coney Island and seeing his mother frequently. I believe I had by then already trained myself defensively to stifle painful emotion. I am walking proof of at least part of Freud's theories of repression and the domain of the unconscious, and perhaps, in writing this way here and in other things I've published, of denial and sublimation, too.

Today, I wouldn't try that swim for a million dollars, tax-free, although I don't doubt I could make it there and back. It's this haunted imagination that's mine still.

My brother had no recollection at all of the episode of the chase and the car when I brought it up some years ago during one of our infrequent spells of hesitant family reminiscence. With the benign revisions made by time in his perceptions, to his ungrudging mind I had always been "a good kid" and, though past sixty, still was. He was proud of me and proud of his son, Paul, who was doing well first as a talent agent and later in television production. Together, we had been fulfilling the dreams of accomplishment that he had no doubt nourished for himself.

But I remember vividly. It was nighttime and dark, and when I saw Lee emerge from the entrance to our building to take possession of me and lead me upstairs to bed or the bathtub, I instantly and recklessly transformed my disobedience into the street game of a pursuit. He was faster, being so much older, but I was swift on sneakers and tricky, and I dodged and faked and led him in an exasperating race back and forth from one side of the street to the other, laughing uncontrollably each time I twisted away to elude him again. And suddenly there were headlights blinding me and a tortured screech of automobile wheels braking, and my merriment ended with both of us stretched out on the bumper of a car that had squealed to a stop against us just one moment before.

I'll mention one other occasion when, speaking metaphorically now, I thought I'd come close to putting two of us in the family away for good, one of them me. This was a prank that none of us ever forgot, but even today it makes a lesser impression on me than it did on the others.

Rising on the sidewalk outside our building, near the curb, was a telephone pole, with spikes sunk into opposite sides on escalating levels to serve as steps for the serviceman to climb to the seat at the repair box about two stories up. They weren't difficult to mount once you attained the starting point at the bottom, a sturdy wedge of wood hammered into the pole for a first foothold about three feet from the ground. I found out how easy it was one day when, given a boost to that bottom wedge by a friend, I began going up the spikes, hand over hand and leg after leg. At the top, when I was at the seat, I discovered with happy surprise that I was gazing right into the open window of our kitchen. And I saw my mother there, busy at the stove inside just a few feet away.

"Ma, can I have a glass of milk?" I asked in my most innocent voice.

The look of bewildered amazement and then stark horror that struck her face when she turned and saw me poised in air just outside the window was so extreme that I feared I, too, might die of fright at just that moment. It could have been about then that my mother made for the first time the remark about my idea of humor that she would repeat many times afterward in maternal surprise and tribute, though often with a dismayed shake of the head:

"You've [He's] got a twisted brain."

One time I saw on her face a look of outrage and astonishment even more distraught, when, while glaring squarely into her eyes during one of my occasional infantile outbursts, I called her a bastard.

My belief, erroneous, was that inasmuch as her command of English was poor, she had not heard that dirty street word before and would have no idea what it meant, no more than I accurately knew then what it meant. At once I saw with terror that I was mistaken. She gasped with incredulity, and staggered back a step. And I knew in instant reflex that I never wanted to see her again with such an expression of deep hurt. I prayed she would never tell anyone.

ONE OTHER TIME about then I had a secret I wanted to guard. Prowling about the kitchen by myself, with a rapacious appetite starting to agitate me as always, I found in the cupboard a bulb of garlic with several of the cloves already broken loose. I thought surely that if I ate one or two, nobody would know. They soon knew. Everyone knew. For the next few days, people even half a block away knew.

3

Sea Gate

SEA GATE, on the western edge of a sliver of Brooklyn oceanfront scraped up and discarded by the receding glacier of the last ice age, remains historic in these annals for two later and more striking occurrences: a fire and a feel—and for an alleged business connection with a dignitary named Alfred E. Smith, a noteworthy summer presence there in the third decade of this century. An earlier celebrity dweller in Sea Gate was one John Y. McKane, political boss and self-appointed police chief on the Island, who saw to it that all things there ran in the peaceful mode he fancied until he himself was scrutinized by a higher authority, indicted, tried, and imprisoned.

The rumor of the involvement of Alfred E. Smith in the development of Sea Gate might be groundless, but he himself was real. Al Smith, formerly the very popular Democratic governor of New York, became the first Catholic candidate—he was defeated—for the presidency. A rarity in office for his unwillingness, I've read, to make use of his public service for his private enrichment, he was later made use of for his prestige and contacts by others more farseeing who were absorbed in the profitable formation of various real-estate properties. One of these was the Empire State

Building. Another undertaking vaguely ascribed to him in local folklore was the formation of the "Sea Gate Association" for the purchase and consolidation of land on the western rim of Coney Island and the conversion of that tidy, choice tract into an elite residential seaside community poking unassumingly out into the entrance to New York Harbor, with the Atlantic Ocean on one side and the tranquil inlet of a bay washing the other. It was a community of homeowners forbidding admittance to nonresidents, with its own uniformed police force guarding the gates at each of the two entrances and a tall chain-link barricade rising on its boundary between the limits of its private property and the rest of Coney Island.

Sea Gate begins where the Coney Island boardwalk and avenues end. The chain-link fence extends all the way down across the sand into the water's edge at both low tide and high, a rampart manifestly differentiating those inside from those outside. No doubt it extends that far in violation of federal law, which conventionally holds beaches to be a public part of the national seashore. In summertime, about a mile and a half away at the opposite end of Coney Island, beat the heart of the respectably notorious amusement section, with its billions of electric lights at Luna Park and Steeplechase and hundreds of other attractions. The newer community of Sea Gate reposed as far from the hurly-burly of the crowds and their seasonal pleasures and as far from the immigrant subcultures evolving in between as it was possible to be without backpedaling away into the water itself.

There, as in other places we know of, the organization of an "association" suggests the dictates of proprietary covenants among the earliest settlers to restrict the ownership and rental of properties to those exactingly approved by the governing body already in place. Probably Jews were not admitted at first, or Italians either. The fence spanning the beach and avenues, and the Sea Gate policemen at the gates, were of course intended to keep curious wayfarers out rather than insiders in. They contributed, as well, to a constant and none-too-subtle semiotic reminder of class distinction. A ban against stores of every kind, apart from aesthetic considerations, implies additionally a rather frigid determination of the early settlers to distance themselves from just about everything else in Coney Island and to persist there independent of the service facilities to be found in the community outside. There were still no stores in Sea Gate, not one, when I, like Columbus in the West Indies, or stout Cortez on his peak in Darién, grew old enough to "discover" this new world, and the inconveniences to families I came to know were many and often strenuous. God knows what these early inhabitants did for their headaches and haircuts. Aspirin could be toted in a pocket, but pockets couldn't hold barbers, and the inhabitants of Sea Gate certainly wouldn't have elected to wander deep into Coney Island to have their hair trimmed by Max the Barber, the father of Danny the Bull. They must have counted on conveying many of life's necessities with them when they came there, for summers or as year-round residents, and they didn't come by subway and trolley car. Before the construction of superhighways and the Brooklyn–Battery Tunnel, the journey by automobile from Manhattan and places still farther would not have been swift.

Their aversion to collegial fellowship with those outside the fence is readily explained by the reputation borne, and earned, by Coney Island as "the playground of the poor." The poor are despised even by their brothers, teaches the Bible in more than one place, and circumstantial confirmation of this truth can be found in the tendency of just about all of us to move out of Coney Island as soon as we could manage to. In general, though, we didn't move far. And we continued to return for our diversions more often than we went to any other place and to focus our social life on our friendships with those still living there and on the remaining social clubs with their phonographs, couches, back rooms, and card tables.

. . .

THE FIRE I SAW inside Sea Gate was my first fire, apart from those regulated small ones, with broken fruit crates for fuel, strung out like signals along the Coney Island beach Tuesday nights in summer acknowledgment of the fire-works shot aloft from the boat anchored off the end of Steeplechase Pier.

At these Coney Island "barnfires" of ours, we ate charred, sandy potatoes, roasted in wood flames and not fit for human consumption, and sizzling burnt marshmallows that blistered the tongue. We called the potatoes "mickeys," although we didn't know why. We cleared our debris from the beach after we had put out our fire and left the spot clean for the next day. We were good little boys when we were good. We were afraid of our teachers, although we liked them all, dreaded displeasing them, and were petrified by the mere possibility of getting into trouble in school.

The blaze inside Sea Gate was a daytime affair, and the real thing.

It was big.

Along with others on our block, I stood on the corner of Surf Avenue and gazed with awe at the broad flush of orange fire and billows of dense smoke, first black, then white, that dominated the horizon of the squat skyline something like half a mile away. What was burning? It was the yacht club, people who were older and wiser kept telling each other. I had not heard those words before. It was, I have since ascertained, the Atlantic Yacht Club, and it was described as "swank." Others are better qualified than I to itemize the traits of what that word signifies in depiction of a yacht club. I didn't even know then what a yacht club was.

Now that I do have some idea of what a yacht club is, I return to the memory of the fire and the presence of a yacht club with a pleased bemusement that never diminishes.

What a yacht club was doing in Coney Island at that time remains a charming mystery I would not choose to unravel by reductive research. My surmises are more intriguing. Certainly, Coney Island was at least as appropriate a location for a yacht club as the building between Fifth and Sixth Avenues on West 44th Street in Manhattan currently occupied by the New York Yacht Club. For one thing, it was closer to water. At the back of Coney Island is Gravesend Bay, which, though rather narrow, is nevertheless a body of water. In grade school there were those who bragged they had walked across the bay on the few days it was frozen in winter. Beyond the bay curves the western shoreline of Brooklyn proper, providing one of the contours shaping the enormous, magnificent, and now largely inactive New York seaport. And beyond that, on clear days, one can easily pinpoint the gray structures of certain of Manhattan's skyscrapers.

In miles therefore, or perhaps "knots," the trip from the city to Sea Gate is shorter by sea than by land, and we know that those oddballs who do enjoy boating, whether by engine or sail, are usually in no hurry anyway and haven't much else they want to do with their time.

Back then there was a company, the Iron Steamboat Company, that ran a regular schedule of shuttle trips from the Battery in lowest Manhattan to the Steeplechase Pier, transporting visitors from the city directly into the amusement area, and these ships seemed to perform prosperously, for they went on operating until Coney Island changed with the war and its alluring mystique of novelty and glamour began irretrievably to wane. From vantage points on our boardwalk and beach we could watch these white sidewheeler steamboats coming and going, and easily spot, as well, the freighters and the giant, international ocean liners, trying to identify the liners by the number of smokestacks as they steamed slowly in and out before us. A luxury cruise ship, the *Morro Castle,* went up in flames one day not far offshore; that would have been my second Coney Island fire, but I was elsewhere when it happened. However, I did go more than once to view the devastated hulk after it had been towed into Gravesend Bay (by name a fitting resting place, it might at first seem, for Gravesend Bay is compounded of grim English words whose portentous message I did not appreciate until I began writing about it; but, alas, I now know that the term arises in nonphilosophical innocence from Dutch words meaning nothing more sinister than "lord's beach"). The journey by water to Sea Gate from some waterway inland was neither treacherous nor long, and it is easy to picture boatmen, and boatwomen, from docking places in the Hudson and East Rivers and even from Westchester, Connecticut, and the shores of Long Island lifting anchor to set course for Coney Island and the Atlantic Yacht Club in Sea Gate.

They had to bring their meals with them or eat in the dining room at the yacht club, if the yacht club had one, for together with the absence of stores, there were no restaurants in Sea Gate. At that time, probably, Jews were not accepted for membership at the club. But Jews were not sailors then, either, not my Brooklyn Jews, so there was no insult to anything but pride. In those preassimilation days, they did not go golfing, play tennis, or ski. And they rarely divorced; if any wanted to, they would have had to learn how.

By the time I found myself old enough to wander about Sea Gate, through the courtesy of one or another school acquaintance who lived there, there was no trace of the swanky yacht club I'd seen burning away or of any other. It had been there, it was gone. The salient landmark now was Lindbergh Park, memorable still for the airplane pilot whose name honors it and, to me, for the milestone event of my first feel. The park is a tiny clearing—the land area of all Sea Gate is small—that served as one of several gathering places for green adolescents of both sexes for giggling hijinks on balmy nights. Word went out from other fellows in my Boy Scout troop that two girls there whom I recognized from grade school would permit you to squeeze their breasts if you waited politely in line with the other boys for your turn in the kissing games. One of the girls was petite and pretty. The second was larger and jolly. I waited my turn and drew the buxom one. The gossip proved true. I felt a female bosom, and I learned something—I learned something fast. I learned that once you had a breast in your hand, there wasn't much you could do with it. Not until the initiating days of my cellar clubs not long after did I begin to comprehend that this first liberty beyond kissing was a step, a passport of sorts, that might, or might not, be a prelude to an advancing stage of intimacies more disorderly.

By that time in Sea Gate, the founding fathers, along with the yacht club, had been removed from the scene by the inexorable stresses of economic and social change and replaced by a different order of landowner with a less demanding ethos. Two-family houses of red brick had sprung up for rental on the idle lots between the capacious wooden summer mansions traditional at seashores. Some years ago, several of these mansions were put to use by the city as dwellings for people on welfare, to the alarm and chagrin of that generation of residents, and this practice may still be in force.

With the change in population, there was no longer much difference in race, creed, or place of national origin between those living inside the gates and those outside. There did exist a presumed financial disparity, but this was something that in childhood we were slow to comprehend and which was not necessarily accurate. The girls and boys of Sea Gate went to the same public school we did and usually had a longer walk to get to it; there was no talk then of any such thing as a private school. They went to the same parties at graduation and to the same movie theaters for Saturday matinees, to the same secondary school by the same trolley cars or school buses. Those fellows who did join social clubs later came outside to join one of ours. Girls I remember—Hannah Tansman and Gladys Simon—did come to classes in grade school wearing fur coats in winter, but memory hints that they were both, perhaps, from families in the fur business. A blond cutie of nine or ten named June Owitz always seemed to be wearing a bright sweater, possibly cashmere. But if there ever was coolness or snobbishness, I didn't notice it, and no one I knew, inside or outside Sea Gate, ever spoke of it. But parents are parents, and in my maturity, I have the feeling that had I been a parent with a daughter living in Sea Gate, I might not have approved of someone like me.

When I entered secondary school, the Coney Island celebrities on the Abraham Lincoln High School football team were largely from Sea Gate: Eddie Mann, Phil Metling, Len Finkleman. When I left, they were from Coney Island streets like my own: Herb Poplinger, Red Goldstein, Richie Wertheim, and others. On my first trip to Lincoln High on a school bus, I had the football lineman Len Finkleman pointed out to me, and with a pang gave up all dreams of even trying out for the football team. He was two years ahead of me in classes and appeared two hundred pounds ahead of me in the evolutionary progression of bone and muscle. In due course I turned out for fencing lessons instead and made the team, but lost interest before even one interscholastic match.

I confess that I loved school, loved both grade school and high school. I loved the vacations and the end of vacations. The thought of playing hookey in grade school hardly ever crossed my mind—I wouldn't have been able to think of a more enjoyable way to spend the time. On days when I was absent with a fever, I would watch the clock until Irving Kaiser from the apartment downstairs and Ira Lopata across the street were due to get home in order to converse with them from my window. Twice in high school I was a truant. I calculated with remorse afterward that I hadn't had as good a time at the stage show and film at New York's Paramount Theater or in Weepy's poolroom as I would have had in the classes, cafeteria, and sweetshop at Lincoln. I had no pleasure in disobedience for its own sake, and I take none now.

I liked school because I was good at it. I took readily to reading, writing, and arithmetic. I even liked the homework, was stimulated to accomplishment by the challenge of each demanding obligation. I liked very much having something to do. I am still less comfortable with unlimited leisure than with the organizing and worrisome feeling that I have something I must get done, like finishing this book, or even this paragraph.

The elementary school year and classes then were divided into halves, into an A section and a B. In my first grade, 1A1, Miss Wolfe one day held up a flash card bearing the word KING. It was our first exposure to an -ing word. I concentrated a moment and raised my hand—I was the first and only child to do so—and when called upon said, "King." Don't ask me how I knew. A day or so later, I was "skipped" half a year, transferred from class 1A1 into Miss Leiberman's "fast" 1B1. There I found myself among a group of students with whom I was to remain all the way until graduation, and then through high school as well. We, the 1 class, regardless of grade, were always the "bright" class, and we advanced together with very few changes in our membership, most of which resulted from new families moving into the district and old ones moving away. Two (2) was the slow class, and 3, 4, and 5 were in between. I was bright, and so were Ruth Gerstein, Hannah Tansman, Gladys Simon, Albie Covelman, Eugene Dolgin, Seymour Ostrow, Phyllis Ritterman, and maybe as many as a dozen others I could name if I put my mind to it. As early as the fourth or fifth grade, Phyllis Ritterman had made it known that she wished to grow up to be a novelist—this before the rest of us knew what a novelist was. She had inscribed as much with her signature in my souvenir graduation album. Almost fifty years after graduation from this primary school, I was invited to speak at a college in Arizona or Texas—I forget exactly where. While the audience was dispersing afterward, a woman facing me squarely as she sat down beside me challenged: "You don't know who I am, do you?" It required no more than a second to summon up the answer. "Sure I do. You're Phyllis Ritterman, aren't you?" From that encounter came my formulation of a theory I find to be generally true: Time may age a physiognomy but doesn't otherwise alter it beyond recognition. (On the chance you may care, I'll contribute the unrelated opinion that psychotherapy doesn't change much either—not character, personality, feelings, or even, in the long run, behavior. I speak here from both personal experience and observation.)

I avidly enjoyed our sessions in the early grades in rapid arithmetic; I naturally would, for these were competitions in accuracy and speed, and I was one of the two, three, or four who were always out in front, and I embraced the chance to show my stuff. In algebra and plane geometry later on, with some tips on attitude from my brother, Lee, I was a whiz kid of sorts in the introductory levels, but not, I discovered with resignation, beyond those. My brother was addicted to mystery riddles. I liked to grapple with them, too. In the Lee Heller fabrication, X was not merely an unknown quantity: X was a slippery party to be tracked down and pinned by the pertinent factual evidence contained in the enclosing data. Included one time on an examination in the 7A or 7B algebra class of Mr. T. D. Bartells was a vexing problem of a peculiarly complicated trickiness. "Only one person in the class got that one right," revealed Mr. Bartells, and then looked my way. "And it had to be you," he added, and threw a stick of chalk at me.

Throwing chalk was his mischievous procedure for keeping control of his mischievous students, of whom I inveterately was one, wisecracking, talking, interrupting, and concocting an occasional practical joke—innocent, I was maliciously inclined to believe—on a fellow student; for example, if the correct answer was two and he didn't know it, I might pretend to help him with the whisper "forty-two hundred and eighty-nine." And surely Mr. Bartells would guess what had happened. I had a million of them. We had been tittering about Mr. Bartells as we advanced each year toward the grades he taught, for T. D. Bartells was known secretly in a punning play on his name as "Titty Bottles." I would be most surprised if he didn't know that, too.

I was never in real trouble in school. The few times a parent was demanded, my sister came. My mother would have been frightened, and I would have felt disgraced by her broken English. My sister recalls intervening only once, and that was over an incident I have forgotten entirely. My offense was not misconduct but boredom. I would clearly be musing on other things in apparent distraction and not be paying rapt attention, but each time the teacher sought to trap me with a sudden question, I frustrated her with the correct answer. I would be gazing out the window, at the wall, down at my hands or feet; sometimes I appeared to be talking to myself, mouthing words. If so, they were probably sentences I was testing for the trick ending of a short story I was already contemplating writing someday, or possibly a phrase with which to begin or conclude my next book report.

Very early, I now choose to think, I was exhibiting a pragmatic fixation on making use of my fantasizing and putting my daydreams to work. The early ambition to become a writer of fiction was one of them.

I was generally at home with the logical and at sea with the theoretical. (I coped with matters beyond my comprehension by taking for granted the truth of what I was told and attempting to go on from there.) In biology in early high school—another triumph—the teacher, in discussing bacteria, raised the question of how we could tell that the process of pasteurization did not eliminate all the bacterial life in a bottle of milk. The answer appeared to me so obvious that at first I didn't even raise my hand. When no one else in the class could give it, I did.

But I lacked innate efficiency when it came to the abstract. My brain went dull with quadratic equations, negative numbers, the multiplication of fractions, trigonometry, beginning calculus. In chemistry, which should have been easy, I often found myself in difficulty with the mathematics of chemical reactions. It was along about this time that certain of my close friends (Marvin Winkler among them) threw in the towel in the struggle with such useless malarkey and transferred out of Lincoln into vocational school. I got by because my memory was reliable and I was able to duplicate through rote the procedures I was supposed to follow. But a logarithm remained unfathomable, and I still haven't solved the eternal mystery of pi (or even understood what the mystery is).

English classes, on the other hand, *were* as easy as pie. I had a surer grasp of grammar when I was learning it than I have now since I've been writing professionally and since my experience of teaching freshman English on a college level. Correcting freshman compositions, with that terrorizing responsibility of always appearing infallible, did much to undermine my assurance about syntax and spelling. So much uncertainty generated by looking things up to make absolutely sure eventually generated long-lived doubts that still obtain.

Reading was exciting, engrossing, and I was doing a lot of it at home on my own. An older brother and sister already working at jobs in Manhattan—it was not a short commute—brought a variety of magazines into the apartment which expanded my mind in a widening radius of common knowledge. There were books, too, from commercial circulating libraries, as contrasted with public libraries—current novels, mysteries, best-sellers that were easy to read, which was not in all respects a very good thing to grow used to. It took a long while afterward for me to relate with patience to literary works in which something more than rapid plots with lots of dialogue furnished the essential components. Magazines like *Collier's* and *Liberty,* which dependably published works of popular fiction, invariably contained in each issue a "short, short story" of a thousand words or less with a trick ending, and the prospect of writing these successfully stimulated my imagination and ambition at an early age.

When I was nine or ten, a visiting cousin on my father's side, Nat Siegel, who might already have completed the course work to become an accountant, brought me the gift of a children's version of the *Iliad*. It was the first work I'd read that truly fired me with excitement and emotion. I could hardly cease reading and rereading it. I couldn't forget it, and I have not forgotten it. It was not only a simplified version but also a narrative version that carried the action to a conclusive finish well beyond the confines of the original. Not until I was almost through high school did I hear that the *Iliad* was not a fascinating small novel for children but a large epic poem. And not until I read it somewhere along the line in college did the knowledge sink in that the subject of the work is the wrath of Achilles and not the exhausting war against Troy. My disillusionment and surprise were not easily overcome. So deeply affected was I by my first exposure to the work in that small volume that I still find it difficult to accept that in Homer's version there is no Trojan horse, no death of Achilles, no final victory and sack of the city. It may say something about my frame of mind that I preferred Hector to Achilles and felt more compassion for Priam than for any of the heroic Greeks, and that in Shakespeare, I liked Hotspur better than I did the prince, and still do, more even than Falstaff—and I like to think that *everyone* of right mind feels the same way.

I wrote my next book report on the *Iliad,* to my delight and to that of my teacher. I decorated the cover with tracings of drawings from the pages of the thin volume. And the month after that, I wrote another, completely different book report on the same work, submitting it with other illustrations. As gently as possible, the teacher took me aside to stress something I had missed: that reading rather than writing was the objective of those assignments and that more than one report on a book was not the practice. It could have been about then that I moved on to *Tom Sawyer,* a work that didn't really please me at all.

The tendency to be unaware of matters that should be

obvious has stayed with me. Going for a master's degree in American literature at Columbia University after the war, I worked for more than a year on a thesis on the Pulitzer Prize plays, a trivial, unfruitful subject that I'm surprised now was approved, without bothering to find out what a thesis was supposed to be. Not until long afterward, when I was asked in conversation what the thesis of my thesis was, did I realize I'd had none. It was accepted anyway. Some time after that, while occupied with writing the latter portions of *Catch-22*, I applied for a job of minor executive status in the advertising-promotion department of *McCall's,* then a women's service magazine with a huge circulation, and was required to submit to a battery of psychological tests that included the Rorschach. I found myself dilating at almost inexhaustible length on each of the whole blots on each of the cards, less volubly on the color ones, barely remarking on any of the details. I scarcely noticed them; I could see only one big picture. If God is in the details, as more than one contemporary authority continues to maintain, I think I've passed Him by in everyone's work but my own. I think it was with intuitive good sense that when I finally applied myself seriously to the writing of fiction, I skirted the requirements of convincing detail fundamental to that genre called realism.

I have one more classroom achievement I'm eager to boast of. In one of my schools, either primary or secondary, we read *Treasure Island* and were assigned to bury a treasure of our own somewhere on a map entirely of our own devising. In my map—inventively, I must say—I marked the various sites with the names of well-known people of the time. I had a Rudy Valley, a W. C. Hill (a well-known radio commentator), a meadow called W. C. Fields, and a forest called Lefty Grove (a famous baseball pitcher on the Boston Red Sox). I would have had a Veronica Lake, if it hadn't been too soon. Certainly I had a Grace or Victor Moore, and other geographical features with place names of that kind. A landmark was a racetrack called Steeplechase. Outside a woods called Helen Twelvetrees (a former screen actress), my treasure was buried in a meadow named Luna Park. It was all in the region of Pancreas, and on the Isle of Langerhans, one in that body of pancreatic cells whose name I had come upon adventitiously in some mystery novel brought into the house shortly before by my brother or my sister. You entered the territory through some mouth or other—I might have used "gorge," too, but I doubt I was that clever—and made your way downward through the alimentary canal. The teacher—named Miss Perks, I remember, a substitute who came for a day and remained for the term—was greatly impressed. I had guessed she would be.

HIGH SCHOOL AND PUBERTY brought significant changes—to our attitudes, responses, and social behavior—and so, as might be guessed, did Hitler, Mussolini, and World War II. We reeled into adolescence with different increments of biological experience and velocity, the girls, naturally, maturing sooner and evidencing signs more prominently: A girl named Sonia showed the fullest bosom in the seventh or eighth grade, whereas a Sea Gate girl named Ruth, whom I had a crush on, slender, dark, and slightly taller, was showing hardly anything at all. But all of us who went on to Abraham Lincoln High School rather than to Brooklyn Tech or to a vocational school began our secondary school education on the same day.

The school was some distance away, and for the first time in our young lives we found ourselves associating closely in classrooms with strangers from other parts of the world, even if those other parts were only contiguous parts of Brooklyn. There were the boys and girls from that second, Italian section of Coney Island, whom we now came to know much better; along with them were pupils from those bordering territories that at first were as alien to us as Alaska would have been. The pupils from Brighton close by, who were Jewish, too, were most like us—the girls on balance a bit better groomed, but the boys no less rowdy and ill-mannered than we were, better at sports because better coached. Naked swimming in the school pool one gym period a week was an indefensible oppression. The only guys who didn't seem to mind were those with very big dicks. The school was just over three miles from where we lived, too far to walk if we didn't want to, and, except for a few revitalizing afternoons each spring, we didn't want to. Our Surf Avenue trolley line bore us into the amusement area, turned up to Neptune Avenue, and dropped us at a corner almost at the school itself. Those from Sea Gate had a longer way to go, for they first had to make their way out of their enclave on foot or by internal jitney. For a few more nickels a week we could journey back and forth by a private bus that departed each morning from a spot on Mermaid Avenue and returned to that same place each afternoon. These buses were individual personal enterprises; the school, though far away, took no responsibility for getting us there. When last I looked, a neighborhood acquaintance from one of the social clubs, Novack by name, was making a good adult living as owner of one, perhaps more than one, of these school buses.

The school, though large and relatively new, was already overcrowded, and for the first year after enrolling, all of us in the entering class were obliged to attend classes in an annex. The Lincoln Annex occupied the top two floors of a typical elementary public school of red brick with white stone trim apart from Abraham Lincoln's main grounds. It was packed with students—boys and girls, young men and women, from a strange and somewhat haphazard assortment of ethnic and occupational backgrounds we hadn't encountered before. Taken all together, we were a motley crew. My recollection is that all of us were white. The school was in an unfamiliar Italian residential neighborhood, and we moved about in it cautiously. Fortunately, we didn't have to move far: The Italian grocery store supplying our first hero sandwiches for a nickel with Italian salami, baloney, or ham on Italian bread was just across the street, and the tracks for the streamlined trolley to which we transferred from our own were just a couple of blocks away.

In the high-school annex and afterward in the main building, we attended classes with students we hadn't, with perhaps a couple of chance exceptions, known before and who hadn't to any fuller extent known each other. Along with the increase in the number of new student-acquaintances, our choice of elective courses further contributed to the diffusion of our Coney Island social sets into the general school population. For a language to study, many of us first chose Spanish in the belief that it would prove easier than French or German; two of us, one the son of the local pharmacist, picked Latin in hopes of becoming a physician, and he eventually did. The boys, with very few exceptions, decided on an academic curriculum, which was meant to guide them toward a college education almost none then desired; the girls, though with many more exceptions, did, like my sister, Sylvia, select a commercial course directing them toward inevitable, traditional jobs as secretaries and bookkeepers. I made room in my program for a class in typing. Although I had no typewriter closer than an old one in Irving Kaiser's apartment downstairs, I felt in my bones that if ever I was to succeed as a hard-boiled news reporter or novelist or playwright—and I expected that to be soon—I might succeed more quickly if I knew how to type. I was one of a handful of boys in a room full of girls I hadn't previously met. I lusted for several who fancied tight skirts and sweaters (I'm afraid I still do, and for those now often pictured in advertisements in slinky shifts) and was in love with none.

It surprises me today to contemplate my complete lack of interest then in working on the school newspaper, the *Lincoln Log,* or contributing to the literary magazine, *Cargoes.* Seymour Ostrow, who also was thinking of becoming a hard-nosed journalist and who later, after the war, became a softhearted criminal lawyer instead, succeeded in becoming a reporter for the *Lincoln Log;* I didn't even try. The few friends I made who also read books and were intensely occupied with the literary magazine spoke effortlessly to each other of writers such as Chaucer, Keats, and Yeats; these were names I don't think I'd heard before. Yet I was preoccupied always, although without remarkable productivity or technical expertise, with the writing of short stories and sarcastic, humorous (*I* thought) nonfiction pieces. These were works I didn't want anyone connected with the literary magazine to know about. Mr. Grumet encouraged such creative efforts in his advanced English course, and with his assignments I was able to hold my own. My favorite author for a time was not Chaucer, Keats, or Yeats but Damon Runyon, of whom not many people, if they know of him at all, are apt to think highly any longer. My favorite humorists later on (recommended to me by Danny the Count as "Benchley" and "Wodehouse," as though every lad in the world routinely knew their Christian names) became Robert Benchley and P. G. Wodehouse, and these were quantum leaps forward to nearly inexhaustible delights. My favorite source for the best in contemporary American fiction was *Collier's* magazine—until a friend of my sister's, who, upon learning from her that I was interested in writing and reading, presented me with a hardbound copy of Irwin Shaw's collection *Sailor off the Bremen,* and then my ambitions turned more serious, and my assumptions of brilliant and immediate fame were moderated accordingly. It must have been about then, after Irwin Shaw, that I began my never-ending tussles with the texts in the magazine *The New Yorker,* where his fiction often appeared.

Notwithstanding a fear of failure at the literary magazine and my facade of indifferent reluctance, in 1939, when I was sixteen, still a schoolboy, and Russia invaded Finland, I wrote a short, short story about that war and a young, heroic Finnish soldier defending his post with ingenious tricks I've forgotten against Red forces overwhelming in mass. I showed this effort to nobody. After hours of hard labor, and with copious erasures necessitated by the constant growth of my vocabulary, I got the story down on white paper on the old typewriter in Irving Kaiser's house. I thought it was great. In fact, I not only wrote the story, I submitted it—I mailed it away—for publication in *Collier's, Liberty,* and the New York *Daily News,* our local newspaper of huge circulation that then also published fiction regularly.

It was not accepted.

Those were my first rejection slips.

No, I don't still have them.

Nor have I kept my first letter or two of acceptance. The first of those came six years later, for a short work written in my tent in Corsica and also tapped out on a borrowed type-writer, this one belonging to a recent replacement pilot who was out flying combat missions while I, my missions completed, sat safely on my ass and wrote stories on his keyboard. The next was for a freshman theme at the University of Southern California—but those can wait until I'm at least out of high school, can't they?

I CAN DIVULGE NOW that during both my early schools, elementary and secondary, hardly a year went by in which I did not for at least part of a term have a secret and serious, nonsexual crush on one girl or another: June, Ruth, Hannah, Gladys, Mimi, Naomi, another Ruth—who can remember them all? Each had what I idealized as an irresistibly pretty face. I used to wonder with dumbfounded amazement why all the boys were not in love with the one I was in love with at the time. Usually, my infatuation was with a girl who sat alongside me at a desk between me and the teacher, so that I could stare at her dreamily, in profile, to my heart's fulfillment. On days these girls were late or absent, I might sink into a miserable dread of disappointment and rejection. These loves were romantic, not carnal, and it was fortunate, so far as I know, that they weren't returned. Otherwise I might have undergone a brief early marriage and a quick early divorce—instead of the long marriage I enjoyed, one of thirty-five years, and the long, unhappy, embittering divorce, which took more than three years to formalize. Luckily, my schoolboy crushes were over by the time I entered college; by then I was already married and spared those heartaches.

On Fridays, I acknowledge now with some pride and shame, with that indelicate pride *in* shame come upon too often in confessional autobiographical pages like this one, I wore to school for a while my official Boy Scout uniform. Troop meetings throughout the various neighborhoods were held Friday evenings, and girls who were Girl Scouts came to classes that day in their uniforms of green, too. It was the fashion. My membership in the Boy Scouts was for me a freak occurrence; mostly till then I had obstinately resisted participation in organizations and organized group activities, and I still do. In grammar school I wouldn't once join the GO (our "General Organization" to help support student activities) and perversely refused to go along on voluntary excursions to zoos and botanical gardens; in high school I passed up the class trip to the 1939–40 World's Fair, and when my team won the intramural softball tournament after a somewhat spectacular outfield running catch by me for the final out with the winning runs on base, I neglected to drop by the athletic office to pick up my PSAL pin, for I knew I would never wear it. I have no idea what happened to my Phi Beta Kappa key or, for that matter, to my Air Medal or bombardier's wings. I never voted in a school election. I don't vote now. I haven't gone to a school or air force reunion and did not attend my college graduation ceremony. For a couple of fruitless years I was enrolled as a voter in the Democratic Party under the gullible impression that I could influence the choice of candidates, an American delusion still besetting millions.

Those two were about my only lapses. But the Boy Scouts for us was more social than spiritual, and I was soon having fun at their games as a patrol leader. In high school, an Italian girl with the shortened name of Mimi was a Girl

Scout. She was different from the taciturn others in my galaxy of stately belles. She was of pale complexion, and she was talkative, witty, and forward, likable rather than beautiful. Direct. We kidded with each other a lot, and we were able to make each other laugh. One Friday, both of us in uniform, she suggested that we plan an overnight hike with just a friend of hers and another boy. Because I didn't quickly grasp what she was suggesting, I declined with some faltering evasions. If I had known for sure what she had in mind, I probably would have declined more abruptly. I was backward that way, she was not. Her warmth toward me seemed to lessen. She knew more than I did, and I was too innocent to learn.

ALMOST WITHOUT PERCEIVING IT, we were growing up. And many of the resulting transmutations were pervasive and subtle.

Earlier, in grade school, a difference of a year or half a year between us meant merely a difference in class level and mattered not at all in the hierarchy of the block and the street; now, the difference in age brought a difference in school locations—with different classmates and acquaintances, different loyalties, different teachers, homework, enthusiasms. Old relationships loosened as new friendships formed. Those left behind had to feel left out of much that was going on. Friends made friends with people from different parts of Coney Island, and they became our friends, too. Boys from different streets soon were coming together to organize themselves into new and better punchball and football teams and grew as interested in girls as in athletics. More and more we tended to hang out with guys who were friendly with the girls we knew; girls, too, became more interested in themselves as girls, and in boys, too. Jeannie Goldman from across the street joined a social club with girls from down the Island who had gone to the public school in the Italian section. She and I never did get to min-

gle socially, to the presumed regret of her mother, who'd
been fond of me through my childhood, and mine, who'd
always liked Jeannie, and later esteemed her all the more
after the accident of the broken hip. Geraldine Scharf on the
next block joined a girls' club, too, and I never found myself
with her at a party again. The boys these girls found were
generally older. Our girls were generally a year or so
younger. I can remember no strong social ties with Irving
Kaiser after I moved into high school one year before he did,
although I continued to use his typewriter and we continued
to know each other until we each followed our separate des-
tinies into military service.

When, while still in high school, a bunch of us finally
got together and chipped in for rent, furniture, and phono-
graph for a social club of our own—my first social club,
Club Hilight, was located in the cellar of a two-family
house—just about all the members were on the same grade
and age level, and close to half were fellows from down the
Island I hadn't known in elementary school. And the girls
didn't have to be from our neighborhood, either. On weekend evenings they came from Brighton, Flatbush, East New
York, and elsewhere and were flattered by invitations to
drop down to our club room to dance and neck. In the summer they'd arrive on the Island from everywhere. I believe it
close to a fact that until I went into the army, I never took a
girl out on a date, and not many of the other fellows did
either. It is still a magic of biology to me how the sexually
advanced of both genders managed from earliest years to
sense each other out, to recognize and acknowledge each
other's mutuality of procreative desires and intuitively come
together for joint satisfaction. Cliques established themselves on that single basis of sexual headway: Periodically, a
special allegiance would form between two or three males
who had latched on to a girl agreeable to putting out for all
of them in sequence on the same occasion, and they, even
when with the rest of us, would cluster together as though
in conspiracy and talk—not only about what they were up

to with her, but also about everything else—furtively. The dedicated marijuana smokers would cling together, too, as did the heroin users later on. To the disappointment of those who were still too young or otherwise excluded from one coterie or another, the old ties of the block and the street were melting away.

And suddenly there were those boys and girls we'd known forever who belonged to no group at all: the boy without personality, the girl who wasn't attractive and couldn't live comfortably with that knowledge, the odd ones, the quiet ones, the nervous ones, even the studious ones, the crippled ones who couldn't play ball or dance the lindy hop. Mursh the Hopper. The stutterer. These were the friendless ones who didn't fit and automatically were being left out of everything, without pity, without attention. It has not been much different since.

Life was turning real in ways we could no longer ignore. In 1939 Germany invaded Poland from the west, Russia invaded from the east, and the big war began. In 1940 our Selective Service Act went into effect, and young men in the neighborhood began to fade from sight and return on furlough in military uniform. George Mandel, a Club Alteo senior while I was still a junior, was called up early, and his gorgeous "wheels" disappeared with him. As an illustrator, originator, and writer in the burgeoning field of comic books, he'd been earning very good money while still very young, and he began to show up in a latest-model blue convertible with automatic top and hydromatic transmission, the first we had seen and the niftiest car we had ever been permitted to caress with our fingertips. Henny Ehrenman, closer to me in age though older, also soon went, to an airfield in Colorado to which I was later assigned for a while. Home on furlough, he described only a good time in the western saloons of Denver with women more permissive than any we had known, or known of. None who were drafted or enlisted seemed to mind. At seventeen I didn't think I would ever have to go. Some of the draft-eligible ones, while they waited, found defense work doing things with a metal alloy called monel; not long after, as I was waiting in turn, I had a couple of defense jobs myself. Others bided their time in a factory manufacturing a fabric called chenille. But a cousin of mine who was only slightly older was killed in a motor accident on an army air base. And after Pearl Harbor they were shipping men overseas. After Pearl Harbor, I smugly took for granted, along with a few million other innocents, that once "we" were in it, the war would soon be over, before I could be called up. "Those Japs must be crazy," I remember saying to the friends I was with on the afternoon of Pearl Harbor day. "We'll wipe them right out."

It was known even before I went overseas that Abie Ehrenreich, an aerial gunner my age who probably had enlisted immediately for him to be in battle so soon, had been in a plane shot down over North Africa and was already a prisoner of war. George Mandel went into Europe with the infantry, succumbing to the allure of the action when he had the option of remaining Stateside as a member of a permanent party unit in an instructional capacity. He will not disagree when I say he should have known better. In Holland he was shot in the leg in an ambush. Recuperating in a hospital when hearing of the Battle of the Bulge, he checked himself out to rejoin his unit and shortly afterward was hit in the head by a sniper. This was a wound whose numerous distressing effects have never entirely left him. General George C. Patton would have been proud of him. My George will not be pleased to hear me say that.

Life was real, life was earnest, and it was turning harsh and earnest for several of us in other ways as well. One boy we had gone to grade school with would finally die of the "weak heart" that had compelled his exclusion from all physical-education classes; I remember another from the Alteo seniors who passed away early from Hodgkin's disease, the first time we'd heard of it (a closer friend, Lou Berkman, was fifty-two when he finally gave in to that one);

a friend from the Boy Scouts died of leukemia. Neighborhood youths would grow up unaccountably mean and
vicious and begin hanging around with toughs from other
neighborhoods. Izzy Nish could be wicked. Smokey was
sweet-natured but could be dangerous. It was best at all
times to keep far away from Louie Schwartz, an inordi-
nately pugnacious young prizefighter. The legend had it
that when he moved far upward in class for a bout with
"raging bull" Jake LaMotta, even his mother went to *shul*
with hundreds of others in Coney Island to pray that
LaMotta would not knock him out quickly but carry him
the distance and pound him mercilessly. Single girls would
surprisingly turn up pregnant when there still was massive
odium attached to that condition and force boys several
years older into unwanted, short marriages to effect legiti-
macy. One girl of sultry, exquisite beauty and a year younger
than I, was so obviously pregnant by the time of her high-
school graduation that the administration was of two minds
about permitting her to take part in commencement exercises. The kid from Brighton we had teased as a sissy would
indeed turn out to be homosexual, before we even understood what that was. Many of us were already working after
high-school classes at jobs we liked only a little—I, an
exception, got a kick out of mine. Others were dropping out
of school as soon as the law allowed, at age sixteen, to go
to work at jobs they didn't like at all. We could stay up
late now, almost all night if we wished, and in summer
in the amusement area we could stay up late enough to
view the overflowing trash baskets as the crowds thinned,
to see the litter of watermelon rinds and chewed corncobs
on the ground amid the ruins of hot-dog rolls, and to comprehend that Coney Island is a rather unclean place when
the ticket booths close and the lights go out.

The aromatic foods that had been fried and grilled
turned greasy. In the early hours of the next day the odors in
the street already signalled decay. Even the fresh breezes
from the sea, which had awakened keen appetites earlier

and stimulated the other senses, could no longer bear away those repellent effluvia of garbage. We had already realized that in winter Coney Island was in the main a lonely, dark, and windy place for people grown too old for homework, roller skating, or playing tag. In winter, marijuana smokers I recognized would often huddle for warmth and each other's company in the lobby of my apartment house, which had no doorman, of course, and was open to anyone who wished to walk in. I knew the smell. I knew them by name. Nobody chased them away.

4

Work

OF THE VARIOUS JOBS I held before going into the army,
just one, that of a uniformed Western Union messenger,
was exotic by Coney Island standards. My post as a blacksmith's helper was the more surprising, but by the time I
became one, at least a dozen other Coney Islanders had gone
south to work in the Norfolk Navy Yard in Portsmouth,
Virginia. Yet not until I tumbled into this new situation did
any of us appreciate that there were such things as blacksmiths still in existence except at a horse track, let alone in
an up-to-date, state-of-the-art, vast American navy yard.
Others from Coney Island, already working in the Norfolk
Navy Yard, were by then in jobs equally remote and un-
foreseen—helpers to steamfitters, machinists, sheet-metal
workers—in an arcane profusion of factory hangars spread-
ing just about everywhere on the level land except the dry
docks, and there painters and riggers were toiling continually at the vessels. An "E for Efficiency" banner floated
above the main entrance to the navy yard. This had been
earned even before my arrival.

We were housed in individual rooms in single-story
barracks, in a stretched-out, labyrinthine sprawl of clapboard bungalows that at times seemed infinite. A Coney

Island man slightly older than the rest of us, who was already a licensed plumber, drove down in his auto. Better paid than we were and more experienced in such matters as mating, he lost little time finding a girlfriend, a cheerful, plump, blond young woman from one of the soda shops in town. He conveyed her into his quarters in our barrack for a little while one evening, and the very next day was directed to move out. A friend I made from a different part of Brooklyn also fell into some kind of trouble over a girl. Late one afternoon after work, the police came and took him away for questioning; the next day all his things were gone, and so was he, back home, without a parting word to anyone. Our friendship had been founded largely on our corresponding developing appreciation for classical music. On calm nights in Virginia we could tease in music on our little radios even from station WQXR in New York. Novices as listeners, we both took indignant and vociferous exception to more experienced critics who extolled Bach and Mozart at the expense of tuneful romantic compositions like those of Tchaikovsky and César Franck, which we then preferred. I would guess that his tastes, too, have broadened by now.

I have to emphasize that it was not insurance against the military draft that drew us southward to war work in the navy yard in Virginia, which afforded no deferments to mere helpers. After Pearl Harbor, almost no one I knew of wanted to evade service. Even pudgy Marvin Winkler took himself into the marines as soon as he was old enough to be vulnerable to conscription. (He married *before* he was old enough, he reminded me recently; because he was under twenty-one, his mother needed to accompany the couple to the marriage bureau at the city hall and with her signature and person provide consent to the union. No such parental authorization was required for the bride.) Nor was it patriotism, either, that led us to Virginia. Neither outside the army nor in do I recall hearing patriotic statements from anyone but our official propaganda sources, and these were issued to us as lessons in "orientation." Rather, we were drawn almost feverishly to our jobs in defense work by the chance of a colossal elevation in pay over what we had been accustomed to making elsewhere: At the navy yard, we would earn a salary of *a dollar an hour* for an eight-hour day in a forty-hour week. On top of that was the boost to time-and-a-half for overtime on weekends: twelve dollars a day for each Saturday and Sunday if we chose to work, adding up to a total of sixty-four dollars for a seven-day week! In our jobs in the city, we had been lucky to make as much as twenty dollars a week; rarely did any of us make more. Thirty was a fortune, and a fortune befalling only those lucky few with uncles or older brothers or brothers-in-law already prospering at something and in a position to hire.

In Virginia, naturally, we chose, starting out, to work weekends, for that was where the big money lay. The toil was physical, and that was new. A snapshot of me I sent home after just a few of those seven-day workweeks was (with some puckish intention) pathetic. The photo caused my whole family to wish I would give the job up and come home even sooner than I finally did. In the picture, I'm just back from another day at the navy yard and even skinnier than I was when I departed from home. In my unpressed, oversized work shirt, trousers, and metal-lined factory cap picked out with a superabundance of caution by my brother, Lee—both of us had absolutely no experience with this breed of outfit—I contrived for the camera to look cadaverous, hollow-eyed, and anguished. With a hint of an elfish leer, I was affecting the remorseless exhaustion of a creature on its last legs. The pose was not altogether fake. Work in the blacksmith shop was truly tiring. The heat was high, the manual labor usually hard, and the smudged sweat soiling my shirt and staining my face in the photograph was the real thing.

Not long ago, my sister was reminded of another, much earlier small drama about my clothes, of which I have no recollection. This had to do with a neatly packed suitcase and a two-week trip from home to a country summer camp to which, startled, I found myself being sent away. The camp operated as a charity for underprivileged city children, and I qualified. Probably it was Lee who learned about it and applied on my behalf. I remember the camp well enough but nothing about the suitcase. What amazed and tickled the others in the family was that upon my return after two weeks away, my suitcase was packed precisely in as good order as when I had carried it off. I simply hadn't thought to unpack it. From the top I had taken my toothbrush and comb and a change of clothes for sports the first day, and I had managed with just those and my travel outfit for the two full weeks. My explanation was that, after all, no one had told me to unpack.

And no doubt it was so much easier to leave the suitcase alone. All my life it's been the same—been so much easier to let other people attend to all such duties for me. In my book *Closing Time* I say of a character, Yossarian, that he couldn't learn to make a bed and would sooner starve than cook. *That* is autobiography.

This summer camp, supposedly a treat, was experienced by me as a lonely and puzzling ordeal pockmarked by ceaseless physical inconvenience: The cot was not my own bed; I had to make it up myself; we got busy each day earlier than I wanted to; the lake was cold and less buoyant than the ocean I was used to; the footing was slimy; there were insects I didn't know about; and I was scared of bees. The ecology of the woods was mysterious and unappealing. Was I glad to get back!

Coincidentally, as I learned much later, Mario Puzo was following a parallel course at approximately the same age, but with a reaction opposite to mine. The camp he attended was a different charity, sponsored by the *New York Herald Tribune* Fresh Air Fund. And he reviews his junket into the woods as perhaps the best time in his whole life—until, I surmise, the success of *The Godfather* was assured (his third novel, by the way). But Mario escaped to country camp from the stifling cauldron and molten cobblestone streets of Hell's Kitchen in Manhattan.

I was from Coney Island.

FLY FORWARD THIRTY YEARS for a possible link between that trip to camp, my first from home, and the leaden gloom with which I have been filled every time I've prepared as an adult for a trip away. There's nothing specific that might account for these emanations of despair. But I do hate packing, the mere thought of it; I loathe unpacking. Weeks before a trip, I find myself brooding in torment over which suit to take, the right shoes to bring for each pair of trousers, the correct tie to match each shirt and jacket, the appropriate shirts. I determine not to take too much and always do. My piercing anxiety when I leave home is that the automobile chauffeuring me to the airport or railroad station will forget to come or break down along the way, that I will misplace or lose my ticket or passport. As a result, I'm usually there at the airport at least an hour sooner than anyone wants me to be, including me. I'm usually prompter than prompt for all appointments. Once aboard a plane and in secure possession of the seat reserved for me, all dread dissipates, and I feel I've already triumphed; whatever venture I am about is already a success. I have no fear of the journey itself, although I will try to make it a point—in a superstition rejected in childhood and thoughtfully reclaimed as a young adult in wartime—to inconspicuously cross the fingers of both hands on landings and takeoffs. I grew very much into the habit of doing this in the air corps as my combat duties progressed toward fulfillment, and I did so in dead earnest on my last flight to Naples for the steamship taking me back. (No one knows I cross my fingers, and I would sooner embrace the tortures of hell than have a single soul find out.)

I suffer none of these forebodings coming home, except perhaps when landing in a thunderstorm, when I am most likely to remember the precaution. But I do hate to unpack, to separate the things to be laundered from those for the cleaners, the medicines from the toiletries, the magazines from the real mail, the real mail from the junk mail. I proceed reluctantly with all this in petite stages spanning at least a couple of days. And I frequently yearn for a mother or an older brother or sister to do it all for me.

PEOPLE IN CONEY ISLAND with work in Manhattan have to travel far to get to it. Not as far as Norfolk, Virginia, but farther than you or I would want to travel today, unless we had to. Then we had to.

First, for about fifteen or twenty minutes, there was the Norton's Point trolley ride to the Stillwell Avenue subway station, the trolley stopping at every corner coming and going during the morning and evening rush hours. People from Sea Gate had to spend another fifteen or twenty minutes just to get to the trolley stop when setting out. Obtaining seats on the subway train in the morning was not a difficulty for us: The last stop on the line coming out, we were the starting point going back and the first ones to board. People coming home who caught the train at Times Square, the start and the finish for the three express lines running back and forth between Coney Island and the city, enjoyed the same benefit at the end of the workday, but the crush of passengers was great and you had to step lively to be among the first to sprint furiously into the vacant carriage nearest you and dash for a choice seat, facing forward and next to the window. Just one station down from Times Square, at 34th Street–Herald Square, where Sylvia got on and off for her job at Macy's department store for nearly forty years, finding a seat of any kind was already a stroke of luck. The seats were usually completely taken by the time the doors closed there and the train was on its way toward the third express stop downtown, 14th Street–Union Square. Those who had no seat when the train left 14th

Street were condemned to stand in uncomfortable close quarters—uncomfortable especially for women—until the train had rumbled across the bridge joining Manhattan to Brooklyn and was rolling deep into different residential areas served by the separate subway lines. Then, people who did have seats began vacating them to dismount. The subway rides in rush hour between Times Square and Coney Island took almost an hour—the Sea Beach line was most direct and lasted a few minutes less, but we tended to go home on the first train to arrive—and were seldom the happiest parts of anyone's workday. It seemed to me then a perpetual tragedy and a scandalous economic outrage—and this idea was not original with me, I knew—that to have to travel so long just to get to work, or even, for that matter, to ever have to go to work at all, was a dismal and unjust fate for enlightened mankind to suffer.

In the mid-1950s, when at *Time* magazine, I discovered without commiserating and with some surprise that many even of my outwardly affluent colleagues faced a journey of some length to their place of labor. I was past the age of thirty but still callow when I began my advertising sales promotion work there, writing copy and producing related visual aids to assist others in the selling of advertising pages. Soon I made the acquaintance of a family member of one of the cofounders of *Time* magazine, the initial venture in what had flourished to become the universally respected publishing megalopolis by which we both were employed. A young man named Britten Hadden, who died very young of a streptococcus infection, had been a partner of the young Henry R. Luce in the creation of *Time*. I was mildly bewildered to find that my contemporary Hadden, Peter, had his home by preference outside the city, in Long Island, in a place called Locust Valley, whence he undertook to travel daily to his work as a space salesman at *Time,* going by automobile to his train station, by train to the terminal in Manhattan, and by taxicab from Pennsylvania Station to the

Time-Life Building (which then rose facing the ice-skating rink in Rockefeller Center), submitting himself with free will to a daily commute whose total time was probably close to the one from Coney Island to Times Square. I wondered why he did that. I learned also from our Research Department, which relied to a heavy extent on statistical information released by the government's Census Bureau and several allied agencies, that there was an established group in their taxonomy known as a Class A suburb, and that Locust Valley was definitely one of them. I, together with my wife and small family (a daughter, Erica, and a son, Ted), was already comfortably ensconced in Manhattan and could get to work easily by subway or on foot, in ten minutes one way and twenty the other. I ultimately accepted the fact that many corporate executives on very high income levels, there and in other companies, *chose* to spend a considerable allotment of their daily hours traveling back and forth to work rather than live in the city. The publisher of *Time* then, James Linen, was among them; so was just about every other person of exalted position there whom I can think of now. I thought it bizarre that people of such means should live where they did when they could easily have afforded to live where I did, in an apartment on the Upper West Side of Manhattan, and get to the office or back as quickly as I could. I felt none of the pity for them I had once experienced for my Coney Island workers of old, and for myself. In fact, I could only think they were nuts.

I soon found one other respect in which I thought them berserk—an obsessive and near-addictive passion for golf. The buoyant enslavement to golf-playing was epidemic in the business departments but mercifully sparing of all us writers and the commercial artists in the Promotion Department (perhaps because we couldn't afford it; it was bruited about, maybe even accurately, that the company picked up all the costs of golf club membership and related expenses for the space salesmen), and it affected me then as a token of some psychological disorder. Today, of course, everyone knows that men drawn to golf are unhappy at home and have difficulty bonding with women.

THE MEMORY I RETAIN most strongly of Pete Hadden hasn't to do with advertising work, mine or his, but with a perfect baseball game pitched by a Yankee named Don Larsen during a World Series—no hits, no errors, no bases on balls, twenty-seven batters faced, twenty-seven batters retired. Such a feat was without precedent in a World Series game—it has not been repeated—and it has been extremely rare anywhere else. In many of the Time Inc. offices each fall during the World Series there were personal table radios brought in and installed for the duration, to enable people to go on listening to every game at work when they could no longer do so at the bars in the nearby restaurants in which they had spent their long lunches. About half an hour after that perfect game had concluded, I recall watching Pete, for whom I was at that time preparing a project, drift as though stunned into the open office in which we in the sales-presentation department worked and draw near me with a reverent expression of awe. "Today," he said, in a hushed voice, "we saw history being made."

It appears to me today in a sentimental mirage that, at *Time* magazine in that golden age of the 1950s, and at *Life,* too, and maybe even at the arid business publication *Fortune,* the World Series no sooner ended in early fall of each year than the Christmas office parties at once began. Or perhaps it was the commencement of Thanksgiving festivities. It doesn't matter. No holiday was needed to replenish the *joie de vivre* that prevailed during business hours in those corridors in those days. There were always sufficient birthdays, anniversaries, retirements, transfers, and whatnots to suffice as a good reason for a party somewhere on our floor. The liquor would flow, the canapés would appear, the socializing would spill over after business hours into small groups in one nearby bar or another. Small wonder we were often reluctant to hurry home. The women at work there were lively, educated, and bright; the only sad faces normally to be found were those on people with a hangover from excessive drinking the night before, or that same day at lunch, or on some man at last drearily aware, in a mood of inescapable self-discovery, that he did in fact have a serious drinking problem and was in truth an alcoholic. It was a rumor then, possibly no more than a rumor, that the company maintained an ongoing arrangement with the Payne-Whitney Clinic at New York Hospital for the discreet admission and treatment of important employees in that predicament as well as of those with various other types of serious depression. There was another rumor that when the company first instituted its most liberal medical benefits program, one that in its introductory phases provided reimbursement for psychiatric care, it transpired that more than 10 percent of the total number of our freewheeling, easy-living Time Inc. employees around the world were receiving one form of psychotherapy or another. The Time corporation was a prodigal and indulgent workplace in which people often broke down (and one of the people teetering nervously on the brink was the character Bob Slocum in that excellent novel *Something Happened*).

An old friend from *Time,* Gerald Broidy, helpfully recounted to me not long ago a business occasion of that period in which he was peripherally involved—organizing a dinner meeting at which a number of highest top-management executives of Time Inc. met with a number of management officials of equal status at the *New York Times*. The dinner was held in the New York apartment of one of the dominant figures at Time, whose wife was a member of the family owning the *Times.* Broidy did not attend. Of course, drinks were served beforehand. Early the very next morning, he learned by telephone from his exasperated counterpart at the newspaper that one of the imbibing nobles from Time Inc. passed out as soon as the meal began and slept soundly through the remainder of the meeting with his head on the table, to the surprise and consternation, I'd guess, only of those dignitaries from the *Times*.

"Which one could it have been?" the man at the newspaper indignantly demanded.

And Broidy, with the habitual laughter that is still his, answered, "Any one of them!"

I believe that it was for a sales call by Pete Hadden that I inventively blended my recent literary education with the immediate business need and devised an opening for his easel presentation that was soon in demand by other space salesmen and is remembered to this day as something of a classic. I forget which product or company was the prospective customer for new or increased advertising, but on the opening board of the easel demonstration, I offered an enlarged copy of the Tenniel illustration for *Through the Looking-Glass* showing the Red Queen skimming over the ground at top speed with Alice in tow, and with her explanation in a caption: "Now, here, you see, it takes all the running you can do, to keep in the same place."

Other salesmen were soon requesting this picture as an introduction for their own sales calls. From me personally there followed new written presentations with this opening, one attempting to persuade the Simmons mattress company to forget consumer publications for a while and employ our newsmagazine to sell mattresses to the hotel and motel owners who subscribed in disproportionate numbers, and another to convince the space buyers for H. J. Heinz to use *Time* to advertise their individual and miniature customer servings of ketchup to the proprietors of diners, coffee shops, and hotels.

It was through such inspired ideas that I received a $1,000 raise at the end of each of my first two years, climbing from my starting salary of $9,000 to $11,000 (if memory serves me correctly). After my third year I received an explanation but no increase: There was a company-wide salary freeze imposed as a consequence of the starting-up

costs of the new magazine *Sports Illustrated.* I did then what
I had done twice before since coming back to New York
City from my teaching position as instructor at Pennsylvania State College. I purchased a new hat—a gray fedora
with a dark band; bought a new white-on-white shirt with
French cuffs; dug out my cuff links; and roamed about
secretly, exploring for a better-paying job. I soon found one
doing the same work at *Look* magazine at an annual salary
of $13,000. A friend from *Time,* Arky Gonzalez, who earlier
had left for more money at *Reader's Digest,* cautioned that
things were very different in the rest of the business world
from what they were at *Time,* and that I might soon miss
being there.

I still do.

At one of the annual sales conventions, to which I was
taken to assist with the projection equipment for the assortment of slide shows presented, I witnessed Henry Luce
himself sternly notify his audience that, to his mind, the
business of the Time-Life corporation was publishing and
that he was not going to fold *Sports Illustrated* merely to
assuage the doubts of the investors on Wall Street or allay
internal concerns about salary increases and the size of continuing company contributions to the employee pension
plan.

At the festive Time Inc. conferences I attended at deluxe
resorts in locations like Florida, Nassau, and Bermuda, on a
table immediately inside the entrance to the dining room for
breakfast each morning were huge glass vats of Bloody Mary
and Brandy Alexander mixes standing ready for all arrivals;
and at the golf course every afternoon, I was told, always
close to the tee at each hole was a large drum of ice with
chilled bottles of beer to fortify the thirsty Time Inc. sports-
men as they braved the challenge of the next fairway. A
young space salesman with a name good enough for John
Cheever or F. Scott Fitzgerald, Seth Bidwell, was head of an
out-of-town office largely, I had heard, because he was a
three-handicap on the links and would cut an estimable

figure with the customers he played with. Another space salesman with a great name was Royal Peterson II; slender, tall, courteous, clad always in suits well chosen and well tailored, he fit his name to perfection. Yet another salesman, I'd been told, had thrown up into the swimming pool at a sales convention I did not attend. With the company so paternalistic, he probably wasn't discharged; more likely, the accident was overlooked, or else he was eased sideways into a new position that precluded his appearance at future conferences. Notwithstanding all the foregoing, the company kept growing in one way or another during the three years I was there—*Time* proudly hailed the milestone of reaching two million in paid circulation—and continued growing hugely during the forty years that followed, despite my departure. It merged ultimately, against my wishes, with Warner Communications, formerly Warner Brothers, a motion-picture entity psychedelically resplendent in its own size and reputation.

But sometimes nothing fails like success. The organization multiplied in value and deteriorated in worth. More money flowed in from television shows and ancillary facilities than from publications. The magazines are today without special dignity or significance, even among other magazines, and I suspect it can't presently be as enjoyable working on them for merger-minded businesspeople whose bristling work ethic, one doubtless beloved by institutional investors, can credibly be refined to automatically trigger the feisty comeback "They're not here to enjoy themselves, they're here to work."

If there are colorful personalities left in management, they are colorful invisibly.

In what seemed a disgracefully rapid sequence not long ago, perhaps the same week, maybe in the same breath, the news-conscious controllers of the company owning the news-sensitive magazine *Time* announced in public forum a single payment of some $70 million to a single executive, one acquired in the merger, and the discharge, for motives purely of economy, of some two hundred employees. Such are the generous freedoms afforded by American free enterprise. And such is the character of the enterprise.

AN ADVANTAGE I ENJOYED commuting from Brooklyn to my earliest job in the city with Western Union was that I started for work directly after my last class at Abraham Lincoln High School. At the end of my schoolday I would board the subway at the Ocean Parkway station of the Brighton Line, and since I was already past the trolley ride from Coney Island and the first two train stops, the time of the trip into the city was shortened by some thirty minutes. And in the early afternoon, when I left school for work, the trains were not crowded and I could pick my seat.

At the first office to which I was assigned, I stored my uniform in a locker in a central changing room for a number of satellite offices in the business districts of downtown Manhattan radiating out from Union Square and from the Flatiron Building on 23rd Street, where Broadway crosses Fifth Avenue. When I was transferred uptown, the uniform hung in a small closet in a single, small office in what was then the General Motors Building, at 57th Street and Broadway. Finally, I kept the uniform at home after I was shifted to an office in Brooklyn not far away in lower Flatbush and worked only weekends. At long last I could sport my dashing Western Union messenger garb right in Coney Island as I rode on my bicycle back and forth between home and office, sometimes even delivering telegrams right in the neighborhood. This never happened, but a hovering dread I forged in my imagination dealt with the risk that sooner or later I would have to deliver to a family I knew a yellow envelope stamped with two red stars. In the days of the telegram, before the facsimile machine and the ubiquitous telephone rendered such swift communications all but obsolete, the two-starred message brought news of tragedy.

In short order I was able to, and I did, ride a bike just

about everywhere without using my hands, even turning
corners into streets broad enough to encompass a sweeping
arc. My bicycle came as a present from my Aunt Esther as
soon as she learned I needed one to keep my messenger's
job. The bike emerged from the stock in the toy store owned
by her and my Uncle Julius in Williamsburg, which itself
was a long haul away. I traveled there by train. I don't
remember on whose borrowed bike I had first learned to
ride and whose I had used to begin at the new place, but by
the time my Aunt Esther came through, I could ride compe-
tently, and no one lacked faith that I could accomplish the
long ride back to Coney Island unharmed. Aunt Esther,
whose personality seemed the dominant one in her family,
mapped instructions directing me to Kings Highway, which
turned out to be a busier and farther-reaching thoroughfare
than I or anyone else but Aunt Esther and Uncle Julius had
dreamed it was. They owned an automobile and drove
when they visited us. A daughter, Janet, was studying medicine, a stark anomaly then for a woman, and a son, Philip,
was soon a lawyer, later a judge. They were relations on my
father's side but remained close to us after he died. All of the
cousins on both my mother's and father's side were considerably older than I but not older than my brother and sister.
That could be a reason I haven't remained close. My brother
was distant from them by temperament; my cousin, Nat
Siegel, also on my father's side, may already have been an
accountant when he gave me the *Iliad*. His older brother,
Morris, was already a physician, and that could have been
reason enough for Lee to remain aloof. Sylvia, on the other
hand, was warm and convivial as always, even to participat-
ing with them in a cousins' club when there were still
enough of them around. Lee seemed always more outgoing
to people he knew slightly than to those he knew well. An
unusually modest man, at nineteen or twenty he took off
from home without warning one day and made his way as a
hobo to California and back over the summer. He didn't
perceive anything extraordinary enough in that feat even to

mention it to his son, Paul, and seemed genuinely surprised that both of us were impressed when I finally brought it up, after Paul was already grown and married. Eventually my mother confided to me with some bitterness that she had been terribly embarrassed in the past by Lee's habit of remaining in his room when relatives were present. Aunts and uncles conversed with my mother in Yiddish when they visited. Only now do I understand that when they spoke of "Itchy," which they frequently did, they were talking of my father, Itchy being the diminutive of the name Yitzak, which is Yiddish for Isaac.

The day I got my bike was the day Lou Gehrig retired from baseball, for I remember listening in Aunt Esther's house on the radio to his tearful farewell as I ate the lunch she had prepared for me. Pedaling away on my new bicycle in a spirit of vigorous exuberance, I began the long ride back through mysterious urban regions I had never been in before. Brooklyn is a vast realm, and the trip seemed an unending adventure through fresh surroundings then presumed to be safe. I drank it all in eagerly. At last, after half an hour or longer and with a pervading stir of relief, I recognized ahead the elevated train station I knew at a familiar strip of Kings Highway, a congested shopping area with all kinds of stores and a Dubrow's cafeteria opening at dawn and serving terrific food into the early hours of the next day. Shortly after, as forecast, I arrived at Ocean Parkway. In ten minutes or so I rolled past my high school. In familiar regions now, cycling the final thirty minutes down the broad boulevard into Coney Island and then home was a triumph.

I have remarked before on a congenital unconsciousness of mine about details: Not until recently did it penetrate my mind that Kings Highway in Brooklyn is really *the King's* highway and that the adjoining borough of Queens is really the Queen's. I don't know which British king and queen they memorialize and don't ache to find out (you can look that one up yourself, if you care more than I do). I would take an offhand shot at William and Mary, because they alone of the kingdom's royal couples seem to go together (Victoria's Albert was a mere consort), and I would probably be wrong.

I do know that in addition to the bicycle, my Aunt Esther gave me a dollar and, as usual, instructions for my mother to feed me more red meat. Either I seemed anemic to Aunt Esther or she was infused with a fear of anemia and convinced that a diet rich in beef would always defeat it. Aunt Esther never failed to give me a one-dollar bill whenever she saw me. At the cemetery, when my father was buried, I remember she gave me a dollar. I remember little more. It was the first dollar I ever had, and I don't know what I did with it. (At five years old, I couldn't do much of anything.) Others, Freud tells me, often unknowingly associate currency with gold and gold with excrement, and vice versa, whether they want to or not. I associate money with life, and an absence of money with death. I can't help it. I, too, can try a guess at the reason. But I still can't help it.

5

On and On

AT THE AGE OF SIXTEEN I was old enough to obtain my "working papers" and seek legitimate employment.

Federal legislation governing child labor enacted not long before proscribed as unlawful the official hiring of anyone younger than that in just about any formal capacity. (Shirley Temple, I must suppose, was a cheeky and heartwarming exception.)

At sixteen one also was allowed to quit school, but I never wanted to do anything like that, and neither did any of my friends. Quitting high school would have been a shame to the family and a scandal in the neighborhood. As it happened, not until I was past twenty-eight and face-to-face with the forbidding requirement of a Ph.D. if I was to continue teaching did I finally back timidly away from further institutional education and take steps to try my hand in the real world. A doctorate in literature is not a simple commitment. By then, I had been married for six years, had one small child, and had served two rather tiring years at very low pay as an instructor in the Department of English Composition at Pennsylvania State College—twelve classroom hours weekly with four sections of Expository Writing, Comp. 5, each of first-year students who, with only a few exceptions, were no more interested in learning the practice of expository writing than I was in teaching it. By then, too, considerably encouraged by the publication in national magazines of a few short stories of mine that were written and had appeared while I was still a college undergraduate at NYU, I had a stronger ambition to write literature than to go on studying it. (I must note here, in an unconvincing pretense of humility, that in 1948, when most of these few stories appeared, Norman Mailer published *The Naked and the Dead;* Gore Vidal, younger than both of us, had given us his war novel *Williwaw* and that year *The City and the Pillar;* and Truman Capote, also younger, had attracted national attention with his *Other Voices, Other Rooms.*)

But back in May of 1939, while still attending high school (and possibly already typing preposterously and zestfully away in Irving Kaiser's apartment downstairs on my short story, which was aimed first at the New York *Daily News,* about my youthful Finnish soldier ingeniously and heroically thwarting the invasion of his native land by Soviet forces), I turned sixteen and set aside my creative passions to rush off enthusiastically to apply for my working papers.

Either Sylvia or Lee had a friend who managed a Western Union telegraph office in the Bensonhurst part of Brooklyn, which is close to Coney Island. In that era just about every residential district had a Western Union office. Through that contact, I secured an interview with a Mr. Shotter in personnel at the Western Union headquarters building at 60 Hudson Street in Manhattan. And through him I was hired as a part-time messenger to work afternoons on weekdays after school and half a day Saturdays when needed. Since the five-day workweek was not then standard, I was wanted most Saturdays to help service the many businesses that stayed open. From a Western Union supply department, equivalent to the kind of quartermaster outlet I was to encounter later in the military, I drew my jaunty uniform. The vision has grown indistinct with the passage of time, but I believe it included brown leather puttees of a type recognizable to us from photos of cavalry officers in World War I and the Spanish-American War. (I am almost positive I wore leather puttees at some stage of my life, and I know it wasn't in World War II and not in the Boy Scouts.) A minimum-wage law was already in effect, and I believe I have it right that the minimum at which I started was twenty-five cents an hour, which increased to forty cents while I was still with Western Union. Working, on average, three to four hours each afternoon and four more on Saturday, but not on business holidays, my take-home pay ranged from five to six dollars a week. When I was let go after more than a year, I took my direction from some older fellows and followed the trail they had blazed to the unemployment-insurance office. To my great surprise, I was eligible. To my greater surprise, I received a hefty, guaranteed six dollars a week, the minimum from that source stipulated by legislation, for thirteen weeks. Here was as much or more than I had been earning by working, and without the unavoidable expense of twenty cents a day for trolley and subway fare.

Oh, what a wonderful world indeed this was that had such blessings in it, I felt like singing out loud each time the postman delivered my six-dollar check—but for only those thirteen weeks.

By agreement at home, whatever I earned was my own for allowance. Lee and Sylvia were both already out of high school and working in the city. And at that time my take-home pay of six bucks a week was plenty.

The assumption in the family when the opportunity for employment arose was that I would be hired for the Bensonhurst office, and it could have been about then that I began training myself furiously on borrowed bicycles. Instead, I was placed in an office in the city, one on East 17th Street just west of Fourth Avenue, a few blocks from Union Square, where I had never been, and a few blocks down from the Flatiron Building, formerly an architectural highlight in the city, of which I had never heard. Manhattan was very different in that period (so was I), and so was the area fronting Union Square. With such bustling department stores as S. Klein's, Ohrbach's, Mays, it was a shopping district second only to the one with Macy's and Gimbel's twenty streets uptown, which in turn was second (if two "seconds" aren't unacceptable) only to the elegant department stores on Fifth Avenue in the fifties. Today, all these stores on 14th Street at Union Square have closed and haven't been replaced. Union Square hasn't nearly the same character without them, and without the fiery labor-movement rallies of the past. But Macy's is different now, too, without Gimbel's just down the street. Fifth Avenue isn't nearly the same today, either, and neither is the Champs-Élysées or, as I found out with sharp pangs of disappointment on a recent vacation trip, the good old Via Veneto in Rome, on which I had spent so many happy, roistering hours during my military service overseas. The spirit of pleasure in which I had luxuriated there during the war and a few times after is still unmistakably the ambience of the city, but it has moved from the Via Veneto to other districts, and I haven't had time to learn where they are.

I believe it was on street level in the Flatiron Building itself that a large, central Western Union office was situated, with a locker room providing space and facilities for forty or fifty of us to change into our work clothes and back at the staggered hours dictated by our different work schedules. I smoked my first cigarettes there—Spuds, then Kools. Prior to my starting work, I hadn't troubled myself to conceive that there might be such things as telegraph offices in the business districts and that there were floods of messengers pacing back and forth on telegraph business. In movies they always pedaled bikes. On the day I began, I walked from school to the subway station as rehearsed, checked in and changed at the one office and reported for work at the other, and my seasoning in the city commenced.

I should explain for out-of-towners that when New

Yorkers speak of the city, they often imperiously mean only Manhattan.

I learned a good deal very quickly. I learned first, as already noted, that telegrams were delivered on foot, that those delivered to offices required no signature of receipt, and that we not only delivered telegrams but were just as often summoned by electrical signal and code to specific reception rooms in office buildings to pick up messages typed on yellow forms to be carried back for transmission by teletype to addressees elsewhere. For those who don't know and do care, I will explain that the words of a telegram came out of a teletype machine on unrolling paper strands about half an inch broad; these were pasted onto yellow forms that were folded into envelopes by the operators and handed to the people working the counter, who assembled them in groups by destination and then handed them for delivery to the next one of us in line on the bench or at the counter. I detected in due course that, as a consequence of our guaranteed hourly minimum wage, there was no longer any real incentive to hurry, unlike the way it worked in the previous epoch spoken about by old-timers, during which they were paid by the number of items handled—piecework, so to speak—and might earn more, if lucky, or might earn less.

I learned, with disgusting effort, to overcome the revolting tastes of cigarette smoking inevitably afflicting the amateur and to acquire the habit. (Sixteen years later, past thirty, I kicked the habit in a squall of pique when the price of a pack rose another penny to twenty-six cents the same week the first of the lung-cancer reports appeared.) I learned that Fifth Avenue neatly divides the East Side of Manhattan from the West Side, a handy detail that once learned is never forgotten, and that the streets and avenues are nicely numbered in consecutive order, until the numbers decline to zero, where streets begin carrying names and the trials to memory begin. Years later, I stumbled across an exception to the methodical numbering of streets, a tangled and astonishing intersection in Greenwich Village where West 4th

and West 10th Streets cross as a result of convoluted deter-
minants that, once understood, are forgotten instantly. I
never learned what most of the offices I regularly went into
and out of produced to justify the cost of their maintenance.
A carpet company was a carpet company, but many of the
others were confusing. The American Woolen Building,
about the biggest and busiest in our sector, was an enigma to
me for the longest time, for it was impossible to believe that
all the companies I called on there were in some way connected with the woolen textile business.

One time on service at another office for two days I discovered the Washington Market, of which I had never
heard, situated then on Manhattan's Lower West Side and
the transfer center for most of the fruits and vegetables
shipped into the city. Thus began my first contemplations of
the nearly countless transactions implicated in the movement of vegetables and fruits from the far-flung acres in
which they had been nurtured into Lily Dashevsky's family's fruit store on Mermaid Avenue in Coney Island, where
my mother could purchase what she needed to bring into
our apartment for us. Another time I worked a bit farther
uptown in a quarter alongside the Hudson River in which
there were establishments committed, believe it or not, to
the slaughter of pigs. I did not believe it, even while there.
This was as startling to me as it was to everyone I told, but I
know it was true. The odors were thick and repugnant, the
workers looked grim as jailers, I soon comprehended what
the squealing noises deep inside the buildings were about,
and I was thankful I didn't have to work there a second day.

My closest acquaintance in this first Western Union
office was a short and slightly older part-timer who lived
in the Bay Ridge section of Brooklyn, where Jews did not
live and would not have lived comfortably if they had
to. Through him, one sweltering summer afternoon after
work, I saw how a nervy, experienced kid his age could go
confidently into a saloon and come out with a cold and
sweating silver pitcher of beer and a couple of glasses. That

day I learned also that few things are as lusciously refreshing as ice-cold beer on a sweltering summer afternoon after half a day's Western Union work.

Riding back into Brooklyn with him on the West End subway line, the only line carrying people to Bay Ridge, I would often witness a mass cultural phenomenon that calls into question the complacent dogma with which we mislead ourselves into believing that we arrive at our biases rationally and independently. At a major express stop, all the people traveling into Bay Ridge and environs left the train for a shuttle extension, and all the copies of the afternoon Republican newspapers, principally the *World-Telegram* and *Journal-American,* got off the train with them; while the liberal, Democratic newspapers like the *New York Post,* and later on a newcomer called *PM,* continued onward with their readers into the Jewish regions of Borough Park, Bensonhurst, and Coney Island.

Excitements and surprises in the telegram-delivery business were few. With one part of my brain I played at walking about my routes at an unvarying pace that would carry me from street to street without halting for a traffic light, adroitly varying my sequence of calls when I beheld the tide of traffic turning against me, and I became quite good at that. There was a thrill one lucky afternoon when, passing the Players Club on Gramercy Park South with a telegram for delivery nearby, I spied and instantly recognized the figure descending the outdoor steps and moving across the sidewalk to hail a taxi: it was Charles Coburn, a character actor familiar on sight from movies like *The Devil and Miss Jones.* There was no mistaking him. The office buzzed with excitement when I hurried back with the news, and I couldn't wait for the day to end and the trip home to Coney Island to be over to tell everyone in my family and on the street that I had seen Charles Coburn in the flesh. I prayed they would believe me.

Another day, an older, full-time messenger—older meant that he was out of high school, about twenty or

twenty-one, and would start worrying about military conscription after the Selective Service Act was passed in
1940—returned to home base from a call to an apartment
near Gramercy Park with the juicy tale confided to the rest
of us that he had been admitted by a man and woman and
been requested by the man to engage in sex with the
woman. He revealed nothing more, other than that, of
course, the woman was good-looking. It mattered not one
whit to me whether he was speaking the truth: In my per-
fervid, young imagination, here was another glittering
reward lying in wait for me as I continued into my maturity.

I am still waiting.

Six years farther on into my maturity, as a sophomore of
twenty-three in my fiction-writing course at NYU, I made
use of the incident in a short story called "World Full of
Great Cities" that never attained publication in a periodical
but has several times been printed in anthologies. The last
time, I recall, it was taken by a Japanese publisher for publication in English for pupils in Japan studying American
ways and literature. For that story, I fortunately hit upon a
point of view that proved apt. By then I was familiar with
Sherwood Anderson's "I Want to Know Why" and Ernest
Hemingway's "My Old Man," and I was deliberately imitat-
ing them in kind: a young man's discovery of something dis-
agreeable in the adult world which he had not expected.
There was this difference, though: In those works, the
reader knows what the uncorrupted and inexperienced
young narrator does not. In mine, the reader has no more
insight into motivations than I, the narrator-as-Western-
Union-boy, had when I first heard of the incident, had when
I wrote the story, or have to this day.

THE UPTOWN OFFICE to which I eventually was transferred lay on a low floor of the General Motors Building,
occupying the whole Broadway block of West 57th and 58th
Streets, near the active traffic crossings of Columbus Circle,

and allowed the three of us there to window-watch the systematic creation of a tall apartment building in the days when construction workers still used red-hot rivets tossed by tongs from the small furnaces ascending punctually with the scaffoldings, glowing bolts that were caught by others in metal cones for hammering into the junctures of the orange-crusted girders hoisted by cranes. The apartment building was at 240 Central Park South, and I know people who are comfortably quartered there today. The trip from Brooklyn to this new place of work was somewhat longer, two local stations past the last express stop at Times Square. But riding home, I was always sure of a seat.

The new office was small, a single room, and served only companies located in the same building, an arrangement chiefly sustained, I judge now, by the volume of business generated in the few uppermost floors entirely occupied by divisions of the General Motors Corporation. Here, too, I worked only half days, changing after school into and out of my uniform in the gentlemen's lavatory on the landing outside our office. I can't remember if I worked Saturdays as well.

Three of us proved enough to handle the work. In charge of the office was Miss McCormack, a blond, pretty woman of small stature, who was enduring repeated problems with a boyfriend about whom Tom Fitzgerald, who'd been there with her awhile full-time, teased her with a friendly, gentle irony. She was the sole operator of the teletype machine, processing incoming and outgoing messages. There was no real need for her at the counter; Tom and I could by turn easily take charge of the telegrams and electrical requests for pickups and organize the routes through the different floors of the building ourselves. Tom Fitzgerald was a tall, equable, taciturn young man of upright posture who moved calmly and was wise, very wise, beyond his years, which were about twenty-one. Soon, certain events outside the office, for which he bore no responsibility, would be causing him to worry about the draft, for the Selective

Service Act of 1940 mandated the registration for active duty of all males between the ages of twenty-one and twenty-six. And before the attack at Pearl Harbor, people did worry about the draft. If they worried after Pearl Harbor, they did so covertly, and males of eligible age still in civilian dress were prompt with apologetic explanations they frequently felt obliged to give.

I'm sure I was there through that summer of 1940, because I easily recall the torrents of telegrams to multiple addressees gushing out from the executive floors of the General Motors Corporation to delegates at the Republican National Convention championing the selection of Wendell Willkie as the candidate to run against FDR for the office of president. Willkie won the nomination and lost the election. Originally from Indiana, Willkie, like Roosevelt, favored support to Britain in the war and opposition to Hitler; in addition, Willkie accepted many of the New Deal programs and therefore had little ammunition to employ against Roosevelt other than the two-term tradition going back to George Washington. That was an election in which employees in Woolworth's stores were compelled by their employers to wear WILLKIE FOR PRESIDENT buttons. He lost anyway, and I was not surprised. A devoted reader by then of liberal newspapers, I couldn't see why anyone would resist Roosevelt for a third term, and later, a fourth. I couldn't believe then, because at the time I hadn't heard of any, that there were such things as human beings of good intention who were Republicans, and I'm still not sure. By now I have the same doubts about Democrats.

The ages of eligibility for the draft expanded progressively in both directions, upward and downward, as our immersion in combat grew greater, and when the government, in 1942, announced the lowering of the draft age to nineteen after I had already passed eighteen, I and a few friends from Coney Island concluded that the time was ripe to enlist. A persuasive enticement was the promise of picking the branch and the division of the service we preferred.

It was a promise kept for those of us choosing the U.S. Army Air Corps; no one I knew personally who chose the air corps was subject to any staggering shock of the kind suffered later by such as Kurt Vonnegut and Mel Brooks, who both were wrenched from one military specialty, for which they were in training, and thrust into the infantry for shipment overseas as combat replacements, for which duty they received no training.

In this new office with Miss McCormack and Tom Fitzgerald the work was more interesting to me because there was so much less of it. I had time for my homework, for extended conversation (which remains a favorite personal recreation), and, by copying Tom, for reaping the fruits of a surprising preoccupation with calligraphy. Working like an artisan of old, Tom was fashioning an elaborate handwriting for himself. Seated beside him as he concentrated, I awaited his decisions on each capital and lowercase letter in our alphabet and labored intently at duplicating his choices when he made his final judgments. By the time I was transferred into the Brooklyn office the following spring, his handwriting had become my handwriting. In time I let myself forsake it, embarrassed by the flamboyant cursives implying deliberate effort and suggesting affectation, and today from Tom Fitzgerald's new handwriting of 1940 I preserve only the long looping sweep under the J in my signature and modified vestiges of the same below my y's, g's, and j's, and in my capital H.

I don't know what happened to Tom in the military or afterward, or to his handwriting, either. He had a Jewish girlfriend he alluded to occasionally. He was friendly with a young, mild-mannered, redheaded, Irish elevator operator who lived near him in the Bronx, and I was friendly with him, too. I was on good terms with all the elevator operators—they recognized me as a fellow workingman. A way to remain in their good graces, I had learned very quickly at the first job after one gruff rebuke, was always to walk down to the lobby from the second floor rather than force an elevator to stop for you there, and always to use the staircase in either direction for a single floor. Today, from the social vantage point I enjoy, and probably from yours, too, it seems almost antediluvian that well-brought-up young white Americans would settle in contentedly to such occupations as full-time elevator operator or messenger; but that was then, and the social world you and I know today is only one aspect of the real world, a single facet, and the rest of today's real world is one more reality from which we, with our privileges, strive to remain safely insulated, and of which we definitely wish to keep ourselves securely ignorant.

I FOUND OUR NEW SETTING in the city more congenial than my first. On the thoroughfare just behind our building, on Eighth Avenue, was a spacious Horn & Hardart Automat. The Automats were favorite eating places of mine then and—a year later—even more so, when I found myself by pure coincidence back in a more exalted job in the same building, with my preferred meal their succulent chopped-sirloin plate, which included any two vegetables and a roll and butter for twenty-five cents. Their baked beans were an exceptional treat, too, as all alive today who have eaten them will attest, and so were their mashed potatoes (I wish I had a plateful of that chopped sirloin with vegetables here right now). I also liked their orange and lemon glacé cakes for a nickel as dessert. A Nedick's was close by, too, for a hot dog and orange drink now and then, and on the corner of West 57th Street was a Chock Full O' Nuts sparkling with cleanliness, at which for a nickel you could enjoy a nutted cream-cheese sandwich on raisin bread. This was not especially filling, but would serve until mealtime and in that respect was more satisfying than a hot dog, whose savory juices and textures always left me wanting another one, and still do.

Inside the General Motors Building was an office run by two youngish men manufacturing formulas for soft-ice-cream machines, and as often as not, when I stopped in with a telegram, they asked for my judgment of a new alteration in the recipe for chocolate or banana which they were seeking to improve. Other times when on that floor I would pop in anyway to offer my help. Another small office, one that functioned largely by telegram, was occupied by a well-mannered and well-dressed horse-race tout. A few times every week he would address the same message recommending the same horse to a few hundred subscribers. I assumed he performed reasonably well, since he stayed in business, but I was too young for bookmakers, and my twenty-five or forty cents an hour didn't yield much room for error. One other venture stood out prominently, occupying virtually an entire floor of the building and called the Manhattan Mutual Automobile Casualty Company. There, a very beautiful, dark, buxom, married, mature woman known as Miss Peck or Miss Beck never failed to greet me with a smile and thank me each time I stopped in on telegram business, and I looked forward to calling there just to experience her welcome and to hear her speak to me again with such genuine, feminine warmth.

When about a year later, through statistical chances long enough for a whopping prize in a state lottery, I reported to Manhattan Mutual from an employment agency to work full-time at the more distinguished job of file clerk, she didn't know me and didn't recall ever having laid eyes on me before.

It must have been the debonair figure I'd cut in my messenger's uniform that had caused her to notice me before.

Clothes do make the man.

6

And On and On

THE TRAFFIC LIGHTS on Ocean Parkway were staggered, our first encounter with this stratagem for allowing automobiles to proceed steadily at a restricted rate of speed. Separating the six or eight traffic lanes were two attractive pedestrian islands. Benches sat every twenty yards or so beneath the foliage of modest shade trees, and these trees and benches and tended pavement walks ran from the lower end of the parkway in Brighton to its farthermost point at one of the grand entrances to Prospect Park. The sylvan aspect of Ocean Parkway, already established by the time I first saw it from my bicycle, likely was a halcyon dividend from one of the public works programs of FDR's New Deal. Ocean Parkway was perhaps the most handsome of the numerous major traffic routes in the borough, if not in all the city, and possibly it still is. A lane for bicycles ran the length of the pedestrian walks from beginning to end, and I was soon making use of it for my telegram business. Stops were dictated only by traffic lights wherever avenues crossed the parkway, and these were mostly a good way apart. To help cope with the predestined boredom that has proved twin to the confidence arising with my successful performance in most jobs I've held—in just about all of them, propelled by anxiety going in, I've done my best work at the beginning—I set my mind to work constructing a diverting challenge: riding the full stretch of Ocean Parkway between the office and home without having to stop for a single red light. That proved easy; much of the time I did better than the mass of automobiles, whose restless drivers were habitually tempted to speed faster than the staggered lights programmed them to do. Because that challenge, once mastered, grew boring in turn, I introduced the daring innovation of performing the same unbroken bicycle journey without using my hands. Frequently I had to veer into the questionable tactic of decreasing speed to allow a traffic light ahead to change before I got to it and could burst safely through. That was permissible under the rules; I made the rules. Soon I was maestro of that undertaking, too, and capering on my wheels, I basked in the admiring scrutiny of the women on the benches—the mothers and grandmothers with children in strollers and baby carriages—as I showboated past them, my arms swinging at my sides or, in a more peremptory bid for attention, clasping my hands across the crown of my Western Union messenger's cap, arms akimbo.

"Look, Ma, no hands!" I shouted silently, heaping laurels on myself as I sped along.

Even after all this while, Brooklyn remains to me a vast, unexplored territory, now enormously more complex culturally than it was, with the surging and discordant infusion of Asian, Russian, African-American, Arabic, and other peoples, together with Hispanic, brown and black, from Latin America and the Caribbean. I am still awed by newspaper accounts of violent happenings in neighborhoods I've been hearing about for a lifetime and am still unable to pinpoint on a map: Red Hook, Bath Beach, Gowanus, Greenpoint, Sunset Park, East New York, and even, to underline the point, Midwood, which when I was in high school and at the Western Union office just off Kings Highway, was close at hand—but where? I delivered telegrams in Midwood, but with the confused notion that I was still in lower Flat-bush, and for all I know now I could have been correct.

When Lee married, he and Perle lived first in an area called Crown Heights. With my mother and sister I visited there several times but have only a nebulous idea of its location. I do know, from the newspapers, that Crown Heights at present is home to a large black community and a large Hasidic Jewish community, who live side by side antagonistically. Certainly, my worries about these two communities would be different, but one group would be no less intimidating to me than the other, and I'm glad I live here now and not there. Take Bushwick. If I were to trouble myself at long last to find out just where the Bushwick section of Brooklyn is, I don't doubt that I'd succeed. But I also don't doubt that I'd soon forget.

I DON'T KNOW what we did at my new Western Union office just off Kings Highway when it rained—I have a dim impression of olive slickers issued by the company, but I wouldn't bet my life on it, or yours—and I can't recall bicycling at work in winter. I have no bad memories of this last, brief tour of Western Union duty. I have no memories at all of the people there.

From this office I would blithely go wheeling off with my telegrams into familiar neighborhoods, even on occasion my own, as well as areas surrounding the office and my high school that were totally new to me, places with names like Flatlands and Canarsie. Small discoveries still titillate me. I knew that Bedford Avenue was beyond the right-field fence of Ebbets Field, the stadium of the Brooklyn Dodgers, and was the place where baseballs struck over that fence for home runs presumably fell. Yet I was really surprised to find Bedford Avenue extending all the way down into residential lower Flatbush bearing its own name, instead of its equivalent, East 25th Street. Coney Island Avenue, so denominated despite its running into the eastern end of Brighton and nowhere near Coney Island, was East 11th Street, and Ocean Parkway I was finally able to fix into place as East 6th Street. Till then I knew only the streets of Coney Island, which were "Wests," and these went reticulating away backward in a contrary direction, my own.

The longest avenue in Brooklyn is probably Flatbush Avenue, extending from the Manhattan Bridge, which indeed connects with Manhattan, down in a straight diagonal through the borough almost to the seashore across the border of Queens. I discovered the long, lower part of Flatbush Avenue on my bicycle; the upper half I traveled ten years later when I lived in Manhattan and drove across the bridge into Brooklyn for visits to Sylvia, Lee, and my mother. Sylvia and Lee, each married, then lived close to each other, near the subway stop at Kings Highway. This was near the Western Union office in which, while finishing high school, I had worked ten years earlier. I liked best of all, after my first odyssey along Flatbush Avenue, the long routes out, sometimes all the way into the distant settlement of Gerritsen Beach, a small cluster of one-family houses standing along canals that connected the waters of whatever inlet comes in from the sea or bay there. I hadn't heard of Gerritsen Beach before and I haven't heard of it since. There the names on the telegrams were not Jewish and not Italian and neither were the faces on the people, who tended to be fair-haired. I never failed to experience a thrill each time I pedaled past the military air-base installation of Floyd Bennett Field, at a time, in early spring of 1941, when nobody I knew had ever been up in an airplane or ever expected to be.

And just three years later, a mere three, in early spring of 1944, I was able to thrill again to Floyd Bennett Field shortly before going overseas, when I landed there in a plane with a flight of B-25s on a training flight from our base in Columbia, South Carolina. (The revisionary idea arises that it could have been Mitchell Field on Long Island we flew to, but the time elapsed doesn't change, and the point is the same.)

Once on the ground we had some time, and I led two surly bombardier acquaintances of mine (I couldn't call them buddies, for we weren't that close), Bowers and Bailey, who'd come in on other planes, into the city for a meal at the famous Lindy's restaurant, then on Broadway and about 50th Street. I had been there before on furlough (and as something of a glorified, though anonymous, serviceman celebrity) right after receiving my bombardier's wings and commission as a second lieutenant. They were both from Chicago—along with the *Chicago Tribune,* their favorite newspaper, they were fervid isolationists and hated FDR, and England, too—and hadn't seen anything like Lindy's before, and they weren't entirely at home with its raucous splendor or mainly Jewish menu. (I forget what they ordered, but my habitual meal there in daytime was a chopped-liver-and-smoked-turkey sandwich on rye bread, along with a sour pickle and sour tomato or two, and straw-berry cheesecake for dessert.) They had both read Damon Runyon, though, and one of them commented that all the men there (including me?) fit the description of Runyon's character Harry the Horse, by which he meant, I was aware, that they all looked Jewish, and of course we did.

In the Italian homes at which I stopped with my telegrams while still with Western Union as I waited for an adult to acknowledge receipt with a signature or to return with a tip for me, I inevitably encountered a strong, pungent odor unmistakably different from the one in my own apart-ment, although of that one, through natural adjustment, I was scarcely conscious. Only lately have I come to realize that the special pervasive aroma of which I speak is Italian and that it was ingrained in wallpaper, rugs, plaster, and upholstery impregnated for years with the steaming fra-grances of olive oil, garlic, and tomatoes.

In those Western Union days I often received a tip in return for my telegram. On birthdays and Mother's Day there was frequently more than one telegram for a single person, and so, too, at the catering halls for weddings. The amount of the tip was most often a nickel, occasionally a dime. My biggest windfall could not have been foretold. Late one afternoon outside a house on Bedford Avenue, returning to my bike after a delivery, I was spotted by a frantic young man who pounced at me as though I were a compassionate angel appearing in answer to a desperate prayer. If he gave me a dollar, he wanted to know, would I go into another house close by and sing "Happy Birthday"—that is, deliver, as a freelance independent contractor, what was officially called a singing telegram—to a girl named Phyllis at a party inside? I said sure, and I did ring the bell, did enter when bade, did advance inside toward a partying group, and did, standing perfectly stationary with shoulders squared, sing "Happy Birthday" to Phyllis, from Eddie. My audience was thrilled and applauded. Returning outside, I signaled to Eddie that the job was done and that his way was clear. I abstained from confiding that an older woman there, likely a mother or an aunt, had tipped me another quarter for my singing telegram.

I found singing "Happy Birthday" easy work—lucrative, too—and regretted that I wasn't able to make a career of it.

In late spring of 1941, with FDR securely back in office, I was scheduled to finish at Abraham Lincoln High School. I had terminated my work with Western Union by the day of graduation. If there was such thing as a prom then, I didn't hear of it; if I had, I wouldn't have gone. To this day, I am leery of group participation and all formalized group activities, and every time I relent I have cause to repent. In protest against the Vietnam War, I went on a march in New York, one in which I was first grouped with other literary people and then ranked in alphabetical order. As a result, I found myself shoulder to shoulder with two literary critics who had already made known their disapproval of me and could correctly adduce, from that circumstance if none other, that I didn't think much of them, either. I was wary of other marches after that and attended only one more, that largest one in Washington, D.C., to which I went in a plane with a group of friends. Erica, my daughter, was there, too, traveling with a busload of high-school classmates. Also on that march was a group of young Catholic college students, all of them females, and the accompanying Sisters from Marymount College in Westchester, where I went to speak about my work as an author the following week, and they were victims of tear-gassing while waiting innocently at a curb for their chartered bus to arrive. I did not even think of going to my college commencement exercises. I did go to my high-school graduation; my mother, Lee, and Sylvia went proudly, too. We had an early dinner together at a restaurant, and after that I took the subway with some friends to a jazz club on 52nd Street to listen to Billie Holiday. We had our own social club by then and knew how exceptional she was.

My first club, Club Hilight, began in a cellar and then moved to a more palatial home, in a storefront on Surf Avenue, just a block and a half away from my house. One day my brother dropped in unexpectedly to summon me home. I was smoking a cigarette. I had kept my smoking secret from the family, and I couldn't say now which of us was the more flustered. I was caught; he had caught me. Each of us was supposed to do something. Neither seemed sure what that something was.

"How long have you been doing that?" Lee finally asked disapprovingly, when we were walking outside together.

I had crushed out the butt. Both he and Sylvia smoked, and I could have retorted by asking how old he was when he began, but I can't be glib when it counts. With a most innocent voice and a most guileless face I can tell convincingly the most far-fetched lie to the credulous, but only when the point is humorous with nothing real at stake. With pressure on, I stammer, I'm dumb.

"As long as you're doing it, you might as well do it at home," he decided. "You should try not to do anything outside the house that you wouldn't want us to know about." And after a pause, he added: "Here, have one of mine."

This was censure that had a positive effect, and a year afterward helped buttress an inhibition already planted in my conscience, one that I credit with vitiating all the narcotic effects of smoking marijuana, apart from a false appetite. Smoking marijuana the several times I did left me with a sore throat and feeling very hungry. Smoking marijuana was something I definitely would not have wanted my family to know about. I couldn't get the least bit high the times I tried, not then or later, a little while after the war, when I puffed only to accommodate close friends while in their company (I didn't want to abuse their friendship as a "drag" or "bring-down.") From lessons learned afterward through that eventual, and inconclusive, couple of years in psychoanalysis, I surmise that I couldn't get high because for reasons nestled deep in my unconscious I simply didn't really want to. In truth, I didn't want to be smoking pot at all.

As for the graduation itself, the festivities had nothing special to do with me. I was not valedictorian (thanks be to God!), won no prizes, and was not singled out by name for any honors other than my diploma. Probably, though, I was the sole possessor of a singular distinction that passed unrecognized. It's more likely than not that I was the only male member of that graduating class named Joey who had received, or was then still receiving, unemployment insurance, raking in my beefy six dollars a week.

There was nothing more by way of celebration than I have related, no thought of anything even remotely like a bonus or vacation. I don't think anyone I knew of then—not Lee, not Sylvia—had ever gone anywhere on vacation. On Saturday morning, I rested. On Sunday, with Lee and

Sylvia counseling over my shoulders, I read the want ads, and on Monday morning, I set out by subway to call on employment agencies and seek my fortune in the city.

MY FIRST EMPLOYMENT AGENCY, the Wall Street Employment Bureau, with a downtown address in the Manhattan financial district on an oblique side street named Beaver Street (it fascinates me that such details take enduring root in the memory), vectored me right back uptown to the General Motors Building for my first interview and onto the payroll of that Manhattan Mutual Automobile Casualty Company, whose comely, maternal, and properly married, dark-haired Miss Beck (or Peck) was unable to believe she had seen me before and signified with a shrug and an unconcerned dip of the head that it hardly made a difference. A new and about-to-be more appropriate crush at the reception desk up front conducted me deep into the back part of the office, where I had never been before. I was spoken to first by Miss Sullivan, secretary to one of the higher executives; she questioned me in kindly fashion, mainly, I judge now, to verify whether I could hear and understand English. After that, her boss needed no longer than five minutes to approve my appearance, I suppose, and I was taken on right then and there to work as a clerk in the file room. My starting salary was sixty dollars a month, which seemed okay. I was elated to have any job at all. I gathered fairly soon that the same wage would be my final salary, too, as long as I remained a file clerk. Had I thought about it, I would have sensed even then that there wasn't much else at Manhattan Mutual that I could quickly learn to do capably, or would want to.

At the time, age eighteen, I doubt I had any inclination to think so systematically. Like my friends of the same age, I was all but oblivious of the future. None of us knew seriously what we wanted to do or would like to become. Descriptive terms for jobs "with a chance for advancement" or "maybe a good future" meant little to us, for we didn't plan; we weren't in a position to. The war was continuing, the draft was a stimulating prospect, and we took what we could get. If one of us ever did receive a promotion, bettering himself with a move from one menial level to one less lowly, we construed the event not as one of destiny or reward but as an astonishing turn of plain good luck. I don't remember how much of my sixty dollars a month I gave to the family to contribute to the general upkeep, but I did give some, whatever amount was requested by my brother or sister. They wouldn't have demanded much.

The file room itself was a spacious cage of chain-wire fence that rose from floor to ceiling and projected into the center of that part of the office floor, a fence through whose square gaps those of us inside could see outside, and people outside could hear and observe us. Because we could communicate freely by voice through the barrier, it was seldom necessary for others to enter our cage, although they often did stroll in.

I learned quickly what the company did: It issued liability insurance to taxis, to fleets, and to independent owners, for claims resulting from accidents, claims for PD's (property damage) and PI's (personal injury), and to limousines as well. I learned quickly, too, and impressed people back home with the knowledge, that at that time the license plates of all taxis in the city began with an "O" and those of the private car services with the letter "Z." Each time a cab or one of our insured limousines was involved in an accident—and in New York City at that busy period when cruising taxis were numerous in all five boroughs, there were collisions of varying degrees of seriousness every day and night—a report was made, and a file containing the report was opened and then filed in one of our numerous file cabinets, to be retrieved and filed again each time a document was added. What we did almost exclusively—and there was a bunch of us to do it—was locate and deliver the file to the right desk each time it was requested and return it to be filed again when it was done with. After a case was closed, usually through negotiation, the file traveled downstairs to a storeroom for dead records and into a place in one of the walls of cabinets there. The file cabinets upstairs were metal; these were of paperboard. After a suitable period, these records were transferred to a rented space in a Manhattan warehouse for dead records that were even deader. One of these dead records, too, would come back to life occasionally, and one of us would be dispatched to the dreary catacombs of the warehouse to fetch it.

There were five of us doing this work full-time, and I became friendliest with Stanley Levy, some two years older than I, who lived far out in Brooklyn near Coney Island, and had, with his black hair and cleft chin, a perceptible resemblance to Cary Grant, and, I conclude from people who knew Cary Grant, was much the wittier. Lou, who'd been there longest, was a slim, friendly Italian from the Bronx; Jerry was Jewish and lived in the Bronx also. Ralph was boss of us all, a spry, springy, hurrying, short young man still under thirty with waxen, wavy blond hair. Ralph, if one went by appearances, always appeared to be doing at least twice the work of any of us, of *all* of us combined—for he sped about to and fro at least twice as fast, always with a sheet of notepaper in his hand, and then one day he was abruptly let go. We were not told why. That slip of paper, Stanley Levy joked after his exit, never had anything written on it.

Entering the file room as boss of us all came Miss Dunbar from another, distant part of the floor, from around a dogleg where the adjusters, legal, and sales people were quartered and tended to keep largely to themselves. Miss Dunbar was a woman of formidable build of about fifty, with a knowing, disdainful look and a derisive half smile. Things were going to be different from that moment on, she firmly let us know when she entered to take charge, and necessary changes would be made. None of us knew what she was talking about; we had no idea what had gone wrong. And, in effect, things were in no way different. We went about our work as before, untroubled and in good spirits, kidding with those girls who kidded back and with the men who encouraged banter—George Schwartz, Mr. Spiese, Harriet Jackman, Miss Beck, Virginia, Eunice. Miss Dunbar's sardonic half smile and knowing look proved to be no more than that: It was just her look, and the only change occurred when Lou's number came up in the draft and he was forced to depart for military service. There was a farewell Italian dinner in his Bronx home for the other three of us in the friendliest atmosphere (a hell of a long subway ride for Stanley Levy and me), prepared and superintended by a beaming, affectionate mother, affectionate to all of us. This was my first Italian home-cooked meal, and I rashly misjudged. Too polite back then to inquire and make sure, I took the meat balls following the soup and spaghetti to be the main course and prudently (better safe than sorry) helped myself to one, maybe two or three extra; and I thereafter had difficulty with the chicken and vegetables and the sausage stuffing that followed before the fruit and cheese and cake for dessert.

The storage room for dead records one floor below us, with its couple of old desks end to end and several discarded swivel chairs, was anything but dreary. For us it was a kind of playground. There was one key, and the file room had it. I ate lunch there with the others whenever I brought sandwiches from home, which was often. My mother would prepare and pack my favorites, along with an apple, orange, or banana: On two seeded rolls, always two and always rolls with poppy seeds, there could be canned salmon with grated onion and sliced tomato or kosher salami or baloney, with plenty of mustard. Another treat of fractionally my own design (I liked to think) was sliced chicken—white meat vigorously preferred, then as today—with lettuce and—this was the magic—mayonnaise lathered on the inside of one of the halves of roll and ketchup soaked into the other. I was on the very threshold of Russian dressing and didn't know it.

There were occasional rubber-band and paper-clip fights in the storeroom or dice games for pennies and nickels or "underleg." (In "underleg," the player swiftly skidded a coin beneath each shoe, so swiftly that neither player could note which side was up. The second player then slid coins of equal value underneath after them. If the coins matched, the matching player won. When they didn't, the first player did. Most times, they split.) You could kill time down there comfortably alone while pretending to still be searching for a file you had already found and go on with the morning's crossword puzzle or complete the entry for the contest in one of the two tabloid newspapers to pick the most winners of the coming Saturday's college football games. Now and then I would choose a file at random to search inside for matters of special interest. I couldn't find any. The storeroom was also a secret trysting place for hasty sexual encounters, for more than one of us, as two of us inadvertently discovered the day I left. So were the two flights of stairs between the floors for even swifter ones. I learned much about office romances from my special friend Virginia, a cheerful, humorous flirt, and exceedingly pretty, too. She was four years older than I and had been through college. Once we were friends, she confided freely about dates with one lawyer there and one adjuster, each of whom threatened to put her out of his car if she didn't prove more accommodating than she chose to be. She lived in New Jersey and did not say she walked back. She also had a sweet and sad nonphysical relationship with a quiet, almost elderly married man, which was confined to a drink after work now and then and an occasional dinner. Nothing could come of this, and neither of them wished that anything more would.

I went to my first opera from the office one Saturday afternoon, a matinee of *Carmen* at the old Metropolitan Opera House downtown somewhere in the West Thirties. I went alone. My choice was a good one. Through weekly and nightly radio broadcasts presenting short sections of classical-music favorites, I had grown familiar with some of

the score—the Toreador melody, the "Habanera," the spir-
ited overture (two of them were already popular in our
streets through corruption by doggerel lyrics: "Toreador/
Don't spit on the floor/Use the cuspidor/That's what it's
for" and "I lost my shirt/I want my shirt"—I've forgotten
the rest; this last was taught me by Lee, from whom I had
also learned all of the stanzas of "Ivan Tzivitsky Tzizar").
At the performance of *Carmen,* I was exhilarated by the
dances, the acting, charmed by the amazing entrance of real
horses drawing coaches out onto an indoor stage in the
colorful procession introducing the final act. I told everybody—real, live horses!

Then I pushed my luck. As part of a naive and eventually futile agenda to initiate my friend Lou Berkman into
the peculiar bliss of musical appreciation, I purchased two
tickets to my second opera, an evening performance, and
brought him along as my treat. Lou was already working in
his father's junk shop in Brooklyn, an arena of enterprise far
more lucrative than the name suggests, and one that sup-
ported two or three of the Berkman families rather well for
as long as was necessary. After work, he came uptown by
subway to my office and kidded with my perky friend Virginia at the receptionist's desk until I was ready to leave. He
paid for my dinner of chopped sirloin, mashed potatoes, and
baked beans at the Automat across the avenue, and we proceeded downtown by subway. My tickets were, of course,
the cheapest, and we finally found our seats very high up
along the side and in the topmost row, from which point we
could not see perhaps a third of the stage. My choice this
time was unfortunate: *Tannhäuser.* I was misled by faith and
inexperience: The melody of the "Pilgrim's Chorus" had
been appropriated for our Thanksgiving song in music class
in elementary school; it is also the melody with which the
overture begins, and I naively thought that such recognition
would make it easier to connect with the rest of the musical
score. For those who may not know Wagner or may not
know *Tannhäuser,* there is a large difference between that

one and *Carmen,* a large difference and a lo-o-ong one. Because of that evening, Lou never attended another opera as long as he lived, and I have never wanted to hear *Tannhäuser* again.

Back at work, with the other Lou gone from the file room and Miss Dunbar, unlike mercurial Ralph, forever stationary and watchful, the atmosphere inside our workplace suffered a gradual shrinking of levity. Lou's replacement did not mesh perfectly with the well-knit camaraderie in which the rest of us had previously flourished. And when Stanley Levy's number came up in the draft, too, and he gave notice of his intention to leave, I gave notice with him. We left the same afternoon. Stanley would be going into the army, I would be going to the navy yard in Virginia. On the day of our departure, there emerged through an amusing coincidence the secret that more than one of us had been making use of the storeroom for dead records on the floor below for speedy, romantic alliances during office hours. There was only that one key to the storeroom, and two of us wanted it. Ever pliable, I deferred to seniority and collected my own farewell cuddle on the staircase halfway down, where once again I could not obtain all that my heart wished for in the way of an amatory send-off. Virginia, as customary, wore a good deal of bright red lipstick, and we couldn't even kiss passionately without smearing both our mouths with inculpating evidence. I was deeply in love with her, which was good. I was no longer in love with her the minute after we parted, and that was better.

7

And On and On and On

IN A FAR SECTION of the long shed of our blacksmith shop, into which I never had occasion to go, a huge sea anchor under construction curved a pointed shank into the air. I couldn't imagine how they were building it. Periodically, I would wheel a barrel of small objects over to one of the circular pools for "tempering," and I would gaze with some wonderment at the thick, colossal arm ascending from the ground higher than everything around it. I puzzled even then over the mystery of the massive links of chain needed to anchor the anchor, how and where these were fabricated and joined. The drop forges in my section were mammoth structures, and these produced only such small items as bolts, rivets, and buckles. I still don't know how these links of chain were made and have stopped wondering. Today I worry instead about tiny jewelry chains, how in the world the minuscule filaments are assembled into those flexible segments.

We swallowed salt tablets all day long. For our health. The population at that time was being urged to consume a lot of salt on steamy days to guard against heat exhaustion. Because of the many burning furnaces in the shop, this seemed unusually important for us. The furnaces were mainly small and stood apart from each other. The cylinders for dispensing the salt tablets were hung like light fixtures all about, on walls and posts. It must have been at least as hot and hard and uncomfortable for the blacksmiths as it was for me, because they worked closer to the fires longer and did the turning and pounding and trimming of the hot metal on the anvils and the dies at the drop forges. My job consisted mainly of carrying one at a time the glowing metal rods from the furnace to the forge or the anvil—I used tongs, of course, and wore the bulky, fire-resistant gloves Lee had picked out for me—each time the man I was delegated to work with that day signalled for another unit, then clearing out of his way the one he had newly shaped. But the blacksmiths were paid much more money than I was, and they were accustomed by life to arduous physical labor. Unlike me, they accepted hard work as natural.

A surprising number of them were from rural North Carolina, the northern border of which wasn't that far away; and a good many of the rest had rambled down to avail themselves of the temporary opportunity of defense work, for as long as that opportunity lasted, from agrarian towns in Virginia. Where else could a worthy blacksmith earn a decent living in peacetime?

I had been prepared by northern friends for the various oddities of speech I swiftly encountered. The most singular of these, unlike any of the exaggerated travesties I had heard in movie theaters, flowed from those who regularly transmuted the familiar (familiar to me) *ou* vowel sound (as in "out") into something else—into *oo*—so that a mouse became a moose (I never thought to probe how a moose was pronounced locally); and so, for example, the sentence "There's a mouse running about the house" became "There's a moose running aboot the hoose." I was much too politic and sensitive ever to joke with the men about this, or even to indicate that I'd heard anything humorously atypical. I have almost always been able (with a sympathetic respect that might be either wisdom or sublimation of cowardice) to at least perceive the basis of the other person's point of view, and to see myself as others might see me. To my mother, and Lee and Sylvia, too, to everyone in our family, it would have been a profound character failing ever to deprecate anyone just for being different or handicapped. Bigotry was a heinous offense.

Because we tried to see ourselves as others might see us, we tended to be a self-conscious bunch. A household anecdote epitomizing that point related to the Jewish holy day of Yom Kippur. My mother, who in general was nonobservant, preferred that I go to one of the two synagogues on our street late in the afternoon to say the *Kaddish* for my dead father, more, I'd guess, to keep up traditional good appearances than from a belief that a prayer from me would be of much help to either my father or the Lord. I attempted to do as she wished for as long as I lived at home, which was until I went into the army. She never insisted; that was not her nature. But in early September of 1949, when I and my first wife, Shirley, were preparing to sail to England for an academic year on one of the earliest of the Fulbright scholarships, she did rouse herself to exhort. By then she had long since broken her hip and was limping about with a cane; that accident befell her while I was still in training as a bombardier. With a diffident urgency that obviously was embarrassing to her, she called both of us aside, a calendar in one hand and in the other a scrap of paper on which the date of that year's approaching Yom Kippur was already noted. We must remember, she emphasized to us, to be sure to find a temple in whatever city we were in when that day came and attend at least part of the services. "Else," she explained in her faulty English, "the people will think you're a 'Comminist.'" It happened that we were in Paris on Yom Kippur, my wife and I, age twenty-five and twenty-six, respectively, and in Paris for the first time, and our attempt to scour the city for a synagogue was not wholehearted. We didn't stumble upon one; yet I don't suppose that many of the people in Paris assumed we were "Comminists." And it is insulting to

God, I suspect, to imagine He cares whether I pray to Him or even knows where or who I am.

On emergency leave after my mother's accident, I was appreciative of the benevolence with which the various bureaucratic desks of the army joined to secure my furlough in what seemed a matter of minutes, certainly less than an hour. I was midway through my preflight training at the Santa Ana Army Air Base in California, a huge installation in which thousands, perhaps tens of thousands, of aviation cadets were received, examined, evaluated, and assigned to classes for preflight training as pilots, bombardiers, and navigators. The telegram had been sent by my sister. My orderly room referred me to the office of the chaplain, which on the spot arranged a loan to me from the Red Cross to pay for the railroad tickets procured for me by the transportation office, which also awarded me a priority rating for the train.

Entering the hospital in Brooklyn by myself some five days later, I had no idea what I would find. For reasons I don't understand and never expect to, I had constructed the bizarre scenario that I might not recognize my mother and feared that my failure to do so might sink her into deep despair. A couple of dozen beds in the open women's ward of Coney Island Hospital stood before me. Facing the entrance when I stepped in was a bed holding a white-haired woman about my mother's age whose attention I captured instantly. She rose on an elbow to observe me more intently. I stared right back with the tentative beginnings of a smile. Her gaze remained fixed on me and I started across to her. I hugged her gently while kissing her once or twice and sat down. I was appalled that she didn't seem to recognize me or respond appropriately to my name. This was worse than I had imagined. It required a few more uncomfortable minutes of awkward talk for both of us to realize that we had never set eyes on each other before. I glanced about wretchedly. At the far end of the ward I then clearly spied my mother practically levitating out of her bed, plaster cast and all, and waving wildly in furious and frustrated exasperation to attract my attention. She looked exactly as I remembered, and she told me yet again that I had a twisted brain. She said it one more time when I revealed that I would soon be flying regularly in an airplane. It went without saying that she feared I would be killed in a crash.

After reading this, anyone who has recently read *Catch-22* for the third or fourth time might be struck by the parallel between the account of my mother I've just given and an episode in the novel in which Yossarian is visited in a hospital bed by a family of tearful strangers, but I don't remember that I consciously had the former in mind when I was devising the latter.

I HAD AN UNCOMPLICATED TIME with my Southerners in the blacksmith shop. It was easy for me to reason from the outset that my own Brooklyn manner of speaking would appear equally quaint and deformed to them, as it well might to citizens of countless other regions all across the continent, and doubtless still does. We seemed eccentric to each other.

To all the white men I worked with then, far back in 1942, the Negroes, blacks, or African Americans also working there, however one chooses to designate them, were held in such irrelevant regard and were fixed so solidly in caste that they were never even spoken about, and those there as helpers in the blacksmith shop were never addressed by anyone but me except in terse reference to work. The one or two in my section I most frequently joined with to cooperate on something and with whom—with what I now properly characterize as no more than a patronizing affectation of acceptance—I tried to establish friendly conversational relationships, intelligently withdrew and kept their distance. What surprised me more than the total absence of relationships between whites and blacks was the apparently uniform virulence with which Protestants regarded Catholics. I first learned about this from a dark and roly-poly Irish blacksmith I worked with often, who'd been reared in Northern Ireland, exposed to the enmity of the Protestant "Orangemen" there—it was the first time I'd heard that word *Orangemen*—and was now in the Norfolk Navy Yard in Portsmouth, Virginia, disapproved of and shunned by the others. Once enlightened by him, I plainly saw how he was mistrusted by his coworkers and coolly boycotted.

The blacks there were disdained and beneath notice, and the Catholics were detested with a touchy hostility. But a Jewish New Yorker like myself was a novel rarity. The local men had never seen one before, and I was the only one in the shop. And I had never been with Southerners. Thus there existed between us a mutual curiosity to be indulged.

At lunchtime and coffee breaks when we chatted in our group, others might drift close to gawk at me and listen with friendly smirks to our conversations. We always got along just fine—almost always—with much courtesy and consideration expressed by them to me about the mechanical mysteries and dangers of this work that to me was entirely new. As the first duty of my first day there, I was directed by the foreman to move a barrel of bolts to the grinding wheels to mill the surplus fringes of metal smoothly from the heads. I looked at the barrel and I looked at the hand truck, and I didn't know what to do. I knew it wouldn't work, but I decided to try: While the foreman and the assistant foreman observed, I squatted, wrapped my arms around the barrel as far as they would go, and tried to lift. The assistant foreman, a man named Beeman, who rarely smiled at me or anyone else, gestured to me to step aside and demonstrated how simple it was to slide the bottom ledge of the hand truck under the barrel and leverage the full weight back onto the wheels for rolling. I got the hang of that one quickly. He led me to the electrical grinding wheels to make certain I knew how to don goggles and to show me what they wanted done. I proved I could learn that one quickly, too.

A single exception to the harmonious relationships I

otherwise enjoyed occurred during one of our daily lunch-time breaks when the general discussion turned to religion and I chose to volunteer the information that Jesus was in fact Jewish and of presumed Jewish parentage. The immediate and united stiffening of the entire circle of white faces was an instantaneous warning that they had never been told this before and did not want to be told it now, or ever. Even my closest pals bristled. And I discreetly chose not to push the point. The symbolic rubric INRI on icons of the crucifixion would not have sufficed to convince them; and besides, I admit, I didn't myself know back then that these letters represented in Latin an abbreviation of "Jesus of Nazareth, King of the Jews."

Years later, in 1962, after the publication of *Catch-22,* I met Mel Brooks on the summer vacation resort of Fire Island, and I heard him joke, in the hoarse shout that is his second nature, that every Jew should have a big Gentile for a friend. My special friend in our group in the blacksmith shop was the biggest one there, a lumbering, easygoing fellow and the son of the foreman of the shop as well. No one would have dared harass me with him as my protector, but even without him I would have been untouched by any kind of bullying or more subtle abuse. There was no Jew-baiting all the weeks I was there, although there was plenty of raillery about my being a New Yorker and my quaint locutions and barbaric pronunciations. And I took care not to make too much of their being rustic Southerners.

One man I worked with often, from a farming community in North Carolina, could count and measure quantities with vertical lines in sets of five, the fifth line drawn sideways to cross through the other four, but he had never been taught the basics of division and multiplication. It was one of my functions to work out for him the number of long bars to be requisitioned for a fixed number of small units to be made from them. But he could do the work: With chalk he would measure and mark the lines for the three-foot lengths to be cut from each rod of perhaps thirty feet. And he would arrange them in his furnace and then pound and fashion them into whatever shape they were supposed to take. One day when I was occupied at the cutting machine and at the same time computing amounts with him while he measured and marked, I luckily turned my eyes back to the machine and just did manage to spy the shearing blade descending on my fingers as they fed in the metal. I pulled my hand back in sudden horror, saving my fingers from dismemberment at the last moment. Never again did I shift my gaze to speak to him or anyone else while at that cutting machine, and to this day I count that near tragedy among the most chilling experiences of my life, more frightening than anything that occurred on my second mission to Avignon or any of the other dangerous things that happened to me in wartime. Perhaps, as is classic in nightmares, what I tremble at most in the memory of the shearing machine is a calamity that never occurred, while everything that happened in combat did. I grade in retrospect those missing fingers I didn't lose right up there with the several times I swam out intrepidly when younger to the Coney Island bell buoy, when I didn't drown, and now am in recurrent fear that I might have.

A jollier episode than that near disaster at the shearing machine involved a working friendship with a young master blacksmith from nearby North Carolina. After a few weeks—after, I conclude, he finally decided he approved of me—he invited me, more than once, to drive out with him on a weekend day to the town he lived in, where, he promised, he would introduce me to some girls who would get a kick out of meeting me and would let me have from them as much as I wanted of anything I wanted.

The temptation was strong. The decisive drawback was stronger: I, fortunately, and unfortunately, too, always look ahead with caution to calculate consequences, even when drunk, and I could clearly see that I would have to give up a day of overtime, more likely two days if I slept over. Whereupon a dispiriting pall settled over my lubricious visions at the thought that afterward I would find myself again doing as much work for eight dollars a day as I could have been doing for twelve.

There was a second factor, a rather droll one, that perhaps also helped me overcome desire. In the country argot of his home territory, the common vulgar term for the primary female genital was the same as the one commonly employed elsewhere for the male sex organ—as I heard with some sense of shock each time he applied it to *them*—and that took a good bit of getting used to. The possibility arises only as I write this that he might have been directing me to males, to boys and men, but I strongly doubt that, for we were all talking as usual about sexual congress with women. And my day and night fantasies about women converged always on what he called a different thing and we called pussy.

Another source of practically daily amusement to my coworkers sprang from the work shoes picked out for me in Manhattan by my cautious brother, Lee. Ever concerned for my safety and everyone else's, Lee sought and found safety work shoes reinforced inside with domed steel shells to protect the toes and the front of the foot against crushing injury by impact from falling weights. Neither of us had the tiniest idea what kind of massive objects in the navy yard I'd be in danger from, and factory accidents do happen. In consequence, the shoes I wore to work were abnormally large and long and very heavy.

As it turned out, there was a tenet of folklore in my Virginia blacksmith shop holding that the size of a man's foot was directly indicative of the mass and range of his penis. None of my coworkers had ever seen, or even heard of, shoes with interior reinforcing structures like mine, and my feet appeared to be the largest, longest, thickest, bulkiest feet that any of them had ever laid eyes on. Much, therefore, was expected of me. It could be that those reinforced work shoes were the reason my colleague had wanted to bring me to his hometown to display to the women he knew there. The continual teasing I was subjected to in the form of mock praise and admiration was baffling to cope with. I was most loath to disappoint them. Secretly, I schemed to use the urinals in the bathroom only when that chamber was vacant, an attempt requiring more luck and craft than I could dependably command, for in the government navy yard, as in all other workplaces in the world, the rest rooms serve not only as toilets but also as sheltered spaces in which to hang out for short respites of recuperation from the unavoidable monotony of work. Rather than risk eventual discovery and bring down upon my head all the taunting, crude, homespun derision that was sure to follow—as though *I* were the one responsible for exaggerated expectations—I soon put myself to the expense of purchasing an ordinary pair of shoes and threw my armored ones away. To those at the fires who noticed the change and commented, I feigned a casual shrug and explained: "Circumcised. You know that."

In actual practice, there appeared to be no greater chance of injury working there than I would today face trying to prepare a hot meal for myself in my kitchen. The work was pretty much as I've said, tending the furnace and bearing bars of glowing metal from the fire to the true artisan; transferring weights from place to place on a hand truck or occasionally by an overhead traveling hoist that traversed the length of the shop on a track near a sidewall and functioned at the touch of button controls like those found today on a remote TV control; cutting metal into specific lengths; grinding bolts into level surfaces at the top, and threading them, too. At the threading machines, almost as a frolic, I devised a speed system of synchronized alternation with the man on the second unit alongside me that allowed us together to thread the bolts at a breathtaking pace unknown before in that shop, a rate that drew admirers and invoked murmurs of amused approbation, even from tight-mouthed Mr. Beeman. But that was diverting only sporadically, for no one was in a rush for the barrels of threaded bolts and we had no true need to hurry, other than to distract ourselves and others.

Now and then I had to work with the heavy sledgehammer. I was not good at that. Luckily, I didn't have to heft it all the way up over my shoulder for maximum power but could let gravity supply most of the needed force as I let it fall with a bang atop some rounding or rimming tool already held in place. Here, the hazard was more to the man I was working for than to me. Apart from that lapse at the shearing machine, I ran no more risk in the blacksmith shop than I had braved as a file clerk or Western Union boy. As a Western Union boy, good God, I could have been struck by a car!

More powerful to me in memory than anything but that shearing machine is a sinister sense of obscure and unnameable risks I might have been running on the train and boat trips I took to get to the navy yard. I am sensitive to such journeys now, when crimes against innocents seem endemic in our national life, although I doubt I was haunted by the threat of such perils back then. If I were, I might not have made the trip, not by myself. I doubt the family would have wanted me to.

The journey took all of one day and the morning of the next. I traveled alone in this first train trip from home, and I remember being silent and solitary for just about all of it. It must have been as forlorn and solemn an expedition for me as the bus ride away to summer camp. I spoke to no one, and no one spoke to me. I'm not good at starting conversations with strangers, and I've never picked up a girl unless the initiating remarks were made by someone else. I was a prisoner of the clock, helpless, a grieving slave to the slow passage of time. I was cut off from everyone. I may by then have already been afflicting myself involuntarily with the gloomy Freudian construct that people who went away from home sometimes did not return.

The train ride finally terminated for me in a place in

Virginia called Cape Charles. There, in compliance with an itinerary of instructions laid out meticulously on paper for me by Lee, I boarded a ferry for a water ride that, to my surprise, consumed another few hours. The length of the boat ride and the enormous expanse of the bay, Chesapeake Bay, were astounding to me—till then, my only ferry rides had taken no more than fifteen minutes, from the tip of Manhattan to Staten Island. Daylight was ending by the time I reached Norfolk. Another trip by ferry would bring me to Portsmouth and the navy yard. However, it had not been thought advisable that I arrive in Portsmouth at night to make my way around a strange city after dark.

On arrival, therefore, I checked into the first inexpensive hotel I could find. It was in appearance . . . unpretentious. The rosy neon lights from a coffee-shop restaurant across the street bled reflectively through my window into the room. I had an uneventful dinner alone there at the counter. I seemed to be the only guest in the hotel. The desk clerk was a skinny, bleary-eyed man of about thirty with a red patch of a birthmark on one side of his chin. I had done a good deal of reading in American fiction by then, and at dinner I had decided that if he proposed sending a woman up to my room, I would brace myself to say yes, but I didn't know how to ask for one. (Now I think I would know how but doubt I'll ever want to.) Waking up early the next morning, I was jittery. I still caught no sign of any other guests, and I was surprised and relieved when I found I had made my way safely out of the hotel with my suitcases and my life.

The ferry ride to Portsmouth was short. On getting off the boat, I asked questions at the dock and proceeded several miles by bus to the office in the bungalow complex in which I would reside, to check in and register for a room, and when finally I spotted some familiar Coney Island faces, I felt myself securely at home.

Upon reporting for work my first morning I learned not only what to do with a hand truck, a grinding wheel, and my barrel of iron bolts too heavy for human arms to hoist, but also how to clock in when arriving. Both the friendly foreman and the uncommunicative assistant foreman were waiting just inside the entrance to the shop, and not only for me. They took notice of every worker coming in, and with eagle eyes kept watch on a large, framed board inside a cabinet against the wall bearing round brass checks arranged in numerical order in rows on separate small rings. I was assigned one of these. Every man checking in on our day shift had, upon entering, to turn his brass check over from left to right to mark his presence. One or both of these supervisors was on station there before eight every morning to make certain that no one man turned over the checks for anyone other than himself. When the work whistle confirmed the end of our day shift, the procedure was renewed in reverse, to verify that someone who'd reported in for the day's work hadn't escaped in the interval. And in the morning, as soon as the work whistle blew to herald the formal beginning of our shift, a hinged glass door was swung closed over the whole display of this version of a time clock and was locked until quitting time.

Anyone not on the premises on time had forfeited not just the hourly fraction of his lateness; he was barred for the remainder of the day, no matter his readiness to work, his skill, or his excuse. It seemed, therefore, that no acute shortage of labor cried out for remedy. It appeared as well that there was no great rush for any of the products that flowed from our shop. We all kept busy faithfully at what we were supposed to be doing, but the rhythm was methodical rather than hurried. When we worked up a sweat it was more from the temperature than the rapidity of the work. People took days off whenever they wanted to. Apart from the occasional assault against boredom at the threading machines by me and a partner, no one ever sped to break records. Periodically, though, a wave of advance warning would circulate lazily through the shop and awake ripples of disturbance vaguely similar to those in an ant colony or a hive of bees when intruded upon: Government inspectors would soon be coming through.

In reaction, the fires in all the furnaces would be turned up, and in each of them rods and strips would be inserted for heating. The drop forges would pump and gasp and pound. Grinding wheels would be turned on and threading machines would thread, even when there was next to nothing to thread. The tapping of hammers would be heard in the land, and all of us were so abnormally immersed in our labors as not even to see the high-ranking naval officers and ill-at-ease white-collar civilians passing through with perfunctory yet discerning pauses, as though they understood what they were looking at and what we were doing and why.

They didn't.

We didn't either.

We worked seven days a week and, except for our licensed plumber with the automobile and his girlfriend from the soda shop and for my acquaintance from a different part of Brooklyn whose unrevealed social activities had occasioned a visit from the police, there was not much for any of us in the way of entertainment. I can't remember going to even one movie during the seven or eight continuous weeks I worked without a day off. After we had showered and rested a little at the end of our day shift, it was time for dinner. To be on the job at eight every morning dictated retiring early, and we were doing that seven days a week. Just outside the entrance to the navy yard, in the diner in which we ate breakfast, we were surprised at first to see that certain kinds of liquor were offered, and more surprised to behold it being consumed at that hour, as though liquor for breakfast were commonplace.

We ate most of our dinners in the boardinghouse of a rather easygoing, voluptuous woman of some years with a shy daughter of about twenty who assisted her in the serving and on whom she kept a vigilant, puritanical eye that did not harmonize with the subtle and perhaps unintended coquettishness in her own sensual bearing. The meals were economical and good, basic: chicken, pork, beef, lamb chops, stews—no fish, thank goodness. The single strange element in her cuisine was something they called corn bread and was not the corn bread we Jewish New Yorkers knew was corn bread. Our corn bread was a plump, hardy, firm, yeasty, East European loaf, and their corn bread was cake. By now, though, I've grown used to their corn bread and wouldn't mind having some right now, with a little raspberry or strawberry jam to go with it. On Passover, all the Jewish laborers in Portsmouth were invited to traditional holiday fare in a large hall rented by members of the Jewish community. It was a happy and novel occasion for us, with much greatly welcomed hospitality, and what we commented most about was the southern pronunciation of both the English and the Yiddish (and the Hebrew, too, in the compressed observances).

In Norfolk, we'd been told, there was a "cathouse" at the address 30 Bank Street. I don't think any of us flirted seriously with the thought of going there; if others went and talked about it, they didn't talk about it to me. Again, a powerful force toward abstinence was monetary, the sobering, unspoken awareness that we would have to atone later with approximately three full days at hard labor for a fling of half an hour in a lewd debauchery that might or might not prove euphorically uplifting. Or worse, might prove ruinously addictive.

At length, I finally did treat myself to a spree of a day off—two full days, I think; a weekend. I forget what I did with it—it could have been a drive to New York packed into the speeding automobile of one of us at a unit cost lower than the normal commercial fare; the memory is a blur. If so, I don't know what I did there. I can remember (or think I do) the address of a bordello in Norfolk I never went to, but nothing of how I passed the time back home in Coney Island or somewhere else after something like *fifty-six* consecutive days of formidable labor. But . . . whatever I did do spoiled me, broke my spirit, sapped my willpower, put an end to my career as a factory worker. Going back to that work even after so short a furlough grew unthinkable, and proved with the passage of the first few days an agony of phobic anguish such that only a man of a steelier character than mine could subdue.

I surrendered with hardly a fight.

I gave notice.

I packed up and left.

Boy—was I happy!

ON MY WAY HOME from Virginia, I stopped in Washington, D.C., for one night and two days to visit with my Coney Island friend Marty Kapp. Marty was from 23rd Street, down in the Italian section. We hadn't met until high school, and he became close friends with the rest of us by joining the first of our social clubs. In our bunch he was something of an anomaly—even his stance was upright and he didn't, like the rest of us, slouch along like a cool hipster when he walked. He didn't twirl a length of key chain or even peg his pants. I believe he was one of the rare ones among us—Sy Ostrow was another—who went directly from high school into college, to Brooklyn College, which was free and near to us. It was from Marty's father, an electrician or plumber, that I obtained the obligatory letter of recommendation for the job at the navy yard attesting to my mechanical experience (which I didn't have) acquired working for him (which I had never done). It was not, alas, the only time in my life I cut corners, as the charitable young lady from California who surreptitiously helped me meet the foreign-language requirement for my master's degree in English at Columbia University can warrant, if she's alive and remembers (if she's alive, she remembers). I'm sorry now I did that. It was my malfeasance then that compelled

me later, with logical good conscience, to show mercy to two
students I caught cheating when I was teaching college in
Pennsylvania.

While I had been laboring away at the navy yard, Marty
was working in Washington in some governmental capacity, either in a civil-service position or perhaps already
enrolled in the navy's V-12 program, an agenda of specialized military education in which he was to spend the duration of the war. He found a bed for me in the communal
apartment he was sharing with a lively group of others
about the same age as the two of us.

The wartime capital city seemed afire with sunshine
and energy that weekend. I spent much of my first day, a
Saturday on which Marty was occupied responsibly with
whatever were his duties, roaming about goggle-eyed in a
state of orthodox reverence. I was appropriately awed by the
Washington Monument and the sleek, domed Jefferson
Memorial, and deeply moved by the solemnity of the seated
figure in the Lincoln shrine. I was as spontaneously thrilled
by all I saw of official Washington as any uncritical first-
time visitor from the hinterlands (i.e., from anywhere outside the District of Columbia) possessing just a superficial
and idealized knowledge of American history and a tangen-
tial, headline-founded awareness of current events. Even
schoolboys now know they can't rely on schoolbooks and
official public statements for any honest grasp of the historical truth. In Lincoln's Gettysburg Address, for example,
once you're past the simple arithmetic at the beginning of
the leading sentence, there's not much left that can be
empirically verified. It's a wonderful speech, one of the best
on record, certainly, and it's mostly a lot of baloney. So much
for speeches!

On Sunday, Marty and I attended an outdoor sym-
phonic concert, my first concert. I remember the featured
work but not the performers; it was the Tchaikovsky Violin
Concerto, which I hadn't heard before. I have a good ear for

music and a magnetic memory for musical phrases. A day or two after I was back in Coney Island, I was fortunate enough to catch the same concerto on the radio. I stopped everything to concentrate, listening intently from beginning to end, and had the feeling when it was over that I had known that music all my life. To this day I can recall and hum the major melodic passages in the openings of all three movements. Also today, the violin concerto of Tchaikovsky, once the most beloved and moving of composers to me, is just about the only work of his I can stand.

BACK HOME IN CONEY ISLAND I was nineteen and at loose ends, carefree, but in the state of boyish lunacy and naïveté still widespread among late adolescents, I'd bet. Though carefree, I was nonetheless in a developmental quandary. Others around me were likewise adrift. Bobby Magrill, the pharmacist's son, was set on becoming a physician. George Mandel, our comic-books cartoonist who was making $300 or $400 a week when I was making $15, already in the army, where he would suffer his serious head wound in the Battle of the Bulge, had attended lessons at the Art Students League. These were exceptions. The rest of us were without concrete direction or motivation.

For us, the military draft looming somewhere ahead was the only certainty in a future that was in all other respects murky. It was hard to give serious consideration to what in later life we intended to do, *could* do. Danny the Count and Sheiky Silverman sold costume jewelry as peddlers outside the busy entrances of the subway station at Union Square. Sheiky also peddled ice cream on the Coney Island beach that summer, 1942, when he wasn't leading the policemen pursuing him in an agile chase through the crowds in the sand. Louie Berkman was in his father's junk shop. We found jobs for each other. Marvin Winkler worked a short while stringing pearls in a factory where Murray "Rup" Rabinowitz already had some standing;

later, Marvin did shipping in the garment center for our Coney Island friend Jackie Sachs.

I looked around for what work I could find and took what work I could get. Davey Goldsmith needed assistance as a shipping clerk during a business rush at the U.S. Hatband Company, and I pitched in with him for a while at $21 a week, learning how to unfold and seal flat corrugated boxes. Now and then, when the need arises, I wish I remembered how. Macy's, through Sylvia, hired me for a couple of weeks to count stock in an inventory period. Someone introduced me to a job in a millinery factory in Manhattan to pack hats for shipping and to keep the floors clean. Until then, I—a fledgling, aspiring author—hadn't bothered to find out what "millinery" was; I'd imagined it was something like lingerie. The millinery we made was of straw, and the scraps of straw nicked my fingers when I did my best to keep the floors clean. Before the first week was out, one of the scowling elderly partners growled at me not to come in any longer. He was telling me I was fired. Lee was no longer a customer's man on Wall Street but somehow the supervisor in a small factory doing subcontracting work for a larger defense manufacturer. I went to work for Lee on a drill press. I adjusted a template over a square of something that was not wood and brought the spinning auger down into each opening in the dotted pattern of the several holes. Doing just this eight hours a day, four hours at a clip, was nerve-racking. Lee was not hurt or surprised when I confessed I couldn't stand it. Along with so many other Americans of my generation in an era of economic depression that had not truly passed, I'd been biding my time, waiting in numb hope for some unknown, defining reality finally to pop up that would clarify the course I should follow, wind me up, and start me on my way.

We had not thought it would be a war.

The announcement by the government that nineteen-year-olds would soon be called up for military service supplied the impetus. We saw no incentive in avoiding the draft. A group of us enlisted—we had nothing better to do. And we were further motivated by the opportunity to choose the branch of service we preferred.

The morning I left for the army, I had orders to report to a waiting room at the Pennsylvania Railroad Station for transportation to the area's military reception center at Camp Upton, Long Island. My mother and Sylvia walked with me to the trolley stop outside Mr. Moses's candy store at Railroad Avenue. We talked routinely as we waited; I promised I would write often and telephone from Long Island if I could. We hugged formally and kissed cheeks automatically as the trolley car drew near and slowed to a stop. Later, many years later, I was profoundly shaken (and tried not to show it) when my sister happened to disclose that my mother dissolved into tears and collapsed with weeping as soon as the trolley car carried me off on my merry way. Sobbing violently, my mother could barely keep standing, and Sylvia strained to hold her erect as they struggled back to the apartment house.

Dope that *I* was, I didn't see that there was anything to cry about.

My mother never mentioned the occasion to me, and I never brought it up with her. Our family tendency to keep disturbing emotions to ourselves has lasted as long as we have.

THE AMIABLE PSYCHOLOGIST Erik Erikson writes somewhere (*Childhood and Society*?) of a "Moratorium" that emerges in the lives of most Western young people between the end of adolescence and the onset of maturity, during which the individual doesn't truly know what he or she is or where he wants to go, doesn't indeed truly know *who* he is, or what he or she should decide to become. It is a season of baffled uncertainty over identity and can lead to grave mistakes. (Witness the skinheads in England, the neo-Nazis in Germany, the neophyte Nazis in Moscow. What is the average starting age of the cocaine or heroin addict? The average mugger?) To the extent Erickson is right, and for those of us Americans in that stage who weren't harmed physically or damaged emotionally by military service, the war came along at just the right time. (For Europeans, there is never a right time for a European war.) It put an end to our confusion and ambivalence, took most powers of decision out of our hands, and swept us into a national endeavor considered admirable and just.

And remunerative, too. My total income upon entering the air force as a private was as much as I'd been able to command outside, and as an officer on flight status was greater than I was able to earn afterward when starting out in my civilian pursuits, first as a college instructor at Pennsylvania State College ($3,000 a year) and next as an advertising copywriter at a small New York agency called the Merrill Anderson Company ($60 a week, $260 per month). But at the Merrill Anderson Company, as an unexpected employee benefit, I drank my first Gibsons with a copy chief named Gert Conroy and learned to love extra-dry martinis in a chilled glass with a twist of lemon peel. (Also, one morning I arrived at work with my pastry and container of coffee and a mind brimming with ideas, and immediately in longhand put down on a pad the first chapter of an intended novel, a chapter that, after expansion and revision, was published in 1955 in the periodical *New World Writing* #7 as the opening of a novel in progress, a work to be titled . . . *Catch-18*. I was at *Time* when a contract for the publication of the novel was offered on the basis of 250 pages and working at *McCall's* magazine when the manuscript was completed at last in January 1961 and published in October. My salary at *McCall's* was good, I had two children, and I was obliged to wait almost a full year until the motion picture rights were sold before I had confidence enough to leave.)

After the war, Marty Kapp continued what technical education he'd begun in the navy V-12 program and graduated as a soil engineer (yet another thing I'd not heard of before). For all his career he worked as a soil engineer with the Port Authority of New York—on airfields and buildings, I know, and perhaps on bridges and tunnels, too—and had risen to some kind of executive status before he died. He did well enough to die on a golf course. Davey Goldsmith went back to work at the hatband company, prospered there, and eventually inherited a division of that company. I was able to go to college. Lou Berkman left the junk shop to start a plumbing supply company in Middletown, New York, and looked into real estate with the profits from that successful venture. Marvin Winkler passed up college, too, and was soon in the photographic film business (his first in a sequence of modest enterprises), converting surplus air corps aerial film into color film for home use. Albie Covelman went to Bucknell and was soon an executive with a coffee-equipment supply company. Sy Ostrow, who was taught Russian in the service so that he could function as an interpreter, returned to college and, with pained resignation, saw realistically that he had no better alternative than to study law. Stanley Levy, from the file room at the automobile casualty company, became an insurance broker and handled what little business I could give him when we at last caught up with each other. Like Marty Kapp, Stanley died on a golf course. It's my opinion they died of boredom.

I was mustered out of the service even before the war was over, demobilized under a point system put into effect as soon as Germany capitulated at the beginning of May in 1945.

But even before the war ended with the surrender of Japan in August, I felt myself walking around on easy street, in a state of fine rapture. What more could I ask for? I was in love and engaged to be married (to the same young woman I was in love with). I was twenty-two years old. I would be entering college as a freshman at the University of Southern California, with tuition and related costs paid for by the government. And I'd just had a short story accepted for publication.

8

Peace

IN DECEMBER OF 1944, when I had completed the tour of duty then defined at sixty missions and was awaiting orders for transportation back to the States, two chaste beginners, both lieutenants freshly shipped overseas, moved into my tent. They replaced a pair who had finished their tours and already left, and one of these new men brought into the tent with him the uncommon personal asset of a portable typewriter. Don't ask me why—I've lost the explanation, though it seems likely he was nurturing the same authorial aspirations I was, and Tom Sloan also.

Tom Sloan, a lead bombardier, who was from Philadelphia, and Hall A. Moody, a wing bombardier from Mississippi, were among the friends in Corsica I was closest to. Tom was a conscientious, quick, and capable lead bombardier in whose formation I found it almost a pleasure to fly. Like Moody, I was merely a wing bombardier and operated only a toggle switch, compressing it in the speediest fraction of the instant after I saw the bombs starting downward out of the open bomb-bay doors in the lead plane. Once overseas, I never made use of the bombsight on which I had been trained, or even had one with me in the nose of my plane. I had a .50-caliber machine gun mounted on a ball swivel instead, and fortunately never had to make use of that implement either. Four of the wing bombardiers in the six planes in each of our formations carried no bombsights but single machine guns instead.

Tom was only a few years older than I, no older than twenty-five, I'm sure, but he was already married and the father of an infant child he'd seen not more than a few times. He was resolutely intent on surviving to rejoin the family he missed so greatly, and he was increasingly and visibly perturbed that he might not succeed. It's a joy to me now to report that he did. Shipping orders for the two of us arrived the same day; not till they were in hand did we truly feel saved.

Hall A. Moody, my age or even younger, was married also, and I relate with pride, not scorn, that neither he nor Tom Sloan ever exhibited even the slightest interest in sex with another woman, not on rest leaves in Rome and not in Sicily, Cairo, or Alexandria. I, unmarried and in depth of experience still almost a virgin, was the boyish and ravenous satyr. Moody was in several ways an innocent: He had never before *even heard* of oral sex, in either direction. He had not heard of it by either the genteel Latinate names we all now know or the vulgar familiar ones we now all use, and the mere suggestion of any such distorted practice was to him an outrageous, debasing horror he declined to envision and caused him to redden and clench his fists in passionate indignation. When Tom and I left together for the States, Moody was still on combat status and I don't know what became of him, but his name doesn't appear on the list of fatalities in our squadron history, and I assume he survived. And Tom Sloan's infant child, the one he missed so dearly and painfully and reticently when I knew him, was about one year old then and now would be past fifty.

With travel orders in hand, Tom and I were flown from Corsica—not to Rome, which I would have favored for a final, farewell, youthful revel—but to Naples on the first leg of our journey homeward. Given the choice of returning by air or sea, I expressed unequivocal preference for the sea, because it had become my furtive and sacred resolve never to go up in an airplane again. (In fact, once back safely, I declined to fly again, as soldier or civilian, for something like the next seventeen years, traveling instead by train to company conventions when at *Time* and *McCall's* and by cruise steamship when the meetings were in Bermuda and Nassau. Not until the stupefying boredom of overnight rail travel ultimately outweighed all fears of dying did I weaken, and by then there were jets.)

After a week or so in Naples, I sailed with a few thousand other servicemen on a converted and highly modern troopship, not long previously the S.S. *America,* I believe I remember, formerly the premier luxury liner of the American passenger fleet. There were six officers in my cabin on two tiers of bunk beds, sleeping, napping, reading, eating, talking, because there wasn't much else to do in the ten days or so we were afloat. None of us had known any of the others before. I cannot imagine now how I spent so much time doing essentially nothing but sleeping, napping, reading, eating, and talking, and I know I wouldn't ever want to have to do it again. We sailed without convoy or other naval escort. Our cabin wasn't first class, because we weren't on deck; but it wasn't steerage either, for we did have a porthole.

We were heading for Boston, but didn't know our destination until we were already in port. From Boston we were transported by rail to Atlantic City for routine processing and reassignment, and from there, on furlough, I traveled home to Coney Island and was triumphantly back with my family as something of a glamorous war hero. I never thought to ask what they worried about and said about me while they waited for my letters, and I still don't know.

Among the first things I did during my medical examination in Atlantic City was ask to be taken off flying status. The doctor was surprised: He found it odd that, after surviving combat duty, I should want to give up half my base pay to avoid only four hours a month of flight time in the

States—there seemed little chance of my being sent overseas again. With the shameless knowledge that I was lying, I pleaded that I was afraid to fly, claiming that the dread I might have was keeping me awake: The mere remembrance of the gasoline fumes inside a plane was sickening to me. By that time there were already thousands of airmen like me who had completed combat duty and were back dillydallying in the States while the government tried to decide what to do with us, and he graciously granted my request. And the lie I thought I was telling him turned out to be true, for by then, I realized, I had genuinely grown terrified of flying.

IN BEING ASSIGNED to my tent, the two new replacements, both of them pilots, lucked into one of the most comfortable and best-appointed pyramid canvas abodes in the squadron. We not only had a gasoline-dripping homemade stove for warmth in winter but a splendid fireplace as well. On the wall of the room in my home in East Hampton in which I am arranging these words—rather, *re*arranging them—is mounted a framed and glass-encased photograph taken inside our tent, lifted from an elegant, bound volume of a squadron history prepared after the war by our squadron public-relations officer, an assiduous captain named Everett Thomas. The page is captioned "The Holidays Corsica 1944" and the photograph highlights a large kitchen knife, a cake, and the five of us then dwelling inside the tent. In the background is a spacious fireplace with blazing flames, topped by a broad wood-beamed mantel fabricated from salvaged railroad ties. We are all posing rather obviously for what professes to be a candid photograph.

A young pilot named Bob Vertrees is shown at a table with a long kitchen knife, and he is slicing into what looks like a Christmas fruitcake that presumably has reached him from home. The two newcomers, seated also, are looking on politely. One gazes from the side; the other, possessor of a sparse mustache and the typewriter, practically faces the camera, but his eyes are properly averted toward the cake. Looking on almost impassively between them is a rather short, high-cheeked pilot named Edward Ritter, short but not so short as to have fallen short of the minimum physical requirements for pilot training. Of those shown, Ritter, arriving overseas after me, has been there in the tent with me longest. I am bending forward in a chair at the right, almost in profile, casually smoking a cigarette and clad in my officer's cap with the wire frame removed, a liberty of fashion conferred on air corps personnel as a distinctive privilege, and a leather flight jacket bearing a round patch of the squadron's insignia, a brazen depiction against a dark background of a slim, well-busted naked female wielding a thunderbolt while her windblown hair streams behind her and she sits suggestively straddling a long, projecting bomb that free-falls forward and downward. On a low table just behind me is the portable typewriter, which I was already, with the owner's permission, making much use of, for letters and for manuscripts. Behind that, at the rear of the tent, are the cozy household flames in the fireplace and the broad mantel of sturdy timber, which had been carpeted for the season with a winding garland of Christmas foliage. And on the wall above the fireplace are a number of large, glossy photographs of beautiful women. They are not exactly of the cheesecake kind, but the one immediately behind my head is of an attractive female reclining on a divan in a becoming dress and a full, silken bosom of a quality that still never fails to provoke in me an intuitive reflection of desire and speculation. Vertrees is grinning as he cuts the cake and both of the new men are smiling, too, while Ritter and I look on, absorbed and content. I've been overseas longer than the others, but we're all about the same age. We're kids not long past twenty, and we look like kids who are only past twenty.

In December 1944 I was twenty-one and a half, and it is hard now, it boggles the mind now, to believe that a young kid like Ritter, whom I'd known the longest and who was somewhat stumpy in physique, was ever, let alone routinely as an occupational specialty, permitted to fly as a pilot at the controls of a twin-engined Mitchell medium-sized bomber that carried a bomb load of four thousand pounds (eight five-hundred-pounders or four of a thousand pounds each) and five other human beings!

How in hell did he learn to do that?

I, who didn't apply for my first driver's license until I was twenty-eight, find it difficult to envision even now that a kind and unaggressive boy, so young, could learn to fly a bomber. And there were others in the squadron of slighter build and even fewer years who were pilots, too.

A little while before, Vertrees, who was a pilot also, had been wounded in the hand by a chip of flak, injured so trivially that he was out of action only a few days and returned to combat duty in almost no time.

Ritter's biography overseas was perplexing. Taciturn, good-natured, soft-spoken, even shy, from Kentucky, he was something of a tireless wonder as a handyman, one with unlimited patience who took pleasure in making and fixing things. The construction of the fireplace was entirely of his devising, if I recall accurately. We have our place in the squadron history book only by virtue of that fireplace. He erected and maintained the stove, too, although by winter every tent contained one like it, a continuously feeding gasoline unit that drew fuel from a can outside and dripped it onto sand in a drum that stood near the center pole and helped warm the interior. We also used the stove to heat our supplementary snacks at night from the boxes of K or C rations that were in abundant supply and the hot water with which we shaved and washed outside in the morning. A flak helmet was our basin. The metal fins on the upright, inverted skeleton of a frame in which unfused bombs were shipped was our washstand.

In combat, Ritter as pilot had ditched safely once into the Mediterranean waters coming back from a mission on which his engine had been shot out, and all the men with him had made it from the plane into the life rafts without injury and had been rescued by air-sea surface craft before nightfall. I remember awaiting their return. Another time, he flew back with one engine feathered and landed safely, and I believe there was one other time he crash-landed without harm to anyone aboard, either at a different landing strip closer to where his crippled plane was in difficulty or at our own, code-named Genoa. ("Hello, Genoa, hello, Genoa" was a pilot's saluting radio call to the control tower of our field at Alisan, Corsica, and the title of a story I once thought I might write and don't believe I ever did.) Hall A. Moody was aboard with Ritter on one of those near disasters, and for that reason, both were awarded a recreational trip to Egypt. Sloan and I went along because we had completed our sixty missions and there wasn't much else for the squadron to do with us as we shambled around waiting for our transfer orders. Also, I suspect there was a forlorn, covert command dream that, refreshed upon our return and intoxicated with gratitude, we would beg to be allowed to fly more missions than the sixty we already had. Neither one of us volunteered to do that.

Remarkably, through all his unlucky series of mishaps the pilot Ritter remained imperviously phlegmatic, demonstrating no symptoms of fear or growing nervousness, even blushing with a chuckle and a smile whenever I gagged around about him as a jinx, and it was on these qualities of his, his patient genius for building and fixing things and these recurring close calls in aerial combat, only on these, that I fashioned the character of Orr in *Catch-22*. (I don't know if he's aware of that. I don't know if he's even read the book, for I've never been in touch with him or almost any of the others.)

In a nearby tent just across a railroad ditch in disuse was the tent of a friend, Francis Yohannon, and it was from him that I nine years later derived the unconventional name for the heretical Yossarian. The rest of Yossarian is the incarnation of a wish. In Yohannon's tent also lived the pilot Joe Chrenko, a pilot I was especially friendly with, who later, in several skimpy ways, served as the basis for the character Hungry Joe in *Catch-22*. In that tent with them was a pet dog Yohannon had purchased in Rome, a lovable, tawny cocker spaniel he bought while others were purchasing and smuggling back contraband Italian pistols, Berettas. In my novel I turned the dog into a cat to protect its identity.

Rome was a wonderful city to go to (and still is), and, given his astonishing achievement, even a limited cast of characters ought to include a tribute to our able squadron executive officer, Major Cover (Major ——— de Coverley in *Catch-22*). Now, I still don't know what an executive officer is or what one does, but whatever ours did, he did exceedingly well. A few weeks after I arrived overseas for combat in early May of 1944 as a replacement bombardier, the Germans retreated north from the open city of Rome (there was no connection between these events, I'm sure). The first American soldiers were in Rome on the morning of June 4, and close on their heels, perhaps even beating them into the city, sped our congenial executive officer, Major Cover, to rent two apartments there for use by the officers and enlisted men in our squadron: For officers there was an ornate four-bedroom suite with much marble and many mirrors in the reputable residential district of the Via Nomentana, with a separate bedroom with double bed for each officer, and a maid to see that the rooms were tidied; for the enlisted men, who came in larger bunches, there was an extended arrangement of rooms on two floors somewhere up past the top of the Via Veneto, with cooks and maids, and with female friends of the cooks and maids who liked to hang out there with the enlisted men just for sport.

Hardly did we learn that the city of Rome was ours than officers and enlisted men who'd been in combat longer were returning starry-eyed from enchanted rest leaves there, speaking, rhapsodically and disbelievingly, of restaurants, nightclubs, dance halls, and girls, girls, girls—girls in their summer dresses strolling with smiles on the Via Veneto. And these fellow fliers taught us the most valuable Italian phrase for just about everything we might want when our turn to go there on a rest leave came:

"*Quanto costa?*"

And thanks to Major Cover and the apartments, we were frequently on leave there.

RITTER HAD ARRIVED in my tent early on in my tour of duty to occupy the cot vacated by a bombardier from Oklahoma named Pinkard, shot down and killed on a mission to the railway bridge north of the city of Ferrara in the Po Valley. There were several of these missions to Ferrara shortly after I arrived, and the target was a much more terrifying one than I was able to grasp in my absence of experience and my idiotic faith in my own divine invulnerability. On another mission to Ferrara, one I don't think I was on, a radio gunner I didn't know was pierced through the middle by a wallop of flak—it was always flak that destroyed, for there were no German fighter planes attacking us the whole time I was there—and he died, moaning, I was told, that he was cold. For my episodes of Snowden in the novel, I fused the knowledge of that tragedy with the panicked copilot and the thigh wound to the top turret gunner in my own plane on our second mission to Avignon. The rest of the details are all pretty much as I related, except that I did not, like Yossarian, discard my uniform or sit naked in a tree, and I was not given a medal while undressed. Back over water on the way home from that mission, a plane with a bombardier friend of mine named Wohlstein in the crew (he could drive, and with a car from the motor pool we would go exploring together through the tiny Corsican mountain villages on our eastern side of the island), pulled out of formation, toppled into a spin, and corkscrewed down to a fatal crash into the water that killed all five men aboard. The pilot in his plane that day was Earl C. Moon, who was copilot in the crew with which I flew in a B-25 across the Atlantic from South Carolina to Algeria and then to Corsica. I didn't witness that crash or know about it until we were back on the ground, for I was entirely occupied ministering to the thigh wound of my top-turret gunner, with bandages, sulfanilamide, and morphine, and with sickly attempts at solicitous and reassuring platitudes while we flew on and on. The aerial gunner and I had not known each other before. When I went to visit him in the hospital the next day, he must have been given blood transfusions, for his Mediterranean color was back, and he was in ebullient spirits. We greeted each other as the closest of pals and never saw each other again.

EXCEPT FOR THE INSERTION into the novel of a radio gunner who is mortally wounded, the incidents I actually experienced in my plane on this second mission to Avignon were very much like those I related in fictional form. A copilot panicked and I thought I was doomed. By that time I had learned through experience that this war was perilous and that they were trying to kill me. The earlier cluster of missions I had flown to Ferrara when first overseas had assumed in my memory the character of a fantasy nightmare from which I had luckily escaped without harm in my trusting innocence, like an ingenuous kid in a Grimm fairy tale. And I also knew from the serious tone in the briefing room and from an earlier mission to Avignon that this target was a dangerous one.

All four squadrons in the group were involved, flying into southern France in a single large bunch, then separating near the city to simultaneously attack three separate targets that were several miles apart. My plane was in the last of the three elements turning in, and as we neared our IP, the initial point from which we would begin our bomb run, I looked off into the distance to see what was taking place with the other formations. The instant I looked, I glimpsed far off amid black bursts of flak a plane in formation with an orange glow of fire on its wing. And the instant I spied the fire, I saw the wing break off and the plane nose over and fall straight down, like a boulder—rotating slowly with its remaining wing, but straight down. There was no possibility of parachutes. Then we made the turn toward our target and we were in it ourselves.

The very first bursts of flak aimed at us were at an accurate height, and that was a deadly sign. We could hear the explosions. I have since read of the tactic developed by the Germans of sending a monitor plane out to fly alongside our bombers and radio our exact altitude and speed to the anti-aircraft batteries below, and it's possible they were doing it that day. Soberly and tensely, I did what I had to—we all did. When I observed the bomb-bay doors of the lead bombardier opening, I opened mine; when I saw his bombs begin to go, I toggled away mine; when the indicator on my dial registered that all our bombs were away, I announced on the intercom that our bombs were away. When a gunner in the rear looking down into the bomb-bay announced that the bomb-bay was clear, I flipped the switch that closed the doors. And then our whole formation of six planes wrenched away upward at full throttle into a steep and twisting climb. And then the bottom of the plane just seemed to drop out: we were falling, and I found myself pinned helplessly to the top of the bombardier's compartment, with my flak helmet squeezed against the ceiling. What I did not know (it was reconstructed for me later) was that one of the two men at the controls, the copilot, gripped by the sudden fear that our plane was about to stall, seized the controls to push them forward and plunged us into a sharp descent, a dive, that brought us back down into the level of the flak.

I had no power to move, not even a finger. And I believed with all my heart and quaking soul that my life was ending and that we were going down, like the plane on fire I had witnessed plummeting only a few minutes before. I had no time for anything but terror. And then just as suddenly—I think I would have screamed had I been able to—we leveled out and began to climb away again from the flak bursts, and now I was flattened against the floor, trying frantically to grasp something to hold on to when there was nothing. And in another few seconds we were clear and edging back into formation with the rest of the planes. But as I regained balance and my ability to move, I heard in the ears of my headphones the most unnatural and sinister of sounds: silence, dead silence. And I was petrified again. Then I recognized, dangling loosely before me, the jack to my headset. It had torn free from the outlet. When I plugged myself back in, a shrill bedlam of voices was clamoring in my ears, with a wail over all the rest repeating on the intercom that the bombardier wasn't answering. "The bombardier doesn't answer!" "I'm the bombardier," I broke in immediately. "And I'm all right." "Then go back and help him, help the gunner. He's hurt."

It was our top gunner who was wounded, and his station was in the front section of the plane just behind the pilot's flight deck. But so deeply, over time, have the passages in the novel entrenched themselves in me that I am tempted even now to think of the wounded man as the radio gunner in the rear. Our gunner was right there on the floor in front of me when I moved back through the crawlway from my bombardier's compartment, and so was the large oval wound in his thigh where a piece of flak—a small one, judging from the entrance site on the inside—had blasted all the way through. I saw the open flesh with shock. I had no choice but to do what I had to do next. Overcoming a tremendous wave of nausea and revulsion that was close to paralyzing, I delicately touched the torn and bleeding leg, and after the first touch, I was able to proceed with composure.

Although there was a lot of blood puddling about, I could tell from my Boy Scout days—I had earned a merit badge in first aid—that no artery was punctured and thus there was no need for a tourniquet. I followed the obvious procedure. With supplies from the first-aid kit, I heavily salted the whole open wound with sulfanilamide powder. I opened and applied a sterile compress, maybe two—enough to close and to cover everything injured. Then I bandaged him carefully. I did the same with the small hole on the inside of his thigh. When he exclaimed that his leg was starting to hurt him, I gave him a shot of morphine—I may have given him two if the first didn't serve quickly enough to soothe us both. When he said he was starting to feel cold, I told him we would soon be back on the field and he was going to be all right. Truthfully, I hadn't the slightest idea where we were, for my attention had been totally concentrated on him.

With a wounded man on board, we were given priority in landing. The flight surgeon and his medical assistants and an ambulance were waiting to the side at the end of the runway. They took him off my hands. I might have seemed a hero and been treated as something of a small hero for a short while, but I didn't feel like one. They were trying to kill me, and I wanted to go home. That they were trying to kill all of us each time we went up was no consolation. They were trying to kill *me*.

I was frightened on every mission after that one, even the certified milk runs. It could have been about then that I began crossing my fingers each time we took off and saying in silence a little prayer. It was my sneaky ritual.

THAT WAS A MISSION on August 15th. A week before, I had seen a plane shot down just after the bomb run on the first of our squadron's missions to the bridges of Avignon. I was in the leading flight and when I looked back to see how the others were doing, I saw one plane pulling up above and away from the others, a wing on fire beneath a tremendous, soaring plume of orange flame. I saw a parachute billow open, then another, then one more before the plane began spiraling downward, and that was all. Dick Hirsch, a fellow from Chicago I'd trained with in bombardiering school in Victorville, California, was in one of those chutes. He came down in a field in Provence, was picked up by the underground, hidden, clothed in civilian garb, and smuggled back through the battle lines into the Allied part of Italy. Once back in the squadron he was rotated home without delay, to his surprise and ours, it being the policy never to expose to recapture anyone who had once had contact with the underground. The pilot killed in his plane was a blond fellow from upstate New York named James Burrhus, and I knew him, too, having flown missions with him. The co-pilot was a younger kid named Alvin Yellon, recently arrived, and I found out more about him fifty years later when I received a letter from his brother asking whether the mission I had described in my writing could have been the one on which his brother had met his death. It was.

It was all very much more dangerous, I realize now, than I had let myself recognize at the time and since. I believe I've read that more than 10 percent of the three hundred thousand American World War II dead were air corps crewmen.

And for those on the ground on the Western Front in Europe that Christmas season, it was even colder and more lethal. I remember seeing in *Stars and Stripes,* the official military newspaper, photographs of bundled-up Americans plodding their bleak way in desperate winter combat clothing through drifts of snow taller than they were. They looked like foreigners in a different, distant war. Theirs *was* a different war. As a consequence of the colossal reciprocal miscalculations by both the Allied and the German high commands, miscalculations historically and endemically inherent in high commands, there ensued that Christmas the disasters of what we've learned to call the Battle of the Bulge. Our generals believed that the Germans could not and would not attack through the Ardennes Forest, and maintained defenses there that were thin and inexperienced; the Germans believed they could indeed break through and that the course of the war would be altered to their significant advantage if they did.

Both were wrong.

The Germans did break through. But the course of the war was altered most significantly, I'd bet, only for the thousands on both sides who were killed, wounded, or imprisoned in that devastating misadventure by aggressive Germans and complacent Americans. My Coney Island friend George Mandel received his head wound from a sniper there, the bullet penetrating his helmet but going into the brain only so far, and my contemporary friend and unintentional contemporary literary rival for attention, Kurt Vonnegut, was among those taken prisoner. Officers at the top, of course, always know much more than those they command at the bottom, but, until it's all over, there's never a way to know if they've known enough.

While combat service in the air corps wasn't altogether the cushy sinecure some might suppose, we did enjoy, together with decent food, enclosed latrines, and heat in our tents, at least one other precious benefit that American ground forces until the Vietnam War did not: a specified tour of duty, after which we were detached from combat, replaced, and rotated home.

I have often wondered whether there were many combat men in our ground forces coming ashore on D-Day who made it through the following eleven months till May and the end of the war with Germany without getting killed, wounded, or taken prisoner.

I wouldn't be surprised to hear there was not even one.

Among the last several missions in my own tour of duty was an especially theatrical one in which I still take both a military and a civilian pride, the civilian pride bred of my sole assertion of leadership and authority as an officer. The assignment that morning was a hurried one. The destination was the large Italian seaport of La Spezia. The target was an Italian cruiser reportedly being towed out into a deep channel of the harbor by the Germans, to be scuttled there as an obstacle to approaching Allied ground forces pressing steadily north. I was relieved to discover myself assigned to one of the planes in a chaff element. The chaff element was a flight of three planes that led all the others in over the target, with their rear gunners jettisoning open bales of aluminized "chaff" from the two side gun ports to confound the radar below that was directing the enemy's antiaircraft fire. We carried no bombs. Because we carried no bombs, we could go zigzagging in at top speed and vary our altitudes. Because we carried no bombs, I shrewdly deduced that there was no need for a bombardier. Therefore, after priming and test-firing the machine gun in the bombardier's compartment in the nose of the plane, I resolved to sit that mission out—literally.

The flight deck of the B-25, that part of the plane occupied by pilot and copilot, had armor plate on the floor and the backrests of both their seats. On that kind of mission in that point in my career, I would take two flak suits with me, one to wear and one to shield as much of the rest of me as I could curl up and cover. That day I took up front with me to the machine gun only the one I wore. After preparing the machine gun to fire and crawling back through the narrow tunnel connecting the nose of the plane with the rest, I retrieved the second flak suit, mounted to the flight deck, and sat down on the floor right behind the pilot, with my back against the back of his chair. I had armor plate below and armor plate at my back, a flak helmet on my head, and an extra flak suit to cover my groin and legs. And as an additional precaution, I sat with my parachute pack already hooked to my parachute harness. This time I had my parachute with me. Normally, the parachute pack was too bulky to fit through the crawlspace to the bombardier's compartment and had to be left behind; there was no escape hatch up front, anyway. I was the veteran of that crew, and the two newer pilots didn't know what to make of me. "It's okay," I assured them crisply. "Let me know if German fighters show up and I'll go back."

When I looked behind us after we had flown through the flak at La Spezia and turned off, I was greatly satisfied with myself and all that I saw, and with all the others as well. We were unharmed; the turbulent oceans of dozens and dozens of smutty black clouds from the countless flak bursts were diffused all over the sky at different heights. The other flights were coming through without apparent damage. And down below I could watch the bombs from one cascade after another exploding directly on the ship that was our target.

And soon after that, I was finished. I was alive and I was well. In that photograph I spoke of earlier of the five of us in the tent exists a huge and invisible divide between me and the others. I was through and they, particularly the two newcomers, now faced more missions to fly to survive, because the official number for those still on combat status, at least in our bomber group, had lately been raised.

How did they feel about that?

As casually oblivious and indifferent, I'd guess, as I had felt in midcourse when the number had been raised first from fifty to fifty-five and then to sixty. For them, it was up to seventy.

WHILE MY COMRADES-IN-ARMS were off flying missions, I hunkered in my tent and played with the typewriter, naturally preferring to do that when alone. Our medium bombers were of medium range, our bomber group a tactical one, striking almost exclusively at rail and highway bridges. The flight time of missions averaged about three hours, though sometimes they were closer to two. It didn't take long to go from Corsica past Elba into central Italy and turn around and come back. I have a log before me that marks the time of missions to Poggibonsi, Pietrasanta, and Orvieto at exactly two hours, to Parma at two hours and ten minutes, to Ferrara, farther north in the Po Valley, at three hours and ten minutes, to Avignon, much farther away in

France in the Rhone Valley, at four hours and thirty-five minutes. Sometimes we—now they—flew two missions the same day.

On the morning of August 15, 1944, the day of the invasion of southern France, we—I, too, back then—bombed gun emplacements on a beach near Marseilles shortly after daybreak (the cannons turned out to be wooden dummies), and in the afternoon we went on that second mission to Avignon, all four squadrons separating over three targets to divide the antiaircraft fire. We divided the antiaircraft fire, but nevertheless all three units suffered casualties.

All that day of the invasion when we weren't ourselves in the air, we watched huge armadas of heavy bombers passing high overhead, higher than we ever flew, from their bases near Naples—hundreds and hundreds of them in their somber, purring formations, more planes on our side than I could believe existed in the entire world. All the advantages in the war now seemed unmistakably ours. But in late December came the German offensive in the Battle of the Bulge, and it took five more months after that for Germany finally to capitulate to us and to the USSR, in the east.

THE SUBJECT MATTER of all the short works with which I was now busying myself and had been busying myself even earlier was not founded on experiences of my own. I hadn't had any then that seemed worth translating into fiction. I borrowed the action and the settings from the works of other writers, who may—I didn't consider the possibility then—in turn have been borrowing from the works of still others. These experiences, which I as author dealt with knowledgeably, were vicarious and entirely literary, gleaned from wanderings as a reader, and they ranged from the picturesque whimsies of William Saroyan to the hard-nosed, sexist attitudes, particularly toward women and marriage, of Hemingway and Irwin Shaw, embodying as well implicit assessments of materialism, wealth, Babbittry, and ideals of masculinity and male decency that I ingenuously accepted as irreducibly pure and nullifying all others.

In the immense replacement depot in Constantine, Algeria, where I spent a few weeks with the crewmen with whom I had flown overseas in our small B-25 before being assigned to Corsica, my primary inspiration as a neophyte writer was Saroyan. He appealed to my taste and seemed easy to emulate and well worth copying. (The stories that seemed easiest to emulate and most worth copying were short ones with few descriptive passages written in literary vocabulary and with a large proportion of vernacular dialogue.) In one of his collections was a story titled (I am working here from memory) "Did You Ever Fall in Love with a Midget Weighing Thirty-eight Pounds?" In one of the stories from my Algerian period (working still from memory) was a young man in New York romantically involved with a girl who walked around on her hands. I have no recollection of my title. (I can imagine now that I imagined then the title "Did You Ever Fall in Love with a Girl Who Walked Around on Her Hands?") Where she walked on her hands and where the story went I have also mercifully forgotten.

By then I was familiar with most of the work of Hemingway, Irwin Shaw, and Jerome Weidman. Jerome Weidman's prewar collection of short stories from *The New Yorker* called *The Horse That Could Whistle Dixie* was another favorite of mine, as were the two novels of his I'd read (which were brought into the apartment by Sylvia or Lee from the circulating library in Magrill's drugstore on the corner of Mermaid Avenue). These were *I Can Get It for You Wholesale* and its sequel, *What's in It for Me?*, and I thought them marvelous, as I did Budd Schulberg's *What Makes Sammy Run?* The Studs Lonigan trilogy of James T. Farrell was another sophisticated favorite of mine and everybody else's, mainly for the realistic action and realistic words. James Joyce's *Ulysses* floated briefly into the Coney

Island apartment also, no doubt borne there, I recognize now, by the notoriety of the court victory over its banning. *Ulysses* sailed back to Magrill's drugstore unread by any of us, although I still can tingle with the *frisson* of astonishment I enjoyed coming upon two forbidden words in the very early pages, one of which describes the green color of the sea, the other the gray, sunken state of the world. John O'Hara was known to me also.

I had a large assortment of other reading to draw upon for stimulation while overseas. Professor Matthew Bruccoli at the University of South Carolina reminded me just a while ago of those plentiful Armed Services (or Armed Forces) Editions, which I had forgotten about. Here— there—was a government publishing venture of scope without precedent and one that probably hasn't been and won't be repeated: editions of more than twelve hundred works in printings of fifty thousand copies each, distributed without charge to American servicemen everywhere. Bruccoli, an insatiable collector, has assembled more than a thousand of these titles. He wants them all and won't ever get them, for I doubt that even he can now locate those missing two hundred volumes.

In one of these paperbound books, a collection of short stories, I found a work by Stephen Crane, "The Open Boat," and in this tale of shipwrecked sailors adrift in a lifeboat is a line of dialogue repeated by a man at the oars like a Wagnerian *leitmotif* (although I did not learn about Wagnerian *leitmotifs* until later): "Spell me, Billy." (I'm not absolutely sure of the name Billy. I no longer have the Armed Forces, or Armed Services, Edition, and Bruccoli might not have it among his thousand, either.)

From this sonorous reiterated chord, which I pondered in my tent, and perhaps from a one-act play of Saroyan's called *Hello, Out There* that I might already have read, could have sprung the notion of the short story to be titled "Hello, Genoa, Hello, Genoa," which would be related entirely in brisk intercom radio dialogue between a bomber pilot, or a few of them, and the control tower at the air base in Corsica. It is (even to this day, I feel) an engaging notion with a beguiling title, and I never tried writing it (or have no recollection that I did).

Instead, I wrote a short story in a day or two that I called "I Don't Love You Anymore." It is about two thousand words long, and like everything from my Algerian and Corsican periods, it is based on things I knew nothing about except from my sifting around in the works of other writers. Consequently, it reflects the style and point of view of many of the malign and histrionic fictions by American male authors of that time and ours: A married, worldly-wise serviceman, with whom we are intended to sympathize, feels temporarily, upon finding himself back home, and offering no specific complaint, that he no longer wants his marriage and no longer loves his wife. (Whatever that last was meant to mean, I truly had no idea. It was a convention.)

I don't know how it happened, but after I was back in the States and just out of the service, the story was submitted as an unsolicited manuscript and accepted for publication in *Story,* a periodical then publishing fiction only and held in very high esteem. By pure luck in timing, the war in Europe being just over, it chanced that the magazine was devoting an entire issue to fiction by men and women from the services.

I was back in Coney Island living in the apartment on West 31st Street when the note of acceptance arrived with the mailman. Overnight, I was, or felt myself, a local celebrity—I saw to that by showing the letter to everyone I knew—and I became talked about, too, in a small social enclave on Riverside Drive in Manhattan, where I was already going steady, keeping company, with a girl I had met not long before and to whom I soon would give an engagement ring and would marry the afternoon of October 2, 1945, just before boarding a Pullman train to California to begin college in Los Angeles.

The acceptance of my story, of course, impressed everybody, although no one I knew of except Danny the Count had every heard of *Story* magazine, and probably it was from Danny the Count that I first heard about it. Possibly it was at his suggestion that I made the submission. The payment I received for "I Don't Love You Any more" was—I had no idea what to expect—twenty-five dollars.

I was soon calculating deliriously. I had spent only two days on the story at a time when I was distracted by the war. Once I applied myself industriously, I figured, I could easily manage to complete four stories a week, approximately sixteen a month, and, by selling them for twenty-five dollars each, I would soon find myself with earnings almost as large as what I had been raking in as a first lieutenant on combat duty overseas.

I had great expectations.

Here was a beginning, a first convincing demonstration of a promising future, and even my prospective in-laws were proudly persuaded. Soon after the wedding and the train trip to Los Angeles, I derived a second and even greater indication of potential triumph from my first-year course in freshman English.

GETTING GOOD GRADES in classes at the University of Southern California in 1945 proved ridiculously easy (Art Buchwald, a student there at the same time, I later learned, conceivably may have floundered in the classroom, but I did not). It was finding an apartment that was impossibly hard.

After luxuriating for a week or more at the Ambassador Hotel for the second part of our honeymoon—it was one of L.A.'s better-known hotels (it was the hotel in whose kitchen Robert Kennedy was shot to death twenty-three years later during his California presidential-primary campaign)—we settled into a large bedroom in a small rooming house downtown on South Figueroa Street, between Washington Boulevard and somewhere else. The costs of the stay at the Ambassador Hotel were met from the cash gifts collected at the wedding, by far the most substantial portion of which flowed into our pockets from my wife's side of the family. The initial segment of the honeymoon was spent in a drawing room of a train going overnight from New York to Chicago and another drawing room of a different train going from Chicago to Los Angeles for three more nights. It was not much fun. We read a lot. The observation car and the club car bedazzled only briefly. A Pullman berth in a drawing room of the *Twentieth-Century Limited* and then on the *Chief* or the *Super Chief* from Chicago to Los Angeles is not ideal as a nuptial couch. There was a beauty shop on board, and my wife, Shirley, went once to have her hair and nails done.

The rooming house into which we moved was obtained through a housing-locating service at the university. It was the property and dwelling of an elderly, shrinking, white-haired couple named Mr. and Mrs. Hunter. A trolley line just outside bore me to the college in one direction and in the other trundled into Pershing Square in downtown Los Angeles and to the pickup and drop-off points of buses going to whichever of the racetracks was in session. There we could find Chinese restaurants and Mexican food, too.

In the household and marriage of our landlords, Mrs. Hunter was beyond doubt the energetic party. Ghostly, tidy Mr. Hunter, in his light-blue or light-gray cardigan sweater, with an ineffaceable and cryptic smile on his trim, pale face, would drift by wordlessly like some harmless spirit whenever our paths crossed during the academic year we lived in his house. In sharp contrast, Mrs. Hunter, when I was away mornings at school, would corner my wife and try to convert her to Christianity, specifically into a California sect to which, she confided with great secrecy, she had already deeded the house and everything else she owned. Some kind of Jewish evangelist was already in the city at the time— formerly a rabbi, she boasted, and of late a proselytizer for Christ—and she thought we would profit greatly by listening to his radio broadcasts and attending his services. On the other hand, she also confided to Shirley that her husband,

Mr. Hunter, was not, or had never been, much good at servicing her sexually and that there were, or had been, periods in her life when her cravings had grown so desperate that she wanted to, or in fact did, seat herself on a cake of ice to cool them. They had never brought forth children.

We had no cooking facilities, and what limited kitchen privileges were offered (refrigeration was about the extent of them) we hesitated to make use of for fear of being trapped in peculiar conversations. On our corner of Washington Boulevard was a good Greek coffee shop, and we ate most of our dinners there and in a few other neighborhood places. On weekend splurges we indulged ourselves in publicized glamorous haunts like the Brown Derby or Romanoff's in hopes of catching a glimpse of some movie personality, any movie personality. (We scored only one, Rosalind Russell, and I would never have recognized her because of her tiny chin, but my Shirley did.) That part of Washington Boulevard near which we lived was also the center of the city's mortuary-monument industry.

Given my wife's rather privileged and sheltered upbringing, I am incredulous now that she succeeded in spending a year with me under such conditions or even agreed to try, and that her mother, Dottie, permitted her to. In 1949, four years later, when I received my Fulbright scholarship to Oxford, her mother's abrupt response to her daughter's exciting news was, I was told:

"You're not going to England!"

We went.

In California, as a married freshman student without friends or family, I found it hard to meet people, and we enjoyed very little in the way of a social life. There was much larking around on campus, especially between the fraternities and the sororities, but we had no part in that. I imagine that an even more confounding time was suffered by the younger male students entering the university, any university, directly from high school. They were very young by comparison to us and they were rendered mute and invisible, were overshadowed by the numbers of veterans crowding into the classrooms, almost all of them my own age, twenty-two, and over. We were older, bigger, and better read and we had experienced more and were zealous to learn (or else we were football players).

It must have seemed a preposterous hope for any of those younger students to succeed in qualifying for collegiate athletics. The football teams consisted mainly of older young men who had been playing on college teams before the war and had spent the years since then growing huger in muscle and bone mass and, often, honing their pigskin skills on one of the service teams. They moved lethargically through classes on a preplanned schedule to conserve their eligibility until they were most needed. The year I attended Southern California, the football team went to the Rose Bowl, with a backfield that was an average age, I'd guess, of twenty-four. I believe the star was twenty-six. The opposing team was Alabama, whose All-American player, Harry Gilmer, had been something of a standout, I think, even before the war. As a student I received two tickets to the big game. Back then, I already detested organized cheering sections and sneered at things like college spirit and cheer-leading squads. Because Shirley had given up trying to grow interested in football and was apathetic about the Rose Bowl, I sold my two tickets for twenty-five dollars each to a couple from Alabama, and we spent that day, and the money, at one of the local horse tracks, Santa Anita or Hollywood Park.

The motives for my decision to go to the University of Southern California remain opaque, but they doubtless included the indispensable one that I was accepted there. I don't doubt that they were also evasive in purpose, intended to delay, to buy time. I didn't want—I felt myself much too young—to have to decide right away what I was going to do for the rest of my life. Once afforded the opportunity to attend college, I decided to make use of it. Going to college was easier and more appealing than going to work and certainly, then, more respected. And what work could I have found that would not have been a blow to the spirit after my jubilant homecoming from the war?

But I didn't know where I ought to try to go. Places on the altitude of Harvard and Yale didn't really exist for me— they were beyond both my grasp and my reach, outside my world and outside my imagining. What would the two of us do with ourselves at Harvard or Yale even if I had applied and been admitted? Who would talk to us? Any concept of higher education as high education was alien to me. I wanted to find out; I wasn't sure I wanted to learn. Anything in the nature of a scholarly love of knowledge was soon cooling realistically with my growing awareness that I would never make the effort to acquire the Greek, Latin, and German referred to so copiously in the illuminating works of literary explication I was guided to. At the same time, the idea was growing stronger that I should strive to make a name for myself as an author of fiction rather than as a critic or some other kind of intellectual. My hyperactive enthusiasm to learn more about just about everything existed principally for my own blissful satisfaction, and still does. (I have given up on Wittgenstein and Sartre and philosophy, but in recent years I have been burrowing into neo-Darwinism, which is congenial to my religious skepticism, and writhing in an exasperating quandary over quantum mechanics, which, to my mind, remains impossible even to define, let alone comprehend.)

I had been stationed twice in lower California during the war and had enjoyed both interludes there. In fact, I pretty much enjoyed everywhere I'd been in the army— Corsica, too, apart from the perils; even San Angelo, Texas, where I was sent for several months after Europe with almost nothing to do almost all the time. I am generally not a hard person to please (although people close to me might find that hard to believe, and distant acquaintances impossible). At the air base in Santa Ana, when I was there for classification as an aviation cadet and preflight training, there were the calm recreations in the town itself on weekends off and the longer, fatiguing overnight excursions by bus from the air base to Los Angeles. At bombardier training school in Victorville in the desert, we could treat ourselves when we desired to the fairly riotous Saturday nights off at Balboa Beach, with its flashy pier and dance halls and bars, and the billions of young girls and women who were also drawn there with the goal of carousing around. For me as for many others, lower California emitted a cinematic charisma as a place of beautiful excitements and charming opulence and opportunity—it still does—and no one expressed reservations about our decision to go there. And, of course, the moderate California weather was always seductive.

This was in stark contrast to the horrible, deeply depressing, incapacitating winter milieu into which I was harshly plunged on my furlough after I'd returned by steamship to the States from Corsica in January and found myself back in Coney Island. I soon knew without need to put anything into words that, given a choice, I would not want to live there again. Coney Island had long before lost its magic for me and for most of the rest of us as an amusement area, and there was nothing but Nathan's open in winter, anyway. It was black and it was bleak. There was no one around and there was nothing going on. There were no social clubs. I had no girlfriend and didn't know any girls I felt I might want to see intimately, or who might want to see me. In Coney Island that winter there was no place but the movies to go to on a date; other places were too far away, and I didn't have a car. If I'd had a car, I wouldn't have known how to drive it. I had nothing to do.

I missed the army, where there was always something to do, even when there was nothing.

In a day or two, sister Sylvia and brother Lee took note of my pathetic inertia, and it was Lee who, typically, came up with a suggestion that was not as implausibly far-fetched as it had sounded to all three of us at first mention. Sylvia and I couldn't have thought of it in a million years, but Lee, the selfless wishful thinker, came up with the proposal that marvelously did the trick: Why didn't I take myself off for a week or so to a long-established resort hotel, not far off in the Catskills, which was relatively fashionable to New Yorkers and known to be popular with people who could afford it, and of which I, in my parochial simplicity, had never heard?

Grossinger's.

We knew I had the money: Allotments from my air corps pay, which we all thought mighty substantial, had been coming to them directly from the start, to be banked in my name. As a serviceman back from overseas I would probably be showered with attention and courtesies. It sounded okay to me. Lee made the reservations and arranged for the van pickup for the trip from Brooklyn to Liberty, New York, and the plan turned out to be a rejuvenating solution not only for the rest of my furlough but also for the shaping of much of my life ahead.

I had never been on ice skates before, but found I could skate capably after the first few minutes, and it was indeed a dashing figure I cut as I circled the rink in my green winter flight jacket with its fur collar and silver first lieutenant's bar. For the evenings I had my officer's dress with my wings and campaign ribbons for overseas service, the only impressive one among them, *I* knew, the Air Medal with a large number of oak-leaf clusters (which came as routine with the completion of every fixed number of missions and not, as others might suppose, for the accomplishment of anything particularly valorous). I had my gleaming Mediterranean suntan, my health, my youth, my good looks, and my modesty. I was Jewish. I could project self-confidence. I was respectful and polite, and I was made much of by the parents there, especially those with single daughters, and by single women unaccompanied by parents. Even I knew it was a sure thing I would win the weekly dance contest on Saturday night, even though I was not then, am not now, and have not ever been anything much as a dancer. As fortune would have it—the kind of storybook good fortune one used to expect to find in romance magazines—I met the girl there, that week in January, whom I would marry in October and remain married to for thirty-five years before we separated.

When I returned to the city we were already going steady.

We dated when I commuted into New York weekends from Atlantic City until I was shipped to San Angelo, Texas. While I was there we exchanged letters. We saw each other again, in New Jersey and New York, when I was transferred in May to Fort Dix to be processed for discharge. And we went on seeing each other when I was out. It was Shirley's mother who took the initiative when I was alone with her one afternoon in her living room and supplied the impetus I hadn't found the power to generate on my own.

"Barney thinks," said Dottie, with the devious premeditation that was second nature to her and occasionally endearing—it was likely that Barney, the husband, had no inkling of what she was up to—"that it's because you don't have the money that you don't give her a ring."

I had never heard such language before.

"Give her a ring?" I inquired, puzzled, for the possibility of my doing any such incomprehensible thing hadn't once entered my mind. "What for?"

"To get engaged to be married."

I had money enough for the ring. She made the purchase and billed me for just $500. Friends and families on both sides were delighted with the match. I was a young and unformed twenty-two and a half; the bride had just passed twenty-one. Almost every fellow I'd grown up with in Coney Island was getting married at about that time: Marvin Winkler and Evelyn, Davey Goldsmith and Estelle, Lou Berkman and Marion, Marty Kapp and Sylvia, Sy Ostrow

and Judy, and others. (As far as I know, mine and only one
other of these early marriages would end in divorce.)

THE MARRIAGE SEEMS to have been a good neurotic fit,
observed the psychiatrist at my introductory consultation with
him in which I tried to present fairly all the imperfections
in me and in my wife underlying the growing estrange-
ment and irreconcilable disputes that had been arising uncontrollably.

It surely must have been a good neurotic fit, to endure
for thirty-five years. Why then did we eventually separate
and divorce? It was a good fit, but, well . . . I doubt either of
us could have said. I don't believe either of us wanted to.

(I found out in ensuing sessions of psychoanalysis that
there was nothing generically denigrating about my new
mentor's use of that term *neurotic*. "All of us are neurotic,"
he erupted one day, after I'd strayed again from my free-
associating into what he called my habit of intellectualizing.
"Only psychotics are not neurotic.")

MOST WEEKDAY MORNINGS at Mr. and Mrs. Hunter's I
spent at school. The thought of cutting classes didn't seriously
occur to me in college any more than it had in high school.
The temptation to do so, had it arisen, would have tormented
me. I enjoyed the work and the classroom competition.

Afternoons and evenings we often roamed about the
city, sightseeing. After all, this was Hollywood, the land of
Mickey Rooney and Judy Garland, Van Johnson, Dorothy
Lamour. Since we seldom had to be anywhere at an
appointed hour, we had time to travel by bus. We looked at
the La Brea tarpits and the house of Hearst's mistress, Marion Davies's house at Santa Monica, at the names immortal-
ized in the pavement outside Grauman's Chinese Theater.
We went to Tijuana one weekend and even ate a taco each
from a street vendor without falling ill. Shirley and I caught

our first sight of shish kebab grilling on a skewer in the neon-glaring window of a restaurant on a pulsating street near the UCLA campus early one evening, and it became a reliable weekly meal, with rice and salad, and a side order of french-fried potatoes, for under two dollars. Our year in Los Angeles was educational: Back in New York, we were the only people we knew ever to have heard of shish kebab, and we boosted it heartily. But grilled lamb is not particularly succulent, and we soon advanced to dishes like beef bourguignonne, coq au vin, cappelletti bolognese, shrimp creole, lobsters broiled or steamed—who can remember them all?

Also in the afternoons and most evenings I did my reading and writing for school and wrote and rewrote my stories and light nonfiction pieces that I mailed away for publication to one magazine after another; they all came back. I had a portable typewriter of my own now, purchased from Macy's through Sylvia at her employee's discount—in the days before discount stores, when a discount was still a discount. Having heard that there existed such a thing as a writer's keyboard, I had ordered it with the idea that my written work would flow that much more swiftly. It had such trivial modifications as quotation marks and question mark in lower case. It made no difference. Typing a little more rapidly only meant that I would have to begin retyping pages, paragraphs, even sentences that much sooner. Both of us read a great deal for pleasure. Shirley read *Wuthering Heights* and was astounded that it diverged so much from the movie. I read everything I believed to be instructive. On our table radio we listened to the one classical-music station in Los Angeles and to the radio-network comedy programs that were already our favorites. Fred Allen was available and Jack Benny was still funny.

Two authors for whom I found myself with a new and fervent enthusiasm were Aldous Huxley, for reasons I now can no longer begin to guess, and H. L. Mencken, whose merits as a thinker and writer are brilliantly obvious to this day: a blunt and mordant dislike for every kind of hokum, a command of American English that is eloquently and indisputably his own, a voice whose surface aspects others might seek to copy but who has not, to my mind, been surpassed in individuality and substance.

I was then among the susceptible many trying to copy him, believing I was the only one. Words like "clodpate" and "bastinado" began showing up regularly in my writer's vocabulary for the scornfully superior humorous pieces I was dashing off at least once a week, interspersed with the short stories I was cranking out at just about the same rate. In the college library I discovered one work of his published in 1919 or so, which, I am ashamed now to say, I responded to with laughing admiration, virtual applause, and which, if in print today and he still among the quick (as he might say, and did), would see him in the stocks for the rest of his natural life, with no fair-minded person dissenting. The volume, a slim one, is titled *In Defense of Women*. The ostensible (and disingenuous) argument is that women in general are the more intelligent members of the human species, and men, in consequence, comparatively stupid. The proof? Women induce men to marry them, to live with them, and to tolerate their presence socially. I am embarrassed to confess that more than Mencken's vocabulary found its way into my literary thinking. It was the fashion, the convention of the time, to present women in a stereotyped way as targets to be patronizingly derided. I am thankful now that none of these efforts of mine found its way into print or even, to my knowledge, still exists.

I had applied to Southern California with a major in journalism, thinking, without thinking clearly, that there'd be a lot of writing and reading involved and that newspaper work by its nature would be invariably arresting, if not always electrifying. While I was registering and noted the required courses, such as copyediting, rewriting, proofreading, and layout, I switched like a fugitive to a major in English and with a deep breath relaxed and blessed my luck. I had a deep feeling of relief that I'd escaped, by the skin of my teeth, an irreparable and very great disaster.

That semester, as afterward, I enrolled in more classes than the stipulated minimum. With all costs met by the government, why not? By attending college summer sessions, too, I managed to complete the four-year curriculum in three years. I finished my science requirements that first year with overlapping courses in bacteriology, botany, and zoology. These were areas of study totally new to me and entirely fascinating. I would have liked an introductory course to physics, too (I still would), but couldn't find the space to fit one in (and still can't). A survey course in the history of civilization—two semesters, I believe—didn't have a minute in it or demand attention to even one item that didn't thrill me. Flashbacks to my elation upon hearing for the first time about the Indus, the Tigris, the Euphrates, the Ganges are still vivid—what resonant sounds these marvelous words discharge—and Praxiteles and Pericles, too. The work in English, freshman composition, was grist for my mill: Punctuation and syntax were easy, the written assignments valued opportunities to show my stuff.

I tried artfully in all my written work to address my subject with a paper that would also, with ingenious alteration, be suitable for publication in one of the popular magazines I knew about. Thus, when research for a theme on paleontology brought me into contact with paragraphs on geological periods with names like Mesozoic and Jurassic, terms I could retain by rote but not aspire to understand, I first met the assignment adequately and next converted the composition into a humorous spoof, presented (I hoped) with the abrasive superiority of an H. L. Mencken, of the deliberate use of unintelligible jargon affected by pedagogues (another word I lifted from Mencken). The new piece, once typed, went out everywhere and went nowhere. It was perhaps not as humorous as I thought.

The short stories I wrote at that time tended to be plotted extravagantly and often to be resolved miraculously by some kind of ironic divine intervention on the side of the virtuous and oppressed. In one I remember, a French farmer in Provence who has secretly collaborated with the German occupiers watches in speechless horror as every one of his ten sons is picked out in a random selection from the village people for reprisal executions. In another, a visitor in search of a persecuted figure in the Christian rural South who has mysteriously disappeared turns out to be Jesus or some kind of avenging angel bent on retribution for his murder. It gives me pleasure to say that these stories went nowhere either.

In an elective course in contemporary theater (I had thoughts of becoming a playwright, too. It seemed easier. There were fewer words) was a blond, outgoing girl named Mary Alden, who early on took a testy dislike to me, which she made little effort to mask. She was my own age, perhaps slightly older, with a couple of years' experience working in the theater. The two of us dominated classroom discussion, and we were on opposite sides of just about every question. She was galled by my contradictions. Having recently come from New York, I had the advantage of referring to people active there in show business of whom she had not yet heard and the teacher had. She found my presumption unforgivable. I was sorry that Mary Alden didn't like me, for I liked her. She held as sacred what I took for sport.

Unfortunately, that has happened with me several times since—with a graduate philosophy major named Norwood Hanson on the steamship carrying a large contingent of Fulbright scholars to England; with a faculty colleague at Penn State named Gordon Smith, when we visited the hallowed battlefield and cemetery sites at Gettysburg; and more than once with a fellow student at NYU named David Krause, but David and I remained friends through college and afterward. The other two refused to speak to me ever again.

My mother could have told them I had a twisted brain.

Finding in my first term in college that I could attain top grades in just about all my courses with little strain, I devised my program for the next semester with veteran savoir faire, coming up with a schedule designed to release me from classes two or three afternoons a week early enough to join my wife downtown and catch the bus that would get us to the racetrack in time to bet the daily double. (This was childish fancy, for neither of us had cashed a ticket on the daily double the several times we had been to the races, and I have never cashed one since.) Dismounting from the trolley car with schoolbooks still in hand after one of these half days on campus, I was surprised by the sight of Shirley waving with one arm and hastening toward me with a face rosy with joy. In her hand was an opened letter that had come in the mail that morning after I had left the rooming house. It was a note of acceptance from *Esquire* magazine for a nonfiction piece I had written originally as a theme in my freshman English class. Assigned the subject of describing some kind of method or device, I had invented a series of sure-fire systems, all of them foolish, for always winning money at the racetrack.

And with the note had come a check for $200!

I was now, at twenty-two, a certified young author of fiction and, with *Beating the Bangtails,* of nonfiction also (an illustrious distinction in 1946, two years before Vidal, Capote, Mailer, and others came rolling onto the national scene and made me feel backward, aged, envious, and derelict).

I was not, however, a certified handicapper of horses, and most of the $200 I earned from my freshman theme on how to win money betting on horses was lost at the racetrack the next half-dozen times we went.

THE VEXATIOUS PROBLEM of obtaining a fitting place to live, which had obstructed the conjugal dreams of us newlyweds in Los Angeles, was brushed away with dispatch in New York by another exercise of the untiring enterprise of Dottie, wielded with Barney's usual reserved and benevolent approval. Friends of theirs were residents and owners of a modernized, narrow, five-story elevator apartment building at a wonderful location in Manhattan, on West 76th Street just off Central Park West, around the corner from the New-York Historical Society and just a few steps from the American Museum of Natural History. When a one-room studio apartment facing front on the first floor became vacant, we moved in.

We were figuratively just a hop, skip, and jump from a couple of subway lines and bus stops and from all kinds of shopping. One subway carried me expeditiously downtown and back to NYU for the next two years; the other rode me uptown to Columbia University for the year of my master's degree. The amount of room at our disposal wasn't notably greater than what was ours in the California rooming house, but here a roll-out sofa bed permitted us to better utilize what space we had. And here we had a compact kitchen area that conveniently held a table for four. We could entertain, and we did. Among the people we had over for dinner once or twice was Maurice "Buck" Baudin, Jr., the instructor in the fiction-writing course in which I and some new friends at NYU were doing so well. Buck was a mere five years older than I, but even after I had moved on from NYU I couldn't with composure bring myself to call him anything but "Mister." The furnishing of the apartment was handled by Dottie and Shirley and was done tastefully and rationally and, I imagine, inexpensively, by their standards. Lee's wife, Perlie, had looked into such things as interior decorating and gushed in praise at the sensible arrangement and the authentic look of several of the almost-genuine antique pieces. Dottie was pleased to have her daughter and her writer/college-student son-in-law installed in an apartment she would be able to display to her friends with pride.

And so, for that matter, was I.

My former mother-in-law, Dorothy Held, was one of those cultivated, modern women who knew the difference between turquoise and aquamarine. On the other hand, she

also knew the difference between sirloin steak and top sirloin, prime rib and top round, and that only first-cut brisket
was suitable for a good pot roast.

My favorite steak before I met her, after I'd left home
and discovered it, was filet mignon, always well done. Not
until I'd met Dottie's daughter and was eating at her table
was I introduced to the joys of rare beef, to the rare sirloin
steak, right up to the bone, and to the heavenly and substantial charm of a standing roast of rare prime rib of beef with a
crust liberally seasoned with garlic, salt, and paprika.
Shirley's family was much better off than my own, with
experience vastly more cosmopolitan: They even read the
New York Times. And her parents found delight in watching
me eat—always a second helping, often a third. They were
generous in other ways, too. They were well off but not
wealthy. Barney—Bernard Held—was partners with a
large company in a much smaller firm manufacturing
dresses. He apparently made a very good income during the
war and for many years after, but the Helds tended, with
Dottie providing the impetus, to spend just about everything coming in and to greatly enjoy whatever they spent it
on—including us. They spent much on us, and it was
largely with their encouragement and help that I was able to
spend almost the next six years of my life, and the first six
years of my marriage, going to college.

A gratifying event in our marriage was the birthday
party my wife made for my sister, Sylvia. Well into the marriage, after some twenty-five years, Shirley was horrified to
hear one day that my sister had never in her life been given a
birthday party, and resolved to make her one. I had never seen
Sylvia so filled with effusive happiness as she was at our house
the next time her birthday rolled around. Tears of laughter
streamed down her cheeks, and her voice soon was hoarse
with her whoops of hilarious reminiscence. With Lee it was
the same; he was talking and chortling and wiping his eyes,
too. I had never before heard either of them, alone or
together, in such exuberant discourse. I listened. I learned.

Among the memories Sylvia recalled with merriment was of her first year out of high school when, at age seventeen or eighteen, she would journey into the city with others to search for a job. This would have been in about 1934, when jobs were not easy to find. She and her female friends would chip in for a pack of cigarettes and pool their money for variety in their lunches in a cafeteria. And at the employment agencies, she remembered, they often were spared long waits in vain by someone appearing from inside to announce that they might as well leave: There were no jobs for Jews that day.

That she could recall this with mirth at her birthday party was testimony to the astonishing good fortune we had all been enjoying since.

Once, in Finland on a book tour, I met a local writer, Danny Katz, a Finnish humorist whose Jewish parents, like mine, had emigrated from Russia. "They weren't too smart," he muttered, chuckling. "They settled here."

Ours were smarter. They had settled in New York.

AT THE END OF OUR first year back in New York, a full apartment just above us with a complete kitchen and large living room and bedroom opened up and was offered to us. Into it we promptly moved, and there we lived until the fall of 1949, when we sailed to England. I've lost track of the numbers, but I'm certain we were helped significantly with the rent and other expenses, for I very strongly doubt that my monthly subsistence allowance from the government while I continued at school would have enabled us to live on a scale that, then as now, seemed lavish. (I did for a while work part-time after school in the circulation department of a magazine called *American Home,* filing and finding the address plates of subscribers, but the hourly income and take-home pay from that would not have been gigantic.) To friends from Coney Island, almost all of whom by then had moved out of Coney Island, and to other friends I made at NYU, our standard of living was kingly.

A commodious, well-furnished apartment in a well-maintained building in a prime neighborhood in Manhattan was as precious then as it is today. We held parties and dinners there often, and it was a good meeting place before going out with friends from locations less felicitous. On balmy nights we served drinks on the roof, where there were comfortable chairs and well-tended plants. In summer, Dottie and Barney always took a country house somewhere or booked space in a luxury hotel for the season—I remember the Lido in Lido Beach, Long Island, and the Forest House at Lake Mahopac, New York—and we would go there on weekends and during other breaks in my summer-school sessions.

All in all, we were living the life of Riley.

And it wasn't costing me much.

Getting high grades at New York University required much more application than had my freshman year at Southern Cal, but I managed in almost all my courses. The competition was tougher. Lacking a campus and a campus social life and no longer an active institution in intercollegiate sports, the Washington Square College of the university was something in the nature of a commuting college. And students who traveled to classes, many from homes quite distant, weren't there to fool around. Especially not the war veterans. Two friends I made in philosophy courses, Edward Blaustein and a student named Kahn, received Rhodes scholarships at a time when few, very few, were awarded to Jews. Eddie Blaustein was later a professor of law, then president of Bennington College (the first Jewish president, he said, of a non-Jewish college), then president of Rutgers University. I don't know what happened to Kahn, but I don't doubt that he, too, did all right. The main lesson I learned in philosophy was to react with skepticism and treat with Socratic malice all emphatic ideological beliefs, especially those of my favorite philosophy teachers.

In the fiction-writing courses of Maurice Baudin was David Krause, who journeyed from faraway New Jersey, journeyed through rainstorms and blizzards—he would, in a figure of speech first coined by Mario Puzo in connection with himself, sooner eat a broom than miss a day of class. He got straight A's, too, and was a professor of Irish and English literature at Brown University all his adult life until his retirement not long ago. David wrote perfect short stories but couldn't be persuaded to submit them for publication because he didn't think they were worthy. And we had Alex Austin, a meager, short fellow who seldom raised his voice above a whisper, even when reading aloud in the classroom. By the time he enrolled in the class, more than two hundred poems and short stories by Alex had been published in "little" magazines most of us hadn't even heard of. It was an essential part of his daily regimen, like brushing teeth, to write at least one short story every afternoon—he would sit down at his typewriter devotionally, often without a thought in mind, and simply begin typing. He had novel-length manuscripts, too, and Baudin was reduced to imploring negotiations with him to limit the number he handed in.

Unlike David Krause, who was a genuine idealist (he saw teaching as a calling; I went into it because I thought it would be easier than a business office), I mailed out everything, worthy or not. When I learned that Buck Baudin was selling stories to *Good Housekeeping* and receiving $1,500 apiece for them, I appended that magazine and all other women's magazines accepting fiction to my list of prospective benefactors. Hardly a workday went by that didn't find the postman delivering to 20 West 76th Street at least a few of my stamped, self-addressed manila envelopes returning manuscripts of mine with rejection slips. *The New Yorker* then was as admirably efficient in editorial procedure as it was superb in editorial content. I used to joke—and it wasn't much of an exaggeration—that a story I would mail to *The New Yorker* in the morning would be back with its concise, slighting rejection slip in the afternoon mail that same day.

Sometime during my second or third semester with

Baudin—I took a third semester without credit because I wanted to keep working with him—he chose four short stories of mine and delivered them for consideration to his literary agent. The reader's report from there said that none in the group was suitable for publication. Of the four, three were subsequently accepted by magazines when submitted by me as unsolicited manuscripts.

Much later, when I taught for four years at the City College of New York between the publication of my first novel, *Catch-22,* and the completion of my second, *Something Happened,* I several times attempted the same thing with my own literary agent for those students whose work seemed especially promising, and was rewarded with the same negative result.

A comment I always seemed to get back from Baudin with each short story, regardless of other notes of praise or criticism, was that I was taking too long to begin, dawdling at the opening, as though hesitant to get going and move forward into what I had in mind. It's a quirk of mine, perhaps a psychological flaw, that has lasted. I have cogitated over it in the closest secrecy, secrecy until now, as a quality that might credibly be described as anal retentive. From the manuscript of *Catch-22,* after it had been accepted, I deleted of my own volition something like 50 of the first 250 pages without loss of incident. (The editor of these very words, Robert Gottlieb, who was also the editor of *Catch-22,* snickers at the words "of my own volition." Okay, it was at his suggestion that I did what I could to move into the middle much sooner.)

In the margin of one story of mine in college, "Castle of Snow," Baudin asked why I simply didn't begin at the top of page four and instructed me to start there when I read it aloud to the class. It went well that way, to my grateful astonishment, and I began on my original page four when I typed a clean copy.

Mailed out by me to the "Fiction Editor" of the *Atlantic Monthly* with that revision, it was rejected, but with a personal letter from a woman there who signed her name and seemed to be implying that with several small alterations it might be accepted if resubmitted. (I wish she had suggested one more, for the choice of Chaucer as the favorite author of an East European immigrant forced to sell his books jars the teeth now with its blatant improbability.) I made the changes, amending what was amiss, providing what was lacking (I welcomed text suggestions then, and I've welcomed them since), mailed the revised manuscript directly to her, and the story was accepted for publication as an "Atlantic First." Coincidentally, in the issue of the magazine in which it finally appeared was a story by the equally young James Jones, also presented as an Atlantic First. (Neither of us was fortunate enough to win the semiannual bonus prize for the best of the Atlantic Firsts in that period.) I was paid $250. With a contact now at the magazine, it was not surprising that sooner or later I would place another work there, and I did. For this second one I received just $200, since it wasn't as long as the first one (and not as good, or even much good at all).

I was a star in the class, and I would have been a celebrity on campus if the Washington Square College of New York University had a campus.

Much the same process was simultaneously going on between me and a benevolent editor at *Esquire* magazine who finally signed his name George Wiswell in elaboration of the initials to the penciled notes of encouragement he had been adding to the formal rejection slips. Eventually he rejected a story regretfully, lamenting some defect in motivation or characterization and virtually pledging that he would recommend it for publication if that fault could be remedied. I made the attempt, the story was accepted, and for this one I received $300. Sometime later they took another one and paid me less, because the second one was shorter than the first (and not as good, or even much good at all). As I advanced in college, I acquired standards and learned to be more critical, and before I finished I also learned that, apart from their being mine, there wasn't much distinctive about all but two or three of the stories I was writing at this time. I now wanted to be new, in the way that I thought, as I discovered them, Nabokov, Celine, Faulkner, and Waugh were new—not necessarily different, but new. Original.

I mention as a public service the amounts I received in payment for these stories, for people generally have a mis-informed notion of the scale of remuneration of successful American authors of fiction, and of freelance writers of any kind. In talking to groups of aspiring authors, I have fre-quently emphasized, particularly when the audience was made up of young people, that unless they had money, would inherit money, or would marry money, they were going to have to work at something else for quite a while, even if everything they wrote from that moment on found publication. Irwin Shaw would have agreed. And so would John Cheever. I used to boast that I could reel off the names of a dozen or more American authors of distinguished national reputation who weren't earning enough from their writing to ignore other sources of income and devote them-selves wholly to their work, and probably I still can. Irwin Shaw could give in an instant the paltry total of dollars he had received for all the short stories he had ever published in *The New Yorker.*

A flattering consequence of my collegiate fame was that I was prevailed upon against my better judgment to submit a short story to the college literary magazine just get-ting started, and I did. For those who care, it was called "Lot's Wife" and was about—oh, never mind that!—the wife was icily indifferent and petty in regard to the victim of an auto accident, the man thoroughly sympathetic but no match for her.

Of more interest is the unflattering aftermath of that charitable gesture, which was a patronizing review of the story in the college newspaper by a fellow student with literary ambitions who condescended to find it pallid, riddled with faults, lacking any compensating merit.

That should have steeled me against unkind critiques in the future, but nothing does.

However, at just about that time I was ecstatic to learn that one of my stories, that same "Castle of Snow," had been selected for inclusion in the Martha Foley annual anthology of best short stories.

That was ameliorating! There was no doubt I was on my way.

And only twelve years later, after working two years at Penn State, one year at an advertising agency, a year at the Army–Air Force Post Exchange System (from which job I believe I was about to be fired), one year in the Advertising Department of the Remington Rand Corporation (which manufactured office systems and equipment and not, as I had feared, rifles), three years at *Time,* one year at *Look,* and three years at *McCall's,* I finished my first novel and saw it published.

AS I'VE SAID AND REPEAT, I wrote the first chapter in longhand one morning in 1953, hunched over my desk at the advertising agency (from ideas and words that had leaped into my mind only the night before); the chapter was published in the quarterly *New World Writing* #7 in 1955 under the title "Catch-18." (I received twenty-five dollars. That same issue carried a chapter from Jack Kerouac's *On the Road,* under a pseudonym.) In 1957, while working at *Time,* when the novel was only about half done, I received a contract for its publication from Bob Gottlieb at Simon & Schuster (providing for a guaranteed advance of $1,500, half on signing the contract, half on acceptance of the completed manuscript). The novel was completed in early 1961, when I was working for *McCall's,* and published in October of that year under the title *Catch-22.* (What you may have heard was true: The number in the title was changed to skirt a conflict that same season with the Leon Uris novel *Mila 18.*)

The novel was not the instant success many people assume it was, not at all on the scale of such immediate national acclaim as greeted the first novels of Norman Mailer, James Jones, and others. It was not a best-seller and it won no prizes. There were reviews that were good, a good many that were mixed, and there were reviews that were bad, very bad, almost venomously spiteful, one might be tempted to say (and I am the one that might say it). In the Sunday *New York Times Book Review,* for example, in a slender notice located so far back that the only people apt to notice it were those friends and relations awaiting it, the reviewer declared that the "novel gasps for want of craft and sensibility," "is repetitious and monotonous," "fails," "is an emotional hodgepodge," and is no novel; and in *The New Yorker,* the critic decided that *Catch-22* "doesn't even seem to have been written; instead it gives the impression of having been shouted onto paper," "what remains is a debris of sour jokes," and in the end "Heller wallows in his own laughter and finally drowns in it." (I am tempted to drown in my own gloating laughter even as I set this down. What restrains me is the knowledge that the lashings still smart, even after so many years, and if I ever pretend to be a jolly good sport about them, as I am doing right now, I am only pretending.)

On a brighter side came generous statements of cheerful approval from a large range of prominent writers—a gratifying and encouraging surprise. Gradually, as reviews continued to appear for weeks and even months after publication, requests for interviews began to arrive, for radio and television too (and all were accepted eagerly). After a first printing of about seven thousand copies, modest additional printings were distributed throughout the year as interest in the work continued and built. I believe there were fourteen or fifteen printings, and sales of the novel exceeded thirty thousand copies before the mass-market paperback edition was released.

My young daughter, Erica, and my younger son, Ted, were mildly baffled to find their father a sudden object of attraction and the recipient of compliments from people we hadn't known. Frequently they were titillated (in short time they found themselves driven to a studio by Tony Curtis himself in his Rolls Royce, to witness the filming of an episode of a popular TV series), but the effects were not always salutary. As the two of us were walking along the beach at Fire Island that first summer, my son of six belligerently thrust himself between me and a stranger who had come up to praise me and asserted stridently, "I'm the one who wrote the book!" (Probably he won't remember that, but I do.)

From then on, I was something of a celebrity presence in the household, and that is never, or hardly ever, an entirely good thing. It would have been witless of me to attempt to ward off these flattering acknowledgments, and hypocritical to pretend I did anything other than lap them up.

In England, where the novel was published several months later, the history was different. By that time, the London literary world was already largely familiar with the work through word of mouth about the American edition and its growing reputation, and its appearance there was treated as something of an event. Best-seller lists were new and rudimentary in England back then, but *Catch-22* was quickly at the head of them. News of this success abroad made its way back to New York and helped keep up the momentum of *Catch-22*'s expanding recognition. In the late summer of 1962, that same Sunday *New York Times Book Review* reported that the underground book New Yorkers seemed to be talking about most was *Catch-22.* The novel was probably more heavily advertised that year than any other, but it was still, to the *Times,* "underground."

And right after that came September and the paperback edition, and a surge in popular appeal that seemed to take the people at the publisher, Dell, completely by surprise, despite their elaborate promotion and distribution strategies. It seemed for a while that the people there could not fully bring themselves to believe the sales figures and that they would never catch up. Still, by the end of 1963 there had been eleven printings. *Catch* was, I believe, the best-selling paperback book that year, with more than two million copies sold.

Sadly, those numbers did not translate into the wealth they might suggest. (The cover prices of these paperbacks was seventy-five cents, the average royalty was somewhere between 6 and 10 percent, and it was divided equally between the original publisher and the author—netting me, I estimate, an unassuming three or four cents a copy.) It was not until the motion picture rights were sold about a year after publication that I felt confident enough, and substantial enough, to leave my job at *McCall's* magazine, where I was in charge of a department of three others turning out advertising/sales presentations, and then I did so cautiously on an unpaid leave of absence for one year. The money from the movie sale totaled $100,000, less 15 percent in commissions divided between agent and lawyer. At my request, payments would be spread over four years, allowing me more than sufficient time to throw myself wholeheartedly into my new career as a novelist and complete another work—I thought.

But not until twelve years later, in the fall of 1974, a mere thirteen years after *Catch-22* (four of those years spent working in the English department at the City College of New York and another teaching year divided between Yale and the University of Pennsylvania), was my second novel, *Something Happened,* completed and readied for publication.

Something Happened was much more successful in its initial edition than *Catch-22* (Irwin Shaw, who had read an advance copy, took me aside at a small gathering to tell me softly, "I think it's a masterpiece." By now I feel free to say I agreed), and since its publication in 1974, I haven't had to work for money at anything I didn't want to work at or associate much with people I don't like. And I won't.

I don't give presents anymore, either, and I no longer observe holidays. I hardly ever hurry.

9

Psychiatry

THE FIRST TIME I met my father face-to-face to talk to him, so to speak, was in the office of a psychoanalyst sometime in 1979, when I was already fifty-six years old. My father had been dead for more than fifty of those years.

For as long as I could recall, I had been the periodic victim of a dream of escalating nightmarish dimensions. It would recur, unchanged, every now and then when I was sleeping at home in my own bed or away from home in hotel rooms, or, almost guaranteed, within the first few nights in strange beds in rented summer places. The dream was always the same in action and emotion. It would always unfold in the identical place, in that same bedroom in the same Coney Island apartment in which I had lived until I was past nineteen and left for the army. I would be in bed in the dream, sleeping, just as I was in bed sleeping when I was having the dream. Unexpectedly, a man would begin coming into the apartment, entering not criminally through the window in my room or through any other in the apartment, but at the front door. His face was in shadows. I would know right off that he was there, and in my dream I would come awake. I was frightened from the beginning and would grow increasingly frightened as I visualized him making his way toward me without hesitation, moving noiselessly past one room after the other along the hallway that ran through the apartment from the front entrance to the last room at the very end, in which I had been lying in my bed, and in fact still was, although in the dream it was always the bed I had slept in while I still lived there. My fear would quickly heighten to sheer horror as I watched myself sitting up in bed and saw the man draw closer and closer. In unbearable dread and panic, I was compelled to cry out for help, and the words would swell in my paralyzed throat and take form as gibberish, they would jam and choke me, I would strain and struggle with all my force, which wasn't much, to shriek out, pleading for safety and survival. And eventually, of course, before he was in my room, before I could distinguish any features of the face that was always cloaked in darkness, before whatever menacing outcome I'd been anticipating with such heart-stopping terror could take place, I would ride to my own rescue by coming awake—as always happens with nightmares, Freud says somewhere.

Or I would be nudged awake with displeasure and rebuked in bad temper by whoever was in the room with me and had been wrested from sleep by my unintelligible gasps and wordless groans.

While recalling and then reminiscing out loud about this dream, with my psychiatrist (psychoanalyst) out of sight behind me as I lay on the couch in his office, I was stricken into silence for a moment by the stunning recognition that I had ceased having this dream, that I hadn't once suffered it for something like the two years past, not since I had entered into the patient-analyst relationship with him. He said nothing. I wondered why it had departed, wondered where that familiar, extremely harrowing, yet completely harmless dream of mine had gone, and as I turned my head to gaze at him, he saw me settle into one of those deliberate, stubborn quiets he'd learned by then meant that I was insisting on some kind of explanation.

"You don't need that dream anymore," he commented

at last, with palpable reluctance. "You have me here now."

I grasped his interpretation with instant clarity and gratification, perceiving its rightness at once.

"Then why," I asked, and it may have seemed I was doubting him, "was there fear?"

"If that wish of yours were to come true," he answered, "wouldn't you be afraid?"

I AM NOT GIVING his name, because I am relying on evocations, and he might not be pleased to see me make public reconstructions that are not accurate, or even some that are. At our second consultation, prior to our formally beginning therapy, he appeared somewhat put out when I responded negatively to his guess that in the interval I had reviewed his credentials. The idea of doing so hadn't crossed my mind; I wouldn't have known how, and I would have felt like a sneak if I had. (On the other hand, he took for granted that I had done so and might have judged me neurotic for *not* doing so.) He was, I subsequently found out, though younger than I, a man of distinguished reputation in his field, greatly respected in New York and elsewhere, and he seemed to want me to know that. He was familiar with my reputation—he was one of those readers I've heard praise *Catch-22* for having had, they felt, a wholesome impact on their thinking when young—so we started out with some kind of equivalence in mutual regard, and it didn't decline.

As fully as I could, I filled him in on everything I felt relevant, doing that with what I thought was commendable objectivity. My language probably was laced with technical terms standard in psychology, because that's the way I am (I suppose there was at least a little bit of showing off). I had read a lot of Freud by then and also had read much about him, and, like all imaginative Americans of my generation who knew about him, had been mesmerized (a term technically medical in etymology) by the egocentric implications

and promises of psychoanalysis. In the course of my program for therapy, which continued with sporadic interrup-
tions into a third year, I confessed willingly to everything I
could remember and guessed at everything I couldn't—
well, almost everything. (I didn't tell my analyst that when I
was young and afraid that my hair would wave or curl, I
would sometimes go to sleep wearing one of my sister's hair
nets, or that one time when my eyes felt sore—they often
still do—I conjured up, entirely on my own, the reasonable
notion of alleviating the irritation with a few drops of olive
oil in each eye for lubrication, and consequently saw the
world through a blur for the rest of the week. There were a
couple of other secrets on that mortifying infantile plane
which I wouldn't want him to know—or you, either.)

I was flattered and quick to agree when he said that any
therapy less than analysis would be kid stuff for me. This
was in the dark ages before Prozac and other mood elevators and stabilizers were at hand and before psychoanalysis,
and Freud himself, had coursed inevitably into the buffet-
ing gales of criticism, denial, and opposition by which they
are mauled today.

He expressed the apprehension that I might exhibit a
tendency to "intellectualize" and thereby obstruct the
process. I told him not to worry about that, although, if
pressed, I would have had to reveal that I wasn't really sure
what either one of us was talking about.

We decided on four sessions weekly when possible; it
often was not possible. There were the ordinary disruptions
caused by things such as colds and intestinal flu. More
unusual and, in time, more tacitly amusing to both of us, I
think, was that frequently he and I would each be tempted
and succumb to attractive invitations to travel. He went
once to China, I went once to a writers' conference at Berke-
ley, and we both acquiesced to frequent requests to speak at
universities and such. Also, I was usually away for the whole
summer with my wife, no matter the intermittent marital

discord—he would be away in August, anyway—and I was not going to give up my July out of the city merely to preserve my sanity or attain the peace of mind I was paying for.

I told him frankly that among my motives for coming to see him (truthfully, I could think of no other real reason) was the tactical wish to have a psychiatric medical authority of my own to quote in comeback during domestic arguments—even to misquote, by attributing to him statements that had not been made. He laughed and was not surprised.

He wanted me to understand that he could be of no help to me with my current emotional problems, a demurral I quickly professed to comprehend. He did believe, however, that a program of analysis might prove of some prophylactic value in warding off that late-life depression that eventually creeps up on so many of the aging and cloistered.

He was mistaken on that first point. He helped me enormously in the matter of day-to-day embroilments at home and elsewhere by being someone impartial and intelligent I could talk to with absolute freedom and who could point out obvious aspects and approaches in each crisis that I could not rationally spot for myself.

As for warding off potential depression, well, because of him or not, here I am in late life, and I'm no more depressed, despondent, dour, morose, cynical, bitter, drowsy, lonely, angry, and all the rest than I've been all along. If I'm gripped at times by the somber realization that I have nothing to do that I would enjoy doing or that not much merry is going on, it's because I don't and there isn't. I feel in pretty good shape as long as I have work I want to do. I know things are going well for me if my first thoughts upon waking up each day are related to what I'm writing. Today, my frame of mind is very good, for I awoke this morning with the idea of putting in right here these two sentences I am putting in. It's when I feel I can't find anything I want to do that I'm inclined to sleep a lot and to imagine I'm being infected by the brooding and miasmic lethargy of what the French call a *cafard* and we used to call "the blues." It grows harder and harder to meet new people you'd like to become close friends with (and the odds are great that you're going to find that out).

He bound me to this: I was not to make fundamental changes in my life once we began—not in my marriage, my work, or other areas—without discussion with him. So obvious was the reasoning underlying this condition that I agreed without hesitation.

And by the end of the summer of 1981, I broke that promise over and over without contrition and without even recognizing I was doing so. I changed accountants, I changed book publishers and instituted a lawsuit against one of them, I left my literary agent, I changed lawyers and then changed lawyers again, I moved out of the marital apartment not once but twice—once in summer, when he was away, and once, this time permanently, during Christmas, when he also was away—and finally, perhaps as a grand and auspicious climax, I unilaterally and abruptly broke off my treatments with him.

That sudden termination followed a disappointing return to the city after a summer away alone, half in Aspen, where I soon made friends, and half in Santa Fe, where I already had some, when I lost all patience and felt myself running out of money. Expenses were building, income was not. A lawyer had counseled me to just relax all summer and assured me that all disagreements relating to the divorce would be peacefully settled by the time I returned. None was. And I had books to finish as well.

And in mid-December of that year I was felled by a rare, paralyzing neurological disease called Guillain-Barré syndrome, whose etiology remains mysterious, and I was pretty much out of action for the next nine months. Stress? Maybe.

From the beginning of the analysis, I tried my best to be a very good patient, one effortlessly surpassing the average, dreaming the dreams I was supposed to, retrieving the memories I guessed he wanted me to retrieve, unlocking all the unmentionable buried wishes I might have surreptitiously repressed, in order thereby to uncover the sources of the doubts, fears, drives, and inhibitions with which I was in blind conflict (although I might not know it). But I couldn't get far. My theory now about psychoanalytical theory is that corrective therapy demands unwavering concentration by a patient of intelligence with a clear and untroubled head who is not in need of it. My head was a swarming fun house of lawsuits, quarrels, work, and too many other distracting entanglements to count. Every day, something new might take dominion in my mind, if not from life then in the concentrated ruminations for my writing. While searching for myself as a fatherless Coney Island child, I had one new novel, *Good as Gold,* published, and another, *God Knows,* was almost halfway completed before I was through. And of course we talked about those and my two previous novels, about their content and what they might reveal about me, and about the little dramas playing out continually around each of them. (In one appalling mental lapse, I failed to notice that the surname of the reviewer of *Good as Gold* in the Sunday *New York Times*—a good review, but not a rave—was the same as that of my analyst, even to the deviant spelling. They were distant relations, it turned out, but that had no effect on either the book review or the extent of my cure.)

I would imagine that in my eagerness to make an excellent impression as a patient, I was not alone among male subjects in a sophisticated hurry to plead guilty to such likely flaws as an Oedipus complex, castration fears, impotence fears, performance fears, ill will, ambivalent emotions toward everyone close to me, latent homosexuality, rage, shame, lustful thoughts, unconscious hatreds and unaccountable losses of confidence, vague perceptions of confrontational inadequacy and abstract dangers, and disguised, subterranean volcanoes of murderous aggression. Had I known then of narcissism as a specific pathology, I might have thrown that in, too. All that serious stuff was easy. It was the simple, unknown stuff that was hard and that eventually proved unconquerable: to go beyond facile academic logic and probe deep into memory for an understanding of feelings and events that might not even be there or ever have occurred, not even in fantasies.

I was blocked often (or thought I was) and freely confessed to that failing even before I could be charged with it. "Resistance" was another of the terms I thought to volunteer. (And I'll freely confess right here that the more than ordinary difficulties I am having with these passages might be arising afresh from "resistance"—from what some might infer in this place as a psychological block and in other sections of this book dismiss as mere writer's block.)

I have always been a fertile dreamer. Now I was giving value to each dream as a treasure of significance. I was intrigued by the way my dreams began to center on our sessions, even to the physical location of his office, and on what I took to be the elusive essence of my monologues. I was beguiled by the frequency with which such details as the number on his office door began appearing in different dream contexts and, when awake, by the cunning and cute lapses in memory, the endearing tricks of the mind that seemed to fit perfectly into Freudian theory. The most dramatic of these occurred on the last session of one season. I was coasting along in the kind of voluble free-association we both believed in when he interrupted brusquely to demand, "Don't you know that you were twenty minutes late today?"

No, I had not known.

During one of the periods of separation preceding my divorce when I was living alone in a sublet furnished apartment, I intrepidly flew off for an unlikely weekend rendezvous, a blind date with a woman I hadn't met or known about before (my most dangerous mission, marveled my friends) and whom nobody I knew had heard of either. (The farcical means by which this unconventional tryst chanced to come about might appear in a sequel, should I ever decide to write one—and I probably never will.) Having arrived, I was at first afflicted by an inability to function sexually, I had to confess to him awkwardly when we resumed on my return (not the only time that had happened to me in my lifetime, I was constrained to admit to him—and to you).

"I wished you were there with me," I said as a joke.

"I was," he said laconically.

"Then why didn't you help?" I said.

"You wanted me to help you do something you didn't really want to do?" he demanded.

From that exchange came much wisdom about the thousand and one other things I often thought I wanted to do but truly preferred not to, and I ceased my regretful wishful thinking about scores of them. I'd never really wanted to live in a house in Tuscany or the French Riviera or have Elizabeth Taylor and Marilyn Monroe in love with me, and I didn't really covet for myself the bolder public life lived by Norman Mailer, although there was much there to envy. People with choices generally do what they want to do and have no real choice but to be what they already are, and I think even my former mentor would agree. I don't actually want to go to the White House for dinner or receive an award of some kind from whichever transient happens to be living there, although I *would* like to get my hands on a Nobel Prize or two.

God knows I deserve it.

Our dialogues were not always so one-sided. From me he first learned the word *catamite*. I was surprised that he didn't know it and he was surprised that I did. I'd found it first long before in a book on forensic medicine that had somehow fallen into my hands in my tent overseas and had taken for granted that it was a technical medical term known universally. And from me came a comment about trying to change neurotic behavior which brought a quick guffaw from him. "It's like asking a hunchback to stand up straight," I said.

He liked that one and said he might use it often. I gave him license, since that clever phrase had originated with a friend, Speed Vogel, of whom and with whom I have elsewhere written. (*No Laughing Matter,* if you're genuinely interested.)

Then there were the dreams.

On days we were scheduled, I usually awoke in a state of high expectancy, especially if I came alive with a sumptuous dream, outlining to myself what purportedly would be spontaneous later, and it dawns on me now that the subject matter of the analysis had in large part become the analysis itself.

"Oh, boy! Have I got a dream for you!" I might say to myself proudly, when I awoke from one with a complete plot, a story line fraught with apparent meaning and latent meaning and replete with the right kind of symbols— symbols of sex and death anyone could recognize: steeples, purses, tearful partings. There was a week in which I heard three jokes all dealing with a shipwrecked man releasing a female genie from a bottle and being granted a wish that was sexual and had been misunderstood. While asleep, I conjured up a fourth that was as good as the others for a joke that was conjured up while asleep. Naturally, I began our day's session with that. Fortunately, he hadn't heard any of the others, and I was able to dispose of much of my fifty minutes with jokes and laughter before I settled down to whatever was that day's most disturbing problem, one that, while perhaps not a choice lode for self-discovery, was uppermost in my mind and couldn't possibly be avoided if I was going to express myself with candor, either by free-associating or in blunt complaint and appeal. (I remember two of the jokes—one involved a large man with a little head walking into a bar, the other a man walking into a bar with a smirking ten-inch mannequin perched on his shoulder. I've forgotten the third one and have no memory of the one I dreamed, either because it wasn't as comical as we thought or because I am again prey to an unconscious and deliberate memory lapse.)

THERE IS A RELUCTANCE to proceed, and it is formidable. It is more than a writer's block. I had forgotten completely, in another memory lapse, that the core of this chapter was to be not my escapades in psychoanalysis at the time of the breakup of my marriage but the death of my father when I was a small boy and the traumatic effects, as all assume, it must certainly have exercised in shaping me. (Rich material, certainly, for the penultimate chapter, and I'm glad I'll never have to review this book—or even write the jacket copy for a book with a passage about how difficult it was to write this passage.) There is a lack of enthusiasm for racing ahead, most rare for me this close to the ending of a book, and it is more likely due to the tender subject matter than to boredom or fatigue or any two- or three-day virus.

Nearly twenty-five years earlier, I'd had my one other personal adventure with psychological investigation, and I talked about that with the psychiatrist often and vividly. Certain impressions left from that encounter have remained ineradicable. In 1958, when I was thirty-five and leaving a job at one magazine for a better one at *McCall's* magazine as head of a small department ancillary to advertising, industrial psychology was much in vogue—at least at McCall's Corporation. I was required to submit to a battery of tests for psychological evaluation before my new appointment could be confirmed. The examinations took up most of one day and perhaps the better part of another and were conducted in mid-Manhattan in the offices of a partnership formed by two professors on the faculty of Columbia University. The procedures were congenial. Most of the tests were new to me, and a couple of them I hadn't heard of before, such as sentence completion, which was both perplexing to me in the range of theoretical possibilities of interpretation and amusing as a guessing game, and the Thematic Apperception Test, the TAT, which, for me anyway, was at times especially challenging and at other times profoundly affecting. The Rorschach test was an immediate catalyst, and I pricked up my senses with the alertness and gusto of, as they say, a cavalry horse at the first notes of the bugle when I saw it coming and we were about to begin.

I charged into the first card. And from then on I talked and talked endlessly about the assorted forces I could easily imagine at work in the individual inkblots in the succession of cards that followed, offering no original responses about any, I'm sure, but dissertating on each until out of breath and the examiner gave evidence of restlessness and we turned to the next. I went gabbing and gabbing away—blithely, inexhaustibly—until I collided with card number 4 or 5, the first of the ink blots in color, and was at once catapulted into a state of startled confusion and silence. My loquacity was annihilated. I was numb. That first color card is labeled the "color shock" card, I learned speedily from a technical book I obtained as soon as I could at the local library, and, for me at least, the card was named fittingly. (For others, too, I must conclude, or where would that title have come from?)

From that point on I proceeded gingerly, far less sure of myself. It wasn't long before then that I had at last taken the trouble to learn from my sister the cause of my father's death. Applying for my first life insurance policy—I had my wife and two children—I drew a blank when I came to the request on the insurance application for the cause of his death. I was jolted with surprise, and disappointed in myself, too, for I divined that the reason I didn't know how he had died was that I had never wanted to find out. The cause of death, as I've said, was internal bleeding following surgery for a stomach ulcer, and I was mistaken earlier when I assumed he had been a ward patient at Coney Island Hospital. I learned just recently from Sylvia that the hospital was Columbia Presbyterian Hospital in Manhattan, a

long, long ride by subway from Coney Island, and it fell
upon Sylvia, then just thirteen, to escort my mother to the
hospital when they received word of my father's death. One
takes the BMT express subway to its final stop at Times
Square and then switches to a line of the IRT. But two IRT
lines are there: One continues up through Manhattan to the
station stop for the hospital; the other diverges into the
Bronx and ends somewhere before the border of Westchester County, which is outside the city. Sylvia had never
been that far from home. It was her macabre luck to choose
the wrong line, and the mournful subway journey of
bereaved mother and teenage daughter to the hospital for
the certification of death took two hours longer than it
should have.

The predominant color on those Rorschach inkblots
that do have color is, I remember (or think I remember),
red, in splotches of different densities and shapes. And on
that first card, after I recovered from my shock, and on the
color cards unveiled subsequently, I could truly see only
blood, blood, and amputated or excised bodily organs,
human organs. Here and there when faced with green I
tried to fake a flower or a fruit, but my heart wasn't in it,
and my soul couldn't follow through. So self-conscious and
embarrassed was I by the consistency of my gruesome
replies that I felt forced to call attention, with a nervous
laugh, to my awareness of their morbid uniformity. (Just as
with the black-and-white blots, I had a lesser dilemma with
genital symbols: I didn't want the examiner to think I feared
seeing any; I didn't want him to think I was seeing too
many.)

After the rite of taking the tests, there was an extended
conversational interview. The mood was relaxed. In the
course of discussion, I naturally mentioned that I was about
halfway through writing a novel for which I already had
been given a publishing contract. What was it about? That
question still makes me squirm (and I'm still tremendously
glad I never had to write a review of *Catch-22,* either—or its

jacket copy). It was set toward the end of World War II—I could be straightforward about that much—and concerned men in an American bomber group on an island off the coast of Italy. And—I swear!—it was only then, in trying to talk about it coherently, that I realized for the first time how extensively I was focusing on the grim details of human mortality, on disease, accidents, grotesque mutilations. I was again awash in the reds and pinks of the Rorschach color cards, in blood, in the deaths of such characters as Kid Sampson and Snowden and even with my colorless Soldier in White. Although I had from the start, from the second chapter on, been dutifully following a disciplined outline, I hadn't perceived till then how much material of a gory nature was embodied in its fulfillment. There was certainly an awful lot for a novel that has since been described by many as among the funniest they've read.

It has struck me since—it couldn't have done so then—that in *Catch-22* and in all my subsequent novels, and also in my one play, the resolution at the end of what narrative there is evolves from the death of someone in the chapter just before, and it is always the death of someone other than the main character. In *Catch-22,* the death of Snowden, who has perished four hundred pages earlier—in fact, before the present action of the novel has even begun—is written about fully only in the chapter before the final one. And in my most recent novel, *Closing Time,* it is the death of Lew as narrated by his wife that precedes the surrealistic catastrophes at the climax, though Yossarian goes on living. And even in the novel before that one, *Picture This,* by which time I'd grown cautiously aware of that undeviating pattern and tried to make an effort to break it, the death of Socrates in the *Crito* as related formally by Plato (to me in translation, of course) is almost against my will the precursor of the final few pages. And—lo and behold—here I am, much to my surprise, doing exactly the same thing with this book! I still haven't broken the pattern. I don't know why this should be so—it reflects no aesthetic or philosophical principle. I would speculate that the individual personality, no matter how protean in creativity, has a character all its own and can construct flexibly only within the parameters of its own nature. The novels of other writers, too, like the mature compositions of classical composers, tend to be more alike than we wish to own.

I've come to recognize something else. Where I stress tender relationships, they are usually most tender between a father and a child, as in *Something Happened,* and also in *God Knows,* where King David's most wrenching recollections are of the death of his son Absalom and of the newborn child who is the result of his transgression with Bathsheba.

The Thematic Apperception Test for the job at *McCall's* provided me with one indelible prototype that still touches me poignantly whenever it comes to mind. In the TAT, one is asked to comment subjectively about simple drawings that are objectively neutral, to project onto the picture a personal vision of what is taking place, to create a text. It was not that easy, and I would bet that there are many people who at times can't bring themselves to fantasize anything at all. The picture I remember, and it's the lone one I recall, is still with me, together with the emotions it aroused at the time, indissolubly joined.

A woman with white hair is in a room with a grown youth with dark hair. That's all. But to me it was a scene of pain, of miserable, unwanted separation. There are no emotions on the faces pictured in the drawing, but I could sense the sadness of a mother and a son. The boy is going away and they are speechless with sorrow. Another person looking at that same drawing, I've since realized, could easily be projecting a scene of triumph and elation—could imagine, for instance, that a boy away from home at college finds pleasant lodgings with a woman who is happy to have him. But I didn't. (I could venture now that the absence of a father in the picture could be the key to my response to the scene, but I didn't think of that then and I would once more be casting about for a textbook psychoanalytical explanation for the grimness I imposed on the scene, and still do. Certainly, in the picture there was no father, only the mother—or rather just a woman.)

I didn't know him. He isn't there. I would not recognize him. I have only a handful of impressions of him—there is only one snapshot, a photograph in which he is younger than I am now but will always seem older—and the authenticity of a couple of my memories is questionable. Allowed in the driver's seat of an auto of his or his bakery delivery van I am encouraged to press the automatic starter and pretend I'm driving at each grinding lurch. He drives me to the Coney Island Hospital to have my tonsils removed. (And that wasn't fun. Lying there alone afterward, I would have given my life for a drink of water to assuage the maddening thirst.) He is playing with me on the sidewalk with an airplane with a wind-up, rubber-band propeller he has bought for me, when Lee comes walking home from the trolley stop after his runaway summer as a hobo, and there is a joyful reunion. ("When you come from California," my mother would repeat for years afterward, "you've *got* to take a bath.") Sleeping in the same bedroom with my mother and father and at least one time being taken into bed with them—make what you will out of that, but I don't doubt it's true. He commands me back from an open window when he spies me making my way out it toward the fire escape. On the day of his funeral, I wouldn't get in the car for the trip to the funeral parlor or the cemetery, and when older boys on the block came after me, I turned the chase into a game.

Sylvia was not at ease answering questions about our father, and I didn't try to extract much. She remembers sitting by the window at night doing her homework by the lamplight from outside, but she doesn't attribute the absence of lighting indoors to any cruel stinginess—none of the families we knew liked the electric company—and after all of us had been driven to wear eyeglasses, she no longer blamed anyone for her defective eyesight. She retains a memory of herself and my mother in the terrible week of mourning that followed the funeral. It was summer and hot. Someone had dressed her, a child of thirteen, in black garments, but my mother advised her to change into something lighter and go outside in the street, where it might be cooler. (I wasn't around for that. I don't know where I was that week, but I doubt it was there. I would remember. In almost three years of therapy I could get so far and no farther.) He was always good to me, Sylvia says—all of them were. His first wife was ill and died and not much later he was ill, too, and he was not always kind to Lee. The youngest in a family of several boys who had emigrated from Eastern Europe to the New York area, he was the least prosperous and the most helpful and cooperative, and was that way with my mother's relatives, too.

Lee talked about him to me one time only and with a mixture of deep and conflicting emotions. His eyes were misty and he kept trying to smile. That conversation took place under unhappy circumstances. In New York from West Palm Beach on a family visit, his wife, Perlie, was troubled by shoulder pain and asked us—me and my first wife, Shirley—to recommend a physician, preferably an orthopedic specialist. The doctor she found took X rays and found advanced lung cancer. During the first program of chemotherapy at Mount Sinai Hospital in New York, Lee and I had dinner alone a few nights in succession at an Italian restaurant just down the block from my apartment— Tony's, on West 79th Street. It was the most time we had ever spent alone together and the longest we'd ever talked. Both of us drank whiskey.

He wouldn't acknowledge himself as a runaway from home that long-ago summer. He had only gone to New Jersey to apply for a job, and when it was clear he wouldn't get it, he had simply decided on the spot to keep going west. He sent postcards home every week to let the family know he was well. His most aching childhood recollection was of riding beside my father winter mornings in a horse-drawn delivery van in upper Manhattan, when they lived there before I was born. On icy uphill streets, my father would have to use the whip on the horse, and people on the street would berate them both for their cruelty to the animal. My father was a good and kind man, Lee said, although he would use his belt to beat Lee for any kind of misbehavior. That sounded brutal to me. "There were lots of Jewish criminals around and he didn't want me to turn out bad." Then he did have a good reason, I said in a conciliatory tone. "Sure. But I was just a little kid. How bad could I have been to deserve that?" Then he wasn't always so good and gentle, was he? "He was always very good. His wife was sick and died and he was sick, too."

Lee did not turn out bad. None of us did. At the age of eighty-four, a widower, he died on the living-room floor of his small condominium in West Palm Beach in a way we would all choose to go, if we were eighty-four and could force ourselves to take leave of life then. Back from a vacation cruise with a group of men and women he'd grown friendly with, he died instantly from a heart attack in the midst of optimistically planning things for the immediate future: He had borrowed some books from the local library that day and had just returned from the supermarket with some staples with which to restock his kitchen.

One more report, from an uncle by marriage in my first wife's family, who'd been a young boy on the block with us when my father was still alive. He described my father to me as cheerful, jolly, friendly, helpful—and so here I am again, as I mentioned earlier, with another book whose penultimate chapter deals with death, the death of someone other than the principal character in it.

THE LAST TIME I was with my father or had anything to do with him was more than sixty-five years ago, on the day he was buried in a cemetery somewhere in Long Island or New Jersey. Sylvia might remember where but would be uncomfortable if I asked her, and knowing where would make no difference anyway. Until now I haven't even thought of asking. I've never grappled much with the idea of trying to find out more about him. I prefer not to. I still prefer not to. And knowing more would make no difference now, either. I know him by his absence. Until just now, if I thought about the day of his funeral at all, I was disposed to remember it as one of the more rewarding in my young life. I sat waiting placidly on a stone bench on a stone patio with a railing, just outside the main office at the entrance to the cemetery grounds. It was summer, I had been dressed neatly, and there was sunshine. People milling about fussed over me. Some handed me coins—dimes, an occasional quarter. My Aunt Esther gave me a whole dollar. I felt rich.

10

Danny the Bull

DANNY THE BULL murdered his mother.

You couldn't ask for a better opening line than that one for a final chapter, could you?

It had something to do with heroin, money for heroin. Either she gave him money, five dollars for a fix, or she didn't, or she had been doing both, giving him when she had it and he demanded it, denying him when she didn't. Not like his father, Max the Barber, who would make a contemptuous, bitter show of disavowal whenever his son came abjectly into the barber shop to implore, who was an awful man (in the judgment of my friend Marvin Winkler, who knew them better than I), a kind of insolent "wise guy," abrasive with unfunny remarks. I know the type, and so do you. His father would make sarcastic fun of Danny before others in the barber shop, renouncing him as "my son, the junkie," and boasting with smug pride that he would not give him a dime.

Danny the Bull's mother and father lived apart; they were no longer married. He lived with his mother down around West 23rd Street, near the big yellow-brick synagogue and the big red-brick Catholic church, where the Jewish sector merged with the Italian. Max the Barber is still the only man I've heard of living in Coney Island at that time who was divorced. He had married again. His second wife was a local woman who also had been married earlier and who brought into this marriage children of her own with the last name of Glickman. In due course, Max the Barber's stepson, Raymie Glickman, fell dead in the street from an overdose of heroin. And Leona, Raymie's wife, also died of a heroin overdose. Max the Barber, the father of Danny the Bull, though a rasping, unfunny wise guy, did have cause for discontent.

Soon after the war, with the social clubs finished and school days past, our gathering places were reduced to a very few for those still living in the Island and for those many more who had moved elsewhere but returned regularly for visits with family and friends. I was already in the city and would travel down from Manhattan.

We were young adults now. On Mermaid Avenue near Happy's Luncheonette was the popular daytime hangout for males—the poolroom belonging to Sammy the Pig. There we could hobnob with lanky Pinya, a rabbi's son with the mien of a hungry friar who was our local bookmaker; with Smokey Bleeker, a well-built, friendly sort of tough guy from an older generation—he was in his thirties; and with Sammy the Pig himself, short and stubby in a porcine way, who didn't gab much and wasn't much fun. In the rear of the poolroom near a large, chalk-lined blackboard mounted to the side was a Western Union ticker-tape machine that typed out up-to-the-minute data on the progress of sporting events nationwide. In season came the inning-by-inning progress of all major-league baseball games. Streetwise sophisticates understood that an unusual lag in a ticker report usually indicated something happening in that half inning of the game; new bets might be made in the delay, odds might change. Bewildering to me still is how some of the guys there who had barely staggered through arithmetic classes for their elementary-school diplomas could now calculate fractional odds and multiple payoffs on parlays with a dazzling rapidity and exactitude that left very little room for betterment by even the swiftest of today's digital computers.

One of these savants had been a fellow student on my own grade-school level at P.S. 188 with the last name Silverman. For reasons known only to himself, he had changed his name to Ershky Jones, and we now called him that. To most of us, the game of checkers was a matter of haphazard luck. But Ershky saw much more than that; somehow he had penetrated to essentials. He won every time against every player, with none of us ever able to spot the things he saw that we didn't.

He could also run up walls. He would run a few feet up the perpendicular walls of apartment houses and rooms, turn, and come back down. He would practice running up walls and down while conversing cynically about things like baseball, politics, and the antiunion and anti–Democratic Party biases of the Hearst newspapers and the New York *Daily News*. He was better than anyone else we knew at running up walls. None of the rest of us had the will to try it more than once.

Smokey Bleeker was almost always around, too, at Happy's Luncheonette or in Sammy the Pig's poolroom, grinning, joking, affable, and crassly unschooled in speech, even in comparison to the Brooklyn articulations of Ershky Jones and me. Loose-limbed, muscular, and agile, Smokey always had coarse, black stubble shadowing his countenance, yet always looked as though he had recently shaved. He had been brought up someplace funny and far away and had once worked on a farm—in Pennsylvania, Poland, or both. By the time I met him he had been in prison and had fought in the prize ring. He and another older neighborhood hard guy named Izzy Nish, this one wiry, had formerly buddied around together in a number of shady, daring ventures, one of which had brought a carload or two of equally dauntless Italians with knives charging down upon them in some other part of Brooklyn. Izzy Nish managed to flee, leaving Smokey behind to be carved up in a doorway. He had narrowly survived. Now the two did not speak and took care not to cross paths. They favored different poolrooms. Smokey's face was gashed with scars, and a circular part of the top of his nose had been sliced out into a hollow. That might be the explanation for his perpetual, neat stubble of beard.

One year Smokey Bleeker enjoyed a season of celebrity because he had a hand, a hand with fingers clenched into a fist, in the genesis of a black eye of a luminous immensity unlike any that people around Happy's or Sammy the Pig's had ever conceived possible before. The black eye was not sported by Smokey himself, naturally, but by a burly fellow of my own generation with a short, thick neck who had been nicknamed—perfectly, and not by me—Quasimodo. Quasi (we sounded the opening consonant like a *k* rather than a *kw*) was a sullen person quick to take offense and accustomed to having his own way. He generally did have his own way, for most of us kept out of his way. After once catching sight of his black eye, we could easily understand why a black eye is traditionally known as a "shiner." Quasi's shiner was of a solar brilliance, an injury mending itself over time in prismatic hues from purple to blue to green to yellow to tangerine, and it glowed like a beacon and seemed to polish the ground in front of him as he walked. People (people like me, who deliberately loitered on Happy's corner in hopes of glimpsing for the first time the shiner I'd already heard of) came there, came to Coney Island, just to see the fabled shiner of Quasi's with their own eyes. Some talk about it still, as I'm doing now, and Marvin Winkler does, too.

That gargantuan black eye came into being as the immediate aftermath of a brief sidewalk fistfight outside the poolroom between Quasi and Smokey Bleeker. I don't have all the details of the provocation. They had something to do with Quasimodo's walking up to where Smokey was seated listening to the radio at the front of the poolroom and changing the station without a word for permission or apology. Smokey, offended, protested that Quasi's action was "rude." (Smokey's employment of that word *rude* was an astounding incongruity for more than one reason, but people on the spot swore it was the one he spoke.) Quasimodo invited him to step outside to settle the dispute if there was objection. Smokey stepped. Outside the poolroom, Quasi, overlooking Smokey's experience in the prize ring, ducked right down to bull forward and seize him around the waist, lift him, and throw or wrestle him to the ground. Smokey, remembering he'd been a boxer and impervious to physical fear, unleashed an uppercut timed to perfection as Quasi's head came down, and that was the beginning and the end of the fisticuffs.

The ambulance from Coney Island Hospital pulled up outside Sammy the Pig's poolroom just in time to save Quasimodo from suffocating, for the gigantic swelling around his nose and mouth was choking his windpipe off from the rest of him.

Of Izzy Nish, Smokey's erstwhile confederate in a miscellany of misdeeds that ultimately landed Smokey in the hospital with knife wounds and perhaps also in prison, I know less. He was not one to hang around with nothing to do and was not inclined to exchange pleasantries with younger kids like me. He was married to the sister of a Coney Island friend by the time he was pointed out to me and probably was employed on a standard work schedule. My occasional random sightings of Izzy Nish all occurred in our other Coney Island poolroom, Weepy's, where a largely different group passed the hours at different times of the day. His taut, tawny-colored face also was marked with a scar or two, but what charisma he possessed lay in his pool playing. He was superb. An expert pocket-billiards player is a miracle to behold to someone incapable like me, and Izzy Nish was among the best I've ever watched. Shooting pool, he was a stolid avatar of that self-possessed, mute, concentrated proficiency that is second nature to the shark and mystifying testimony to the maze of intricate nuances inherent in so pacific a competition. For those who don't know, foresight in billiards directs the player not to the billiard ball that is safest to sink but to the one that will leave him and the white cue ball in the best position to sink the next, and the next, and the next. And finally the last, which should be left in a position enabling you to sink it forcefully at the end of a rack while enabling you to break apart the new rack with your cue ball in the same shot, and thereby continue. It was like chamber music watching Izzy move smoothly and wordlessly through one rack of billiard balls, two racks, and sometimes three.

Weepy himself, Murray by name, the owner of this poolroom, was a family man with daughters. Unlike Sammy's, Weepy's had no bookmaker and no ticker machine. There were salami sandwiches on a roll for a nickel each and chocolate-flavored drinks in cold bottles. Women were welcome at Weepy's but were rarely present.

Blackie the Pinochle Player, in a more retiring way, was another local personality. He was a champ at cards, though not at picking horses. I'd laid eyes on him only a few times, never at play, but I'd heard, more than once, the anecdotal account of one tormenting game he'd played at high stakes and the renowned remark he'd made immediately after it. When the bidding was over and he was about to begin play, he calculated with distress that he had drastically overbid. In pinochle, unlike bridge, the player in command has no partner and doesn't play with the support of a dummy hand; he faces two opponents united against him. Blackie, caught between folding the hand and paying up or playing the hand and paying double if he lost (quadruple, for his trump would have had to be spades), reckoned despondently that he needed to take every one of the fifteen tricks, every point left in the deck, to make his bid. He chose to play. He played slowly, and slowly he made all the tricks. Closing in toward the end, when he could guess with assurance where the rest of the cards lay and realized that he was certain to make the hand, his muscles went slack and he drooped with the strain. Looking down with an unhappy sigh and shaking his head with dismay, as though he had lost, not won, he moaned out loud:

"I played the game all wrong."

HAPPY'S LUNCHEONETTE, on Mermaid Avenue a few blocks from Weepy's poolroom, was a lively, clean, well-lighted place, a safe and convenient setting in which to meet with our wives if it was that kind of evening or to hang around in with just the fellows. There were no longer many other spots. It opened early and went on serving very late. Lounging around doing nothing before we went where we were going or after we had been, we could easily put away as a snack a tuna sandwich or two on white toast with a leaf of lettuce inside and a slender length of pickle alongside. Before the war, tuna salad hadn't been heard of. Now a simple tuna sandwich went down as easily as a potato chip or a salted peanut. I told you we liked to eat, all of us, and those of us I still claim as friends still do. We've never regretted a mouthful. For a true hunger, Happy's pork chops were good, and his hamburgers, too. Our drinks of preference were chocolate egg creams or malted milkshakes of any flavor, or in winter a hot chocolate. A taste for coffee takes time to mature.

Happy's, together with the street corner outside, was also a clustering spot for the neighborhood's many surreptitious "vipers," a commissary of sorts where the dedicated marijuana smokers could buy and sell and borrow and swap, and a couple of years later on, when they evolved as a subculture, for the junkies to drift into and linger idly in their auras of furtive and suspicious confidences.

It was around the corner from Happy's and down the side street one night that observers caught their first sight of heroin in use. A friendly generous pusher showed up to coach a bunch of those there, at no cost, how to mainline heroin. Of the dozen or so willing to accept the injection directly into the vein, every one was quickly retching violently and vomiting into the street. You would have bet that not a single one of them would ever want to go near the stuff again. And you would have lost. All did and all were soon addicted.

One more watering place for spring, summer, and autumn socializing was a roomy square bar on the boardwalk in our Jewish neighborhood. A bar was an uncommon place for us then, but this one fronted wide onto the boardwalk, projecting the airy character of a resort, and was run by someone we knew. The atmosphere was of a spacious café, a cabaret without live entertainment. Women came there, too, with escorts or with each other. Everyone there knew everyone else, at least by sight. I had long since been living away from Coney Island, and I was led to this place by Marvin Winkler after one of my visits to my mother. It was there that I bumped into Howie Ehrenman from West 31st Street whom I hadn't seen in so long a time, ever since we had departed separately for the war. He, with his brother Henny and the family, now lived somewhere else in Brooklyn. Howie had grown taller, and was quarreling confidently with an adoring girlfriend at the bar. She was a stunning beauty—an Italian girl with lush, olive features and blond hair that glittered—and I thought her ravishing. I haven't seen him since. Marvin directed my attention to a fresh-faced, pretty girl of a different complexion, peaches and cream, who sat facing us at the opposite side of the rectangular bar, pert, laughing, gleaming. She looked, said Marvin, "like a bottle of milk," didn't she—that figure of speech was his—and you would never guess, would you, he confided, that she was being treated for gonorrhea. My instant reaction was to scan enviously the male faces in the room—I was younger, of course, and a romantic even then—for sight of the likely guys, the lucky, likely ones, who might have contracted that disease from that cheery doll. She did indeed look as clean and pasteurized and homogenized as a wholesome bottle of milk. Ever since I heard that simile from Marvin I have been waiting for a chance to use it in my writing, and now I have.

LIKE SOME I KNEW in the neighborhood and others I heard about, Danny the Bull had acted more than once to commit himself voluntarily for treatment in the federal drug rehabilitation facility in Lexington, Kentucky. A quirk in the law then (perhaps still) left a person free to use drugs but decreed it criminal to possess them. In seeking help, one could admit to use and addiction without incurring arrest, and many, perhaps all, of these desperate Coney Islanders did.

At Lexington, Kentucky, the treatment was "cold turkey"—immediate, total withdrawal. It was from those coming back that we first learned the term. This was before the development of methadone and similar alleviating pharmaceutical substitutions, and going cold turkey on heroin was an excruciating ordeal, or at least was said to be by any who had endured it. Leaving Lexington at the completion of a program of treatment, the subject could, if he (or she) wished, obtain from an orderly in an underhanded way a list of sources of supply for the illegal drug of choice on the route home from the institution. What made the outlook for almost all of them dismal was that when the time arrived to go back home, they had no place to go *but* back home.

For a very short period I was acquainted with a minister involved in drug rehabilitation work for the East Harlem Protestant parish in New York. The population of his parish was predominantly Hispanic, mostly Puerto Rican. He was a ruddy, buoyant man of a likable disposition, but his pessimism about his work was total: He felt the futility of bringing the weak-willed, damaged addict back into the same situation from which he had come and expecting him to overcome the numerous psychological, social, and environmental influences that had lured him into his addiction to begin with.

A couple of us were witness to a striking and depressing illustration of this fragile despair. We met Danny the Bull by chance one day outside Happy's while he was killing time and waiting, maybe, for another look at Quasi's black eye. The Bull had just come back from another stay in Lexington. He was animated, convinced, firm, almost chipper. Suddenly, he stiffened; then he was quivering, and looking elsewhere. His trembling appearance now was one of agonized indecision and terror. We gazed in the direction he was staring. On the sidewalk across Mermaid Avenue stood an inert, huddling figure one of us recognized as another neighborhood junkie, always a likely source of supply and information about supply. Danny the Bull held out against temptation for not even one whole minute, withdrew from us, and crossed over again.

In California there was Synanon House, an organization much publicized for successful work with addicts. So celebrated was its reputation for dramatic successes that a film director for whom I was doing some rewriting on a slight sex comedy (*Sex and the Single Girl,* and the title is more risqué than the content) assigned a researcher to Synanon to give him material for a feature film to be set there that would have a happy ending and great commercial possibilities. And for all I know, he made it. Danny the Bull knew of the place, too. With a friend who was also a junkie, he flew out to Santa Monica to apply for admission. The verdict of doom handed down to him there was that they might succeed in helping his friend but they could do nothing for him. How they could tell I don't know. Danny came back alone to Coney Island and into the apartment on Mermaid Avenue in which he lived with his mother. A short while later, he burst through a door and choked her to death with his bare hands as she lay in her bathtub.

He insisted afterward in an incoherent explanation of his rage that he had done it because it was all her fault, that she had kept him a junkie by giving him money, and that if she had acted as his father, Max the Barber, had done and given him nothing, he probably would have been cured. He was consigned to a hospital for the criminally insane and if he's still alive he may still be there.

About the thunderstruck, horrified, immigrant Jewish woman who was his mother, I would submit that she had not the smallest idea of what was happening to her as she was being strangled to death by her son in her bathtub, or why. And I assume she had been just as helplessly dumbfounded by the addiction and the miserable, weird changes it had produced in her young boy's behavior about which she understood nothing—unlike mothers today, and laudable public officials, who know a great deal about the drug problem, and still can do nothing.

Another neighborhood heroin junkie with whom I had been much better acquainted was a kid named Solly. We had been through grade school together and sometimes played in the same games on the same team. I don't remember what happened to him in high school, but I doubt that he finished. He had been to Lexington, too. He was like Mark Twain, who found it easy to give up smoking, having done it so many times; Solly had kicked the heroin habit more than once. Marvin Winkler pitched in to assist him after the last attempt. He provided Solly with steady, regular employment in a pastry-baking venture newly begun in New Jersey. Solly strived happily and industriously and took pride in his work. He kept clean. "I make the best honey-glazed doughnuts in the world," he would boast with sincerity. "People come from all over New Jersey and Connecticut to eat my honey-glazed." Soon he had a girlfriend, and the last I heard was that they were talking of marriage. Then Marvin had to close the business to move to California. We don't know what happened to Solly after that.

I can say with some pride that not one of the friends in the three distinct social groups I ran around with in Coney Island (in general, the people from one didn't cotton to those in another) became an addict or thought for a second of ever yielding to anything so self-destructive or in fact to anything over which they had no control. (As with LSD much later on, there was no longing in any of us for that rarefied state of mental elevation about which users bragged.) My conviction is strong that those who did give way to drug addiction were individuals without any compelling attributes of personality.

SPOOKY WEINER was not a junkie and not likely ever to become one. However, through peculiar physiological attunements of unknown origin, he ripened for a while, strangely, into the local authority on gage, or pot (by later generations called "grass"), and was the regnant arbiter on "garbage." He had a gift, an unerring flair, for the detection of inferior or adulterated seeds of marijuana. This genius did not pass unnoticed by older hands, members of the bygone Alteo Seniors social club with whom we were still in contact. They would take him along on drives into the city to Harlem or Greenwich Village for major purchases. There, in murky hallways, the suspense would thicken as Spooky sampled and tested. Others in the close crowd of prospective buyers and hopeful sellers would cease to breathe as Spooky inhaled deeply from a stick, or reefer (later a "joint"), rolled by his own hands. They waited on tenterhooks for the effect to register and for the squeezed-out verdict to emerge from a throat disinclined yet to exhale. As often as not, the verdict would come with that one word: "garbage." When the verdict was garbage, the transaction was canceled and they would have to search about for a better connection with a better grade of hemp, or gage, or pot, or grass.

Spooky's famous sensitivity to garbage eventually bore him into a scrape with the law that many of us in whom the incident lives, including himself, still find humorous. There came a Saturday night when I was scheduled to meet with him early the next day at my apartment in the city to aid in the launching of a business enterprise of his having to do with the early-morning home delivery of Sunday morning breakfasts of bagels, lox (smoked salmon), and cream cheese.

I had, as a charitable service, written the advertising copy for the direct-mail solicitations already distributed by him with a bold headline of his own creation. (That headline read: SLEEP LATER SUNDAY MORNINGS! The company name, with offices on Surf Avenue in Coney Island, was Greenacre Farms, Inc.) Early that Saturday evening, I received a telephone call from Danny the Count in Coney Island advising me with some glee that the appointment for the next morning was off; Spooky wouldn't be there.

"Why not?" I responded, and I was already chortling along with the Count in anticipation of his reply, for I was not unaware of the mishaps with which Spooky's business career had been continually and supernaturally blotched. "Where is he?"

"He's in jail," said Danny, with a burst of a bronchial laugh that sent me off laughing, too.

"What happened?"

What happened was that Spooky, with his exceptional devotion to the good in marijuana and his sensitive antennae for "garbage," had been delegated to go into the city to buy a large quantity of rolled reefers for which four or five others had chipped in. The purchase completed, he returned to Coney Island to Weepy's poolroom to await the arrival of his partners. Hardly had he seated himself on the brim of a pool table in the rear than he spied a posse of plainclothes policemen flooding in from the front. In those primeval times in Coney Island, plainclothes police officers in warm weather could be easily marked by two distinguishing traits: by the shirts worn outside the trousers to conceal the tools of the trade at the belt, and by the Celtic-pink and Saxon-white skin of their faces, which were definitively Gentile. They were there looking for someone else, but Spooky couldn't know that. Deftly, he flipped his packet to the floor into the shadows near a wall, praying no one would see.

"Pick up the package, sonny," said the officer who saw. "Or I'll peel that mustache off your face."

Spooky accompanied them to jail with his mustache on.

The fix went in, the judgment was mild, the arresting officer couldn't be altogether positive that he actually had seen the suspect toss the goods away.

Sometime later, Spooky found himself filling out an official application for something like the renewal of a driver's license, and he was faced with the query of whether he had ever been arrested. Fearing a penalty of fine and imprisonment, he decided to make a clean breast of things and answered yes. The follow-up question, though, required him to state the cause. Here he allowed a spasm of humor to override his prudence. With a lightened heart, he wrote:

"Failure to dispose of garbage."

OUR PUNCH BALL GAMES were over. There was no longer amusement for us in the amusement area. We were moving away to live in other places; no one I know of who lived there has moved back or would want to. We were used to the rides and the games and we went there now only to shepherd others who had never been or, lacking any better diversion, to eat. When Nathan's, which was open winters, too, introduced pea soup, it was the best pea soup in the world, singularly so on frosty, stygian nights, and when they began selling pizzas, the pizza was the equal of the best in the world. (As with Solly's honey-glazed doughnuts, people who knew came from far and wide to savor Nathan's delectables and were never disappointed.)

Luna Park had already declined into an unruly and disintegrating relic and was gone; Steeplechase was ailing, sluggishly deteriorating, although we couldn't see that. Observing the gaiety of people less jaded than ourselves cheerfully moving about inside brought a complacent satisfaction. What we definitely were not used to and quickly embraced were the advantageous circumstances our American society was affording us and into which we were advancing with eagerness.

My trips into Brooklyn after our return from California were irregular. We went as a married couple, or I went alone. Often we journeyed to Brooklyn but didn't go to Coney Island, and much of what I learned I heard from others, mostly from Marvin, who remains the oldest of my very close friends (although we haven't seen each other now in two or three years), and also from Louie Berkman and, news about a different set of people, from Davey Goldsmith, Danny the Count, Harold Bloom, and others. Bulletins of another character came to me from my mother, who remained in the Coney Island apartment until her intestinal surgery rendered her too dependent and impaired to continue living alone, and from Sylvia and Lee, who had their separate apartments nearby. As a married couple, my wife, Shirley, and I socialized most agreeably; we had Marvin and Evelyn, Lou Berkman and Marion, Dave Goldsmith and Estelle, later George Mandel and Miki; still living in Coney Island was Danny the Count, always funny; Evelyn's girlfriend Maxine, married to a former prizefighter; and Maxine's limber older sister, June, an excellent lindy-hop dancer (a very infrequent thing in a white woman) who fell in love with Danny the Count and in order to marry him divorced a husband to whom she had been married early. We mixed easily and we normally could meet as conveniently in the city as in Coney Island.

In Brooklyn when we had no special plans, where we went and what we did often depended on who had the car. One night Heshie Bodner had the only car, and an older eminence of considerable substance and brawn named Scarface Louie decided that he and his large dog had a number of business calls to make in other parts of Brooklyn and lower Manhattan.

"Whose station wagon is that outside?" Scarface Louie inquired, leaning into Happy's.

Heshy made believe he didn't hear.

"Heshy's," a younger innocent named Spotty Dave volunteered, helpfully pointing.

And Heshy for the next several hours was off on a dis-
quieting and perilous journey.

By occupation, Scarface Louie had something to do with
the union workers in taverns and small restaurants; either
he ran the labor unions or he busted them. That evening he
needed meetings with people outside one barroom after
another, while Heshy and the dog were ordered to wait in
the car. The conversations were quick and quiet but vehe-
ment, too. Once or twice they picked up someone else at one
place and dropped him off at another. When another rider
was in the car, the big dog sat on the front seat beside Heshy.
Outside one dark saloon a man was slapped around on the
sidewalk, with Scarface Louie looking on collectedly, making gestures of approval. There was even a robbery before
they were through. At a gas station where the attendant was
less than courteous, Louie and a friend decided they might '
as well take the cash. Heshy and the dog didn't step from the
car during the long trip except for Heshie and the dog to pee
against the tire now and then. The dog was a Great Dane.

"Thanks, Heshy," said Scarface Louie when he was
dropped off at Happy's. "We'll do it again soon."

THE MOVEMENT OUT OF Coney Island after the war
wasn't then, not at first, an incidence of white flight before
an influx of people who were of darker skin and of even
poorer economic station. That came later (and continues
everywhere, and the apprehensiveness and prejudice at
work appear to include social and economic anxiety along
with the racial). Rather, the migration away was an optimistic drive toward betterment in response to the multitude
of captivating opportunities that flowered in the wake of
our victory in the war. Among the richest and most sensible
and far-reaching was the G.I. Bill of Rights: Along with the
obvious good of making available a higher education to
those like myself who'd never hoped realistically to acquire
one, it detained several million of us from pouring all

together into the workforce and inciting unrest by over-
flooding it. Conjoined with this powerful impulse toward
upward mobility was the allure of the suburbs to many in
the overcrowded cities (to many in the same suburbs and
outer districts the longing was to transfer into the overcrowded heart of the cities) and the easy fulfillment of a
newly awakened aspiration of families to own their own
homes. Shortly after the war came the first Levittown, out
in Long Island, in what was then open farmland, followed
soon by scores of similar construction developments, advertising attractive houses at fabulously reasonable prices, with
paltry down payments, low interest rates, and government
financing through G.I. loans. Willie Siegel from my own
street in Coney Island (already as a young adult called Bill
Siegel, just as I was no longer Joey but Joe) was the first contemporary I knew of to buy his own house in a suburb and
perhaps the first to make that quantum growth in maturity
of wanting one.

I was gone from Coney Island permanently with my
marriage in October of 1945, five months following my discharge from the army. After the year in England and the
two years of teaching in Pennsylvania, we settled into Manhattan in an impressive, rent-controlled apartment building
with elevators, doormen, and elevator operators, and I went
on living in that building for the next twenty-eight years,
until the final separation leading to the eventual divorce.

Davey Goldsmith had soon moved away into an apartment in Brighton, still close enough to all he knew; Marty
Kapp was first in Riverdale, just north of Manhattan, next
in New Jersey; Lou Berkman started his plumbing-supply
business in Middletown, New York. All of us married, all of
us in our twenties. Lou's family, like mine, was still in
Brooklyn, and we would see each other there as well as in
Manhattan. Marvin Winkler had moved with his family
from Sea Gate in Coney Island to Ocean Parkway even
before the war. Albie Covelman moved away with his family then, too, to somewhere close in Bensonhurst, I believe. It

was just after a four-handed pinochle game at Albie's house one lazy Sunday afternoon in December that we heard the news of the attack at Pearl Harbor and declared categorically that the Japs had gone crazy and would be slapped down in a week or so. That Hitler then declared war on us before we did on him was a momentous event that seemed to elude my notice. (Had Hitler not blundered that way, there might have unfolded in the European Theater an alternate war in which . . . ?)

George Mandel had also earlier moved with his family into a different part of Brooklyn. After the war, while I was still at NYU, he already had a large, bohemian, bachelor loft in Manhattan, where he could paint and write. He was near Greenwich Village and near my school, and I would drop by there often, as would Danny the Count and Marvin Winkler. All of us were ecstatically astonished when the paperback reprint rights to his first novel, *Flee the Angry Strangers,* published in 1953, were sold for a price of $25,000! His share of half that seemed a fortune. And $12,500 then *was indeed* a fortune to someone living largely on disability payments for his war wound, and to someone like me, who had worked as a college instructor and next as an advertising copywriter for the same small salary of sixty dollars a week. I thought I, too, might try a novel of my own one day when I felt myself competent to complete one. As it turned out, I didn't feel competent to begin one until I was already past thirty.

I DON'T GO THERE anymore. From my home in East Hampton to Coney Island is a long drive. I wouldn't want to go even if I lived closer. My friends are scattered. Their parents are dead. The only people I know who still live there are Sandy Kern, the widow of Ira, a boy who was a classmate in grade school and high school, and Frances Goodman, a friend of my sister's of her own generation. But they both live in Sea Gate, behind the fences and the private security forces. (And I've just learned that Sandy has moved, too.) The beach is near, the ocean is there, the weather is more clement in winter and summer than the extremes in the rest of the city, but they are there for the soothing feelings of safety and peace of mind that a homogeneous haven provides as much as for anything else.

There is not much of a Jewish neighborhood remaining outside the gates. Twenty years back, sometime around 1978, I made a trip back into the residential area of Coney Island for my novel *Good as Gold,* just to note the changes. That Marvin and I met in a bar on Mermaid Avenue in itself signified a large change—a change in us that we met in a bar, and a change in our old neighborhood of Coney Island, in which a bar, that particular bar, was the only place left for maturing people in the old crowd still living there to gather feeling safe. Smokey was there that evening, and that was the last time I saw him. He was getting old, he admitted, grinning and laughing as always, and he told me how he had found that out. That summer he'd been peddling ice cream on the beach, and he and an Italian kid in his twenties from down the Island had crossed into what each wanted to think of as a monopoly domain. Neither liked the competition. And the other, like Quasimodo in a different time and place, invited Smokey to settle it with fists under the boardwalk if he had a mind to. "And," said Smokey, putting his head back with a grin and basking in the tale and the memory, "he beat the hell out of me—so easily." Smokey hadn't been able to see a single punch coming, he related to me, practically boasting. "And I'm the guy that used to chase away all the other peddlers!" And that's how Smokey could tell he was getting old. (I included his account of that incident, name and all, in *Good as Gold,* as I also used Sylvia's birthday party, and the torturing wounds—not scars, unhealing *wounds*—of Lee's lifelong ambivalent love for our father.)

I also went back for an afternoon to look around, and afterward I recorded these impressions of mine of Coney Island in that work of fiction:

Four springy, dark-skinned bloods in sneakers were coming his way, and he [Gold] knew in a paralyzing flash of intuition that it was ending for him right then and there, with a knife puncture in the heart. . . .

They passed without bothering him, deciding to let him live. His time had not yet come.

Gold had noted earlier all the boarded-up, ruined shops on the three major lateral avenues of Coney Island and wondered where all the people went now to buy food, have their suits and dresses mended and dry cleaned, their shoes and radios fixed, and their medical prescriptions filled. In his rented car, he drove alone one more time the desolate length of Mermaid Avenue to the high chain-link fence of the private residential area of Sea Gate, where owners of the larger houses were now accepting welfare families, turned left toward the beach and boardwalk, and made his way back slowly along Surf Avenue. He did not see a drugstore. Behind the guarded barriers of Sea Gate, which once grandly sported a yacht club and was restricted to well-off Christians, younger Jewish families now congregated for safety and sent their children to whatever private schools they could. Elderly men and women, as always, probably still crept forth from secret places each morning and prowled the streets and boardwalk for patches of warming sunlight, conversing in Yiddish, and Raymie Rubin's mother had been killed one day on her return. [A true event: Raymie Miller's mother had been murdered by an intruder in her ground-floor apartment in the building on West 31st in which we had first lived.] Gold did not pass a single Jewish delicatessen. There was no longer a movie house operating in Coney Island:

drugs, violence, and vandalism had closed both garish, overtowering theaters years before. The brick apartment house in which he had spent his whole childhood and nearly all his adolescence had been razed: on the site stood something newer and uglier that did not seem a nourishing improvement for the Puerto Rican families there now.

The newer, high-rise apartment building in the public-housing project there doubtless had elevators, better plumbing, and central air conditioning. I preferred my old apartment house, with its window in the bathroom and a kitchen roomy enough to hold a table at which a family of four could sit comfortably for meals.

Farther down the Island, the Italian section appears compressed but pretty much intact, with the landmark restaurants of Gargulio's and Carolina still functioning. And the Steeplechase Pier, with Steeplechase long gone, was recently officially christened with the name Auletta Pier, to honor a citizen prominent in that section—also, incidentally, the father of the journalist Ken Auletta.

But when last I was there, the fishermen out on the pier with lines down for crabs and their bobs and sinkers out wishfully for whatever small fish might be hooked were almost entirely Hispanic, as were the women and men with small boys and girls romping delightedly around the pier in the sunshine. All were overjoyed to see me, and the group with me, for I was there with a British film crew for a television show of which they all now felt themselves selected to be part.

I HAD BEEN BACK only a few times. There was the occasion in the sixties mentioned previously when George Mandel and Mario Puzo and I relaxed in Steeplechase and found pleasure in watching our small children scampering about the grounds. And there was an afternoon and that one evening for on-site research sometime about 1978, when I spoke with Smokey in the bar.

Early in 1982, while a patient in a rehabilitation hospital, the Rusk Institute in New York, recuperating from the muscular weakness of my Guillain-Barré syndrome, I went again. Then I was the accomplished native guide on an abbreviated autobiographical tour with Mary Kay Fish, a physical therapist from upstate New York who had never been to Coney Island; Valerie Jean Humphries, a nurse; and Jerry McQueen, my friend with the car who was then a homicide detective with the city's police force, and a very good one. Valerie Humphries was one of the covey of nurses I fell in love with during a confinement lasting almost six months in two hospitals. We were married in 1987, and she still seems to like me.

Since then I've gone back to Coney Island only three times, and always with television film crews from Europe who wanted to shoot footage for their programs of the place from which I had come, especially since it was a place with a world reputation and so tellingly visual.

The first group was from England, the next from Germany. This last time I was again with a production group from England. As before, all of the Europeans had heard of Coney Island, and their faces were alive with expectation as we arrived and made ready to disembark from the van and the car. Doubtless they had all been to playlands more modern and luxurious in a variety of cities and countries. But this was Coney Island, and to their minds Coney Island was a luminous myth of which they had long heard and which emitted the animating mystique of legend.

Their enthusiasm was infectious; I turned eager, too, and proprietary. And at Nathan's, the rallying place I had selected, I charged with more ravenous hunger than the others to the griddle for hot dogs and to the next post for the fried potatoes (with extra salt, please). They progressed to the food counters with the timidity of reverence. The food at Nathan's has never failed to impress my Europeans, and *most especially* those from Britain, where the bland sausages they put up with have been the topic of caustic jokes since the days of rationing in the last world war.

This was in May 1994, and the experience was again exhilarating, an adventure for all of us. A complex of apartment houses rose where Luna Park had stood, and the former location of Steeplechase was a vacant area of several blocks, but they didn't seem to mind.

The defunct Parachute Jump was to them an Eiffel Tower of reddened steel.

It was midweek, a schoolday in early spring. There were no large crowds. The only high attractions left in operation in Coney Island were the Wonder Wheel and the Cyclone. They hardly noticed the difference.

They had never, it seemed, laid eyes on such a boardwalk, such a broad, long, sand beach, so sweeping a seascape of the ocean to the horizon at the vast opening into New York Harbor. Unpopulated, the spectacle was serenely perfect, sublime, eternal.

On Surf Avenue, where games and rides and confectioners and shows had once raucously functioned, one alongside the other almost to infinity, the numbers were cramped into a contained area, and most of the stalls were now the spilling retail counters of a flea market. That was okay with them, too.

They didn't object. Of the mechanical attractions in operation, a greater proportion than ever before were miniaturized rides for children, but the Europeans with me, of course, didn't miss the ones that were gone. And they didn't care when I spoke of the changes. For them, it was a rapture to be there—if only for that first time.

We—Valerie and I—rode the Wonder Wheel with them while they taped footage from our swaying gondola on high. But the Wonder Wheel is tame. The Cyclone is not. Jittery beforehand with trepidation, a soundman and a young British woman who was assistant to the producer determined together to brave it; they were shaking when they staggered off afterward and wobbled back to the rest of us, pale with incredulity and jabbering with exultation from the thrilling ordeal. Although it was a schoolday, the rides for the children were full. Buses from a number of schools were parked on the side streets. The children had been brought from their separate schools for a day's outing in spring. They varied widely in their distinct groupings, black, brown, white, Asian—one cluster obviously was from an Orthodox Jewish institution—and their gleeful shrieks of laughter echoed everywhere as they tore around in the orbits of the different mechanisms, definitely having fun (as all children everywhere should always be allowed to do).

I may be kidding myself, but I think I had more.

IRWIN SHAW IS GONE and is very sorely missed by all those who knew him and gloried in his large mind and bois- terous generosity of spirit. James Jones is gone, too. Both already were famous novelists when *Catch-22* came out, and—unacquainted with its author—praised it before pub- lication and helped lift it off to a fortunate start. And we had become friends. Mario Puzo's legs are troubling him. Mine are still weak from that neuropathy of fifteen years ago (and from those fifteen years of aging, too). Speed Vogel has become susceptible to respiratory infections and takes Coumadin for blood clots. Julie Green takes Coumadin now, too, and so does David Goodman and my sister, Sylvia. Lou Berkman did die of Hodgkin's disease, as related in *Closing Time*. My first wife, Shirley, is gone, too—lung can- cer, like my sister-in-law, Perlie. George Mandel is still actively around, good-humored as always and growing at least as hard of hearing as the rest of us. Marvin Winkler hangs on, though gorgeously overweight in face and form, as does his wife, Evelyn, who works in California as a teacher of preschool children, and he marvels each time we talk by telephone that the three of us have lasted this long and seem to be mostly in good health. On the first day of

May every year he telephones from California to wish me happy birthday. Every February I try to remember to telephone him on his birthday, which falls late in the month. (In Eugene, Oregon, there is a man I've never met or spoken to named Bradford Willett. For something like thirty-five years now, starting soon after the publication of *Catch-22*, he has sent me a birthday card. Through several changes of address they have managed to catch up with me. Probably, he was in his twenties when he began, and I am delighted and touched deeply to receive them.)

It is sometimes hard now to look back, to take stock, and to realize, to truly believe, that I have been to college—that was not a common thing in my youth, as I've said, and movies about college life were very popular, and were always comedy romances; to know further that I have even taught at colleges—daydreaming of that would have been a lunatic fantasy at the beginning; and that, further yet, I studied on a scholarship at Oxford University in England for one year, at St. Catherine's College, and that after a term there in 1991 as a Christiensen Fellow, I was appointed an Honorary Visiting Fellow.

Just think: I am an Honorary Visiting Fellow of St. Catherine's College of Oxford University!

I have much to be pleased with, including myself, and I am. I have wanted to succeed, and I have. I look younger than my years, much younger to people who are young, and I am in reasonably good health. My appetite continues hearty, and is complemented by a sterling digestive system that almost never lets me down. I still have most of a good head of hair and probably I have sufficient income and money to go on living as well as I want to, with enough left over, I feel, to please my few heirs (Valerie, sister Sylvia, children Erica and Ted). I am in love with my wife, still find other women appealing, enjoy a good many close friendships, and I have just finished writing this book.

It will take about a year to be published, and I expect much of what I've just said to still be true when it is.